Political Crisis / Fiscal Crisis

POLITICAL CRISIS / FISCAL CRISIS

The Collapse and Revival of New York City

MARTIN SHEFTER

Basic Books, Inc., Publishers   New York

Library of Congress Cataloging-in-Publication Data

Shefter, Martin, 1943–
    Political crisis, fiscal crisis.

    Bibliographic references: p. 237
    Includes index.
    1.   Finance, Public—New York (N.Y.)   2.   Default
(Finance)—New York (N.Y.)   I.   Title.
HJ9289.N4S54   1985   336.747′1   84-45315
ISBN 0–465–05875–2

To Sudy and Elizabeth

CONTENTS

PART IV

THE POLITICAL IMPLICATIONS OF URBAN FISCAL CRISES

ACKNOWLEDGMENTS

THE MOST fundamental contribution to this book was made by the teachers and colleagues who helped shape my understanding of politics. My interest in urban politics was originally stimulated by Edward C. Banfield and James Q. Wilson, and though I never formally studied with Barrington Moore, Jr., or Samuel P. Huntington, they also deeply influenced my work. After receiving my doctorate, I obtained a second education from a remarkable group of friends and colleagues on the Harvard junior faculty—Martha Derthick, Peter Gourevitch, Robert Jervis, Stephen Krasner, James Kurth, Peter Lange, Charles Maier, Theda Skocpol, and Paul Weaver. In recent years I have also received intellectual sustenance from Amy Bridges, Walter Dean Burnham, Stephen Elkin, Thomas Ferguson, Benjamin Ginsberg, Peter Katzenstein, Ira Katznelson, Isaac Kramnick, Theodore Lowi, John Mollenkopf, T. J. Pempel, and Sidney Tarrow. This book is the most fitting expression of gratitude I can offer these teachers and friends.

Many other people have contributed specifically to this book. My understanding of New York City's fiscal crisis was deepened by a series of seminars on urban political economy at Cornell, involving Tom Boast, William Goldsmith, Raymond Horton, Patricia Leeds, Peter McClelland, Carol O'Cleireacain, Frances Fox Piven, George Roniger, and Julia Vitulo-Martin. A number of research assistants helped me gather information about New York City's government and politics—Nancy Love, Paul Pescatello, Helene Silverberg, and Samuel Swersky. Grants from the Jonathon Meigs Fund enabled me to hire these assistants.

All students of contemporary New York are indebted to the policy analysts of the Setting Municipal Priorities (SMP) project for their first-rate research on public policy in the city. This book draws heavily on that research. I also wish to thank the project's directors, Charles Brecher and Raymond Horton, for providing me with unpublished data they had compiled on recent New York City expenditures, and for inviting me to participate in SMP conferences.

The Institute for Advanced Study in Princeton, New Jersey, was the perfect milieu in which to begin writing this book. For the opportunity to spend a year in that intellectually stimulating environment, with no competing obligations, I am indebted particularly to Professors Albert Hirschman and Clifford Geertz. I am also grateful to Isaac Kramnick for bringing my work to the attention of Martin Kessler, the publisher and president of Basic Books, and to Kessler himself for his sound advice, his patience, and his prodding.

James Q. Wilson, Peter Katzenstein, and Tom Boast read a draft of this book, and their suggestions and corrections helped me improve it. I alone, of course, am responsible for any errors that remain.

My wife and daughter contributed in very different ways to this book, and in gratitude and love I dedicate it to them.

INTRODUCTION: THE POLITICS OF URBAN FISCAL COLLAPSE AND REVIVAL

IN 1975 New York City experienced a severe fiscal crisis. During the early months of that year it became known that the municipal government was financing many of its annual expenditures with borrowed funds, and that when the notes it sold for this purpose fell due, they were redeemed by borrowing yet more money. When these unorthodox financial practices became general knowledge, the capital markets closed to the city. This held the potential of catastrophe because the city could pay its employees, suppliers, and creditors only by borrowing additional funds. Without financing, New York's government might cease functioning, and the lives and property of the city's residents would be imperiled.

To prevent such a disaster, the state and federal governments arranged new sources of financing for New York's municipal government and transferred ultimate authority over the city's financial policies to new agencies that were not responsible to the city's electorate. In the 1977 municipal elections Abe Beame, the mayor who had been in office when the fiscal crisis erupted and who ran for a second term with the support of the city's Democratic machine, was defeated by Congressman Ed Koch, who had long been associated with New York's Democratic reform movement. Once in office, however, the new mayor reached an accord with machine politicians, and his campaigns for reelection in 1981 and 1985 were backed by them. Equally remarkable, although Koch had had one of the most liberal voting records in Congress, after entering City Hall he got into a series of bitter disputes with New York's racial minorities and municipal employee unions, and his bids for reelection received substantial support within the city's business community. Perhaps most remarkable of all, although Koch was a life-long Democrat, he made an arrangement with the city's Republican party after he became mayor that allowed him to run for reelection in 1981 as the GOP nominee as well as the nominee of the Democratic party.

Though remarkable, the political events surrounding New York's fiscal crisis are revealing, for they illuminate what in normal times cannot be directly observed in American cities—the boundaries within which the game of urban politics is played and the imperatives confronting the players in that game. This book attempts to gain a better understanding of these boundaries and imperatives by analyzing the political sources and consequences of New York City's recent fiscal crisis.

Many observers of, and participants in, American urban politics have sought to analyze the causes and consequences of New York City's fiscal crisis. The most commonly offered explanation for the eruption of the crisis is emphasized in a report on New York City finances issued by the Congressional Budget Office (CBO) in 1975—namely, that the migration to New York of more than one million poor blacks and Puerto Ricans during the three decades following World War II coincided with the decline of the city's manufacturing sector, which traditionally had employed new migrants to the city, placing upward pressure on municipal welfare expenditures. At the same time, the CBO report noted, the movement of many middle-class taxpayers to the suburbs reduced the capacity of the local government to finance these expenditures. Other observers have emphasized the role that public employee unions played in the genesis of the fiscal crisis by driving up the city's labor costs. Still others have argued that the fiscal crisis was engineered by leading bankers and businessmen to compel the municipal government to implement the financial and developmental policies they advocated.[1]

Regarding the aftermath of the fiscal crisis, a commonly expressed view is that New York's financial and corporate elite seized control of the municipal government through the agencies created in 1975 to supervise city finances, and that since then local officials have been required to pursue tax and expenditure policies reflecting the preferences and priorities of that elite. And the remarkable set of alliances with established economic and political interests that Ed Koch cultivated in the wake of the crisis has generally been attributed by observers to the mayor's personal opportunism.[2]

Although there are elements of truth in each of these accounts of New York City's fiscal crises, they suffer from a common problem: presupposing that the financial difficulties the city faced in 1975 were unprecedented. The events of 1975, however, were only the most recent of a series of fiscal crises that for well over a century have erupted periodically in New York: in 1856, 1871, 1907, 1914, 1932–33, and 1975. In these crises the city was unable to sell its bonds in the open market; it faced the prospect of having no funds to pay its employees, suppliers, and creditors (with the accompanying danger of a disruption of municipal services); and in most instances the city was saved from bankruptcy when a consortium of banks agreed to bail it out, after extracting some stiff financial and political concessions from City Hall. Following all but one of these crises, the incumbent administration was driven from power by a coalition of political forces that attacked City Hall in the name of "reform." Eventually, however, many supporters of these reform administrations entered into tacit or explicit alliances with the machine politicians they had recently attacked.

It should be noted that the five fiscal crises between 1856 and 1933 all erupted prior to the decline of New York City's manufacturing sector, the suburbanization of middle-class taxpayers, the migration of large numbers of nonwhites to the metropolis, the unionization of municipal employees, and the appearance of Ed Koch on the city's political stage—that is, prior to the developments most often cited to account for the 1975 fiscal crisis and its political aftermath. This, in turn, suggests that these explanations may be inadequate or incomplete—that the proximate causes and consequences of the 1975 fiscal crisis may be manifestations of recurring tensions in the city's political and economic systems. This book analyzes the political antecedents, aftermath, and implications of New York's 1975 fiscal crisis in the context of these recurrent tensions.

Such an analysis has implications extending beyond New York City. New York is by no means a typical American city, but it often is prototypical and at no time has its influence been more evident than in the past fifteeen or twenty years. Many of the programs and practices that led New York's expenditures and indebtedness to grow so rapidly in the late 1960s and early 1970s were adopted by other major American cities, and a few years after New York's 1975 crisis several other cities experienced similar financial problems. The financing arrangements and monitoring agencies that rescued New York from bankruptcy were then imitated in varying degrees by other cities.

More generally, a brush with bankruptcy, the suspension of "politics as usual" (that is, the imposition of restrictions on local self-government and the installation of an administration pledged to the "reform" of municipal government and politics), and, finally, a tacit agreement between supporters of these reform administrations and the machine politicians they had castigated for driving their city to ruin is a cyclical pattern that has characterized the history of other American cities. Indeed, these episodes occur with sufficient regularity that fiscal crises should be regarded not as aberrations, but as an integral part of American urban politics.

By analyzing the similarities and differences between the politics of New York's recent fiscal crisis and earlier ones, this book attempts to discern the extent to which the city's experiences in recent years are a consequence of circumstances unique to it in the 1960s, 1970s, and 1980s, and the extent to which they are manifestations of more enduring features of the political systems of major American cities. Chapter 1 discusses the forces that shape the politics of cities and analyzes why cities periodically experience fiscal crises. Chapter 2 explains how the political conflicts associated with fiscal crises in New York City came to be expressed as struggles between machine politicians and reformers. Chapters 3 through 5 analyze the political sources of the 1975 fiscal crisis. Chapters 6 through 8 analyze the impact it has had upon the conduct of politics in New York City today, and explore directions in which the city's politics might change in the future. Chapter 9 assesses the extent to which the patterns of fiscal politics prevailing in New York characterize other major American cities, and discusses what the periodic eruption of municipal fiscal crises and the periodic suspension of "politics as usual" imply about the prospects for democratic government in urban America.

PART I

MACHINE POLITICS, REFORM MOVEMENTS, AND URBAN FISCAL CRISES

1

The Political Economy
of Urban Fiscal Crises

FISCAL CRISES are distinctively urban phenomena. Although the federal government's expenditures have exceeded its tax revenues much more often than not since the 1930s, Washington has never faced the problem of being unable to finance its deficit. That American cities have confronted this problem many times raises the question of why there is such a difference in the nature of the fiscal problems faced by Washington and those faced by urban governments. Moreover, because municipal fiscal crises erupt periodically, a pair of puzzling questions are raised. If cities periodically face severe fiscal problems, why aren't these confronted on an ongoing basis? And, if cities are able to maintain a balance between their expenditures and revenues during the decades between fiscal crises, why does this equilibrium periodically break down?

The answer to these questions lies in recognizing that city officials are subject to a variety of imperatives. The necessity of winning votes and maintaining civil order can lead city officials to increase public expenditures at a rapid pace. However, under normal circumstances the necessity of preserving the municipal government's credit and promoting the health of their city's economy compels them to restrain the growth rate of locally financed municipal expenditures.

3

Because cities have considerably less autonomy than does the national government, economic and political developments occurring beyond their . borders can easily upset the balance between municipal expenditures and revenues, as can changes in the structure of local political coalitions and organizations. Since municipal governments, unlike the national government, cannot print money, a city can only finance its deficits as long as investors are prepared to purchase its securities. If investors fear that a municipal government lacks the economic ability or political capacity to redeem its securities, they will not lend it more money— precipitating the sort of fiscal crisis New York City has confronted a half-dozen times in its history.

Fiscal crises characteristically discredit the city's top elected officials and lead to their defeat. The shock of defeat often convinces local politicians that they must acquiesce to changes in the political practices and public policies that enabled their opponents to triumph. The political alliances local politicians engineer, and the fiscal policies they pursue to regain and retain control over the city government, can then endure until further changes in the national or international economic and political systems again tempt them to increase municipal spending more rapidly than municipal revenues, which will spark yet another fiscal crisis.

The Imperatives of Urban Politics

If they are to gain and retain power, city officials must heed a variety of imperatives. Urban politicians have compelling incentives to pursue policies that will (a) generate votes, (b) maintain the health of the local economy, (c) preserve the city's credit, and (d) regulate and contain conflicts among the city's residents.[1] These are not imperatives in the sense that public officials cannot but heed them, but the penalty for failing to do so can be severe. The imperative of vote generation is the most obvious of these—elected officials must win more votes than their opponents if they are to gain control of the municipal government and hold on to the perquisites of power for themselves and their political allies.[2]

Another imperative for an urban regime is securing sufficient revenues to finance the operation of the municipal government. Local taxes are a major source of municipal revenue, and their proceeds vary with the health of the local economy. If local businessmen find that municipal

4

taxes are too high, or if the public facilities and services the municipal government provides to their firms (or to their customers and employees) are inadequate to make the city an attractive place in which to do business, they may close down or leave town. Other firms, for the same reasons, may not take their place. Consequently, the city government may be deprived of revenues sufficient to finance its current activities—a problem in itself for public officials and a threat to their ability to continue providing their political supporters with the public benefits they expect. Beyond this, employment opportunities, income, and the general well-being of city residents are tied to the vitality of the local economy, and voters are likely to reward elected officials who can claim to have contributed to that vitality. In seeking to serve a variety of interests, then, public officials are driven willy-nilly to pay heed to the interests of the city's most substantial taxpayers and its major employers.

Similar considerations lead mayors to be concerned with whether their city is regarded as creditworthy by the municipal capital market. Cities sell notes and bonds for two crucial purposes. One is to cope with short-term divergences between municipal revenue flows and expenditure obligations. Municipal tax revenues and grants from the state and federal governments generally flow into a city's treasury at widely spaced intervals—in many cases only once a year—whereas every month cities must pay their employees, suppliers, and often their creditors. To meet these obligations, cities sell short-term notes backed by the revenues they are scheduled to collect later. Money is also borrowed to finance the construction of public works (such as bridges, water and sewer systems, and schools) and the purchase of capital equipment (such as police cars, fire engines, and sanitation trucks). Selling long-term bonds for this purpose enables a city to pay for these projects and equipment over the life of the items in question. Investors, of course, will only purchase a city's notes and bonds if they are confident that any money lent will be repaid, which requires public officials to conduct the city's financial affairs in a manner that will instill such confidence. Failure to heed this imperative would deprive the municipal government of the credit needed to pay its monthly bills and acquire facilities that make the city a place in which families can comfortably live and firms can profitably do business.[3]

City officials must also contend with conflicts arising from disagreements concerning the entitlements and obligations of members of the community vis-à-vis their fellow citizens and the municipal government. These conflicts can be fought in the streets—in the form of crime or riots—or in the electoral and policymaking institutions of government. City officials

5

generally seek to control conflicts occurring outside the established institutions of government because they generally regard the protection of life and property as a primary mission of government, and because their failure to do so would alienate many voters and investors and encourage higher levels of government to intervene in the city's affairs. City officials also often have an incentive to reach compromises with their opponents that will limit the intensity of conflicts occurring within the institutions of government. By doing so, officials can reduce the costs and uncertainties inherent in all-out electoral battles and discourage the losers in policy conflicts from calling upon outside authorities to reverse decisions made locally. Finally, because urban regimes characteristically do not incorporate every interest in their city as full partners, their stability depends in part upon their ability to forestall or cope with opposition from these excluded groups.

The Open City

Municipal officials can find it difficult to meet these imperatives because cities lack autonomy juridically, economically, and politically. In the juridical realm, cities do not have the legal authority to issue visas or impose quotas on immigration, to enact tariffs or manipulate interest rates, and, of course, to use military force to defend themselves against outsiders who wish to intervene in their affairs. Because they cannot insulate themselves from various national or international developments that have important implications for the interests of city residents, the claims made by city dwellers upon municipal governments in an effort to defend their interests are greatly influenced by such external developments. For example, because municipal governments cannot regulate the flow of people across their borders, events occurring elsewhere in the nation or world may alter the very composition of a city's population. The potato famine in Ireland in the 1840s, the anti-Jewish pogroms in Russia in the late nineteenth century, and the mechanization of agriculture in the American South following World War II, led millions of Irish, Jews, and blacks to move to American cities. This had major consequences for the size and character of the labor force available to employers in large cities, for the competition faced by long-term residents for public jobs and services, and for the problems with which municipal officials had to contend if they were to maintain public order. The efforts of both old-timers and newcomers to protect or advance their interests in the face of these developments shaped the agenda of politics in America's largest cities for well over a century.[4]

Commodities and capital, as well as people, can move easily across the boundaries of cities, and the limited economic autonomy of cities can have important consequences for urban politics. A substantial proportion of the business firms in any large city compete in national or international markets, and the prosperity of even those that do not is dependent upon sales to firms (or to the employees of firms) in the city's "export" sector. As conditions in national or international markets change, the businessmen operating in these markets are likely to want to alter municipal policies in directions that will enhance their firms' competitiveness. They may seek improvements in the facilities for transporting goods and people to and from work sites, shifts in the character of the services the municipal government provides to business firms and their employees, reductions in municipal tax burdens, and so forth. But even in the absence of any overt pressure, city officials can ignore the effects of municipal policies upon the standing of local firms in wider markets only at the peril of seeing these firms leave town or go out of business, depriving the city's residents of jobs and decimating the municipal government's tax base.[5]

The political system of a city is no more autonomous than its economy. Participants in local politics often seek power in cities in an effort to increase their influence in national politics. Conversely, groups that have allies at the state or national levels may be able to draw upon the legal authority or material resources of these higher levels of government to enhance their power locally. Finally, the views of various actors in city politics concerning the purposes and the proper domain of government, and their entitlements relative to it, are shaped at least as much by national political currents as by local ones. Cities are components of a broader political regime, and there is a two-way flow of political ideas across their boundaries, just as there is a flow of people, commodities, and capital.[6]

Political Coalitions and Regime Capacity

Politics influences a city's response—or lack of response—to external forces and imperatives in a number of ways. Although city officials may face dire consequences if they fail to heed these imperatives, some

7

officials lack the political vision or the ability to alter established patterns of behavior, and hence suffer those consequences. If the incumbent political leaders in a city fail to satisfy a majority of the electorate, they will be defeated at the polls. If they fail to pursue policies that enable local firms to adjust to market changes or policies that encourage new firms to set up shop in their city, the local economy will decline. If they are unable to preserve public order, higher levels of government may intervene and reduce the authority of the municipal government. And if the municipal government does not remain solvent, it may be placed under some form of receivership.

Political factors influence not only whether municipal officials will successfully respond to the imperatives confronting them, but also the precise manner in which they will respond. There are a variety of ways to match municipal expenditures and revenues, establish a balance between the local public and private sectors, and resolve conflicts among a city's major social groups. Opting for one or another of these alternatives will win officials the approval or the enmity of different interests in the city. The choices public officials make among these alternatives are influenced by their judgement concerning whom they can least—or most—afford to alienate. These decisions are influenced by the leverage that various interests are able to exercise in their dealings with the city government—for example, the number of voters sharing that interest, or the assistance that interest is able to provide to public officials, or the injury an interest is able to inflict upon City Hall by virtue of its control over capital or credit.

There is one qualification that must be made to the last statement, but it is one that, if anything, further emphasizes the important role that political choices play in the fiscal affairs of cities. Although elected officials must win more votes than their opponents if they are to gain and retain power, they have some leeway in determining how to put a winning coalition together. A voter can perceive his or her interests in a variety of ways—as a consumer of this or that municipal service, as someone who is saddled with paying one or another local tax, as a member of an ethnic group or social class, or as a resident of a particular neighborhood. Politicians thus have some freedom in deciding *how* they will appeal for the support of a given group of voters as well as in determining *who* to appeal to for political support. They can assemble majority coalitions by seeking to win the support of any one of many possible combinations of voting blocs, while conceding the others to the opposition.[7]

The responses of an urban regime to the imperatives confronting it are a function not only of the strategic choices made by its top leaders, but also of the regime's institutional and organizational capacity to enact and implement decisions made at the top. If a regime is to enact a consistent set of policies it must be able to overcome, regularly and reliably, the dispersion of authority among public officials. To implement these policies, it must be able to influence the behavior of the "street-level bureaucrats"—policemen, teachers, clerks, and others who actually perform the tasks of municipal government—and give them the legal authority and material resources necessary to perform their jobs. Finally, if a regime is to mobilize a reliable electoral majority, it must have the means to communicate with voters and induce its supporters to go to the polls on election day.[8]

It must be emphasized that these preconditions are not always fulfilled. Officials in policymaking positions may regularly fall into deadlock; they may be unable to control the behavior of their nominal subordinates; street-level bureaucrats may be incapable of performing the missions they are assigned; and elected officials may be unable to turn out a reliable majority of voters on election day. In any of these events, the behavior of a municipal government will be influenced by whatever pattern of relationships does emerge among the city's political actors, institutions, and organizations. Such a regime, however, is not likely to navigate easily through the cross-currents that could capsize it.

City Politics and Urban Fiscal Crises

For all of these reasons, those who govern a city must engage in a delicate juggling act. This act is not impossible to pull off if voters recognize that they reap benefits, such as jobs and lower taxes, from policies designed to bolster the local economy, and if members of the business community recognize that their ability to recruit skilled employees and to attract prosperous customers depends in part upon the municipal government's providing a level of public services that makes the city an attractive place for such people to live. Moreover, in cities that rely upon the real property tax for the bulk of their locally generated revenues and in which home ownership is widespread, voters may be, if anything, *more* tax-conscious than local businessmen. Local officials are likely to find that by keeping municipal taxes and expenditures at a minimum, they can simultaneously please the city's voters, businessmen, and

9

creditors, and avoid sparking any rancorous political conflicts.[9] But even when there are conflicts among these constituencies, municipal officials may arrange compromises that the major social forces in the city may not regard as ideal but are prepared to live with. Under certain conditions, however, it may be difficult for city officials to keep aloft all the balls they juggle. A possible consequence of this is a municipal fiscal crisis.

Cities face fiscal crises when two conditions prevail. The first is when changes in the economic, demographic, or political environment make it difficult for local officials to meet the most immediate of their imperatives without spending more money than they collect in taxes and intergovernmental aid. The second condition is when the city's creditors refuse further financing of the resulting budget deficits.

Cities are prone to run budget deficits when cyclical downturns in the national economy, structural changes in a city's economy, or the emergence of competing centers of manufacturing or commerce lead to widespread unemployment. Municipal officials may then find it politically advantageous, or necessary for the sake of preserving public order, to provide some form of relief to the unemployed and their families. The very economic conditions that lead to such expenditures, however, may make individual taxpayers and local businessmen loathe to pay higher taxes to finance them.[10]

Unless local officials are able either to get the state and federal governments to finance relief for the unemployed or to make compensating cuts in expenditures for other municipal programs—which is difficult to do even during a depression—the combination of higher expenditures and declining revenues will produce a budget deficit. New York provides a striking example of how difficult it is to cut existing expenditures, even during a severe depression. Although the real income of the city's employees rose as prices fell in the early 1930s, the administration found it politically impossible to cut the nominal wages of municipal employees in order to cover some of the costs of unemployment relief. Indeed, cutting municipal expenditures is so difficult that declining revenues can lead to budget deficits even in the absence of a municipal effort to provide relief to the unemployed.

Another circumstance in which municipal expenditures increase more rapidly than revenues is when local officials, in an effort to mobilize political support (or to forestall opposition) among an ethnic or racial minority whose members previously had received less than their proportionate share of public benefits, increase the flow of benefits to the group in question. Alternatively (or simultaneously), a change of national administration may enable newly powerful political forces to press City

10

Hall to channel additional public expenditures to their local allies. In either of these cases, the political weight of the group receiving benefits may not be great enough to enable local officials to finance these increased expenditures by reducing expenditures that benefit other constituencies or by raising taxes. At this point, City Hall might be tempted to engage in deficit spending.

Under a number of circumstances, then, city officials may want investors in municipal securities to finance some of the costs of meeting the imperatives of vote generation, order maintenance, and protecting the strength of the city's economy. Under what conditions are potential investors likely or unlikely to play this allotted role? The limited juridicial autonomy of cities makes this more of an open question for municipal governments than it is for the national government, which has the exclusive authority to create legal tender. The federal government can borrow whatever is needed to finance its deficits, because if necessary it can print money to prevent a default on United States Treasury securities. By contrast, because cities cannot create legal tender, they *can* default on their loans. If potential creditors doubt that a city will be able to repay the money it borrows, they may refuse to lend the funds the city may require to continue functioning.[11]

What occurs—or fails to occur—at each step in the sequence of events precipitating a municipal fiscal crisis is influenced by the structure of a city's political organizations and institutions, the strength and composition of prevailing political coalitions, and the content of prevailing political ideologies. It is not the case, for example, that all cities will respond to an increase in unemployment by providing relief financed with borrowed funds. Whether a rise in unemployment will generate significant pressure for a relief program depends on the views of the unemployed regarding the government's obligations to persons unable to work and their capacity to disrupt civil order or defeat elected officials if these obligations are not fulfilled to their satisfaction. Whether an urban regime finds it necessary to respond to demands of the unemployed depends on the ability of its top leaders to prevent their associates or subordinates from taking up the cause of the unemployed, the willingness of other political forces to coalesce with those advocating a relief program, the vulnerability of incumbent officials to an electoral challenge by the proponents of the program, and, in extreme cases, the municipal government's ability to quell disruptions by the unemployed.

Whether local officials finance relief by increasing taxes, reducing expenditures on other programs, or borrowing money is determined not only by the legal and financial feasibility of each of these courses of

11

action, but also by the relative political costs they would incur by pursuing each alternative. Finally, whether potential creditors are prepared to finance a city's deficits depends upon their estimation of the likelihood that the municipal government will repay the money it borrows. This judgement inevitably is colored by politics. If investors believe that local officials would find it politically impossible to slash public services and cut the salaries of municipal employees for the sake of repaying them, they will refuse to purchase that city's securities, precipitating a municipal fiscal crisis.

A fiscal crisis usually convinces economic elites that the politicians in power are misgoverning their city and discredits incumbents in the eyes of many voters. This often contributes to the formation and triumph of political coalitions that attack these politicians in the name of reform. In most of the nation's largest cities, however, reform administrations have generally been short-lived, because losing control of City Hall gives urban politicians a strong incentive to come to terms with various supporters of the reform coalition. A typical component of such a "postreform accommodation" is a renewed commitment by these politicians to balance the municipal budget and maintain the city's credit. Subsequent changes in the wider economic and political systems in which cities are embedded, however, can upset this fiscal equilibrium. If it again becomes difficult for municipal officials to meet the imperatives of vote generation and order maintenance without accelerating the pace of municipal spending, the stage may be set for another fiscal crisis.

2

Fiscal Crises and the Machine/Reform Dialectic

FOR MORE than a century, the political conflicts and compromises that generated fiscal crises in major cities in the United States were bound up with struggles between machine politicians and political coalitions rallying under the banner of reform. This chapter analyzes the role that conflicts over fiscal policy played in the development of New York's Tammany machine and in the emergence of periodic challenges to the machine by municipal reform movements. It concludes with an analysis of how these conflicts and compromises created the institutions and patterns of political conduct that ultimately generated the city's 1975 fiscal crisis.

Fiscal Politics and the Emergence of Tammany

Over the course of the nineteenth century New York's Tammany machine became the most powerful political organization in the city. This development can be explained by analyzing the changes occurring during this period in the three major forces that shape urban politics—the national economic and political systems, the imperatives of urban politics, and the organizations politicians construct to meet those imperatives.

Changes in the External Environment

In the eighteenth century and the early years of the nineteenth century, New York City was governed by members of its mercantile elite. As political scientist Amy Bridges has brilliantly argued, members of the city's mercantile elite were able to monopolize local offices because they and the city's artisans (who comprised a majority of the electorate) had complementary views of their rights and obligations. The artisans conceded control to the merchants, who organized the commerce upon which the prosperity of all New Yorkers depended, and in return the municipal government actively regulated the local economy to protect the artisans' way of life.[1]

Economic, demographic, and political upheavals during the second quarter of the nineteenth century destroyed the foundations of this regime. The transportation and industrial revolutions created a world market for manufactured goods, making it impossible for the upper class in any one city to grant greater concessions to the working class than did their counterparts in other cities, as the additional costs would price their goods out of the market. The concurrent spread of the economic ideology of *laissez faire* led members of the upper and middle classes to deny that they or the municipal government had any obligations to those beneath them in the social structure. In conjuction with the reorganization of production and residential patterns in the industrializing city—both of which reduced direct contacts between the members of different social classes—this destroyed the dense network of ties that had made it possible for New York's mercantile elite to govern with the consent of the working class.

At the same time, the influx of hundreds of thousands of immigrants into the city in the 1840s and 1850s—the chief source of labor for the new industrial system—increased the city's ethnic heterogeneity and created the potential for new bases of political cleavage and alignment. Furthermore, during the Jacksonian era national political parties were organized, linking different segments of the city's population to allies elsewhere in the state and nation. This generated additional divisions within and between various social groups in New York and provided contenders for office with an incentive to mobilize new voters into the electorate, thereby swamping the old merchant-dominated regime.

Meeting the Imperatives of Urban Politics

A class of professional politicians who sought, in sociologist Max Weber's words, to "live off politics" constructed the party organizations— most prominently, Tammany Hall—that supplanted New York's regime of notables.[2] (New York City's Democratic machine came to be known as Tammany Hall during the early decades of the nineteenth century, because the General Committee of the city's Democratic party met in a hall owned by the Tammany Society, a local fraternal organization.)[3] These politicians were prepared to make concessions to important social forces in the city in order to obtain the votes, revenues, credit, and civil harmony that are requisites for gaining and retaining power. The rise of machine politicians came at the expense of other competitors for the leadership of the city—among them, more radical contenders for the leadership of the city's immigrant and working-class population and the mercantile elite, whose control was not happily relinquished.

There was nothing automatic about the support that Tammany received from the lower- and working-class immigrants who composed the bulk of New York's population. Machine politicians periodically faced serious challenges from more radical competitors for the leadership of the city's immigrant subcommunities. In the case of Irish-Americans, for example, Eric Foner notes that there were

two overlapping but distinct centers of power, or poles of leadership, within the Irish-American community.... [One was] a nexus composed of the Catholic Church, the Democratic Party, and the Irish-American middle class. The social dominance of this triple alliance was challenged in the 1880s by the organized social radicalism articulated and institutionalized in the Land League's radical branches and the Knights of Labor. Here were the only organized alternatives to the Tammany-oriented saloon and local clubhouse as a focus for workingclass social life in the Irish-American community.... [They] embodied a social ethic that challenged the individualism of the middle class and the cautious social reformism of the Democratic Party and the Catholic Church.[4]

A direct confrontation between these two sets of contenders for the political leadership of New York's Irish-American community—as well as its other ethnic communities—occurred in 1886 when the city's Central Labor Union and the Knights of Labor organized the United Labor Party and nominated social critic Henry George for mayor. George won a larger proportion of the vote in poor neighborhoods inhabited by second generation Irish-Americans than did Tammany's candidate, and he also did very well in German neighborhoods.[5]

One way the Tammany machine responded to such competition was by enacting some of the policies advocated by its opponents. After Henry George's strong showing in the 1886 mayoral election, for example, the machine's delegation in the state assembly and senate supported legislation prohibiting the coercion of union members by employers and creating a Board of Mediation and Conciliation to resolve labor disputes. In addition, machine politicians created an unofficial welfare system which provided a modicum of relief to the poor at times of individual need and collective distress and distributed thousands of public jobs and other forms of patronage to voters. So extensive was this patronage system that in the 1870s one out of every eight voters in New York City held a public job.[6]

Tammany also appealed for the support of immigrants by defending them against assaults upon their political rights and civil liberties. The machine fought against the efforts of Republicans, upstaters, and upper-class New Yorkers to reduce the political influence of immigrants by altering election laws and restructuring the institutions of municipal government; it opposed the efforts of Protestants to proselytize the children of Catholics in the public schools; and it defended its constituency against the efforts of prohibitionists and sabbatarians to enact legislation regulating the sale of liquor. The machine also nominated members of the city's largest ethnic groups for public office.

Most upper-class New Yorkers did not approve of how machine politicians mobilized popular support and governed the city. The public treasury—and, ultimately, the municipal taxes they paid—financed the jobs and other benefits that Tammany's precinct captains and district leaders so magnanimously distributed to their followers. Nonetheless, the behavior of machine politicians was less dangerous in their eyes than some of the alternatives. For instance, the practice of distributing patronage to voters in exchange for political support was less costly and less inconsistent with the principles of *laissez faire* than would be the municipal government's responding to certain demands of the city's labor movement. At mass meetings of the unemployed during the depressions of the 1850s and 1870s labor leaders demanded that unemployed workers be provided jobs on municipal public works projects as a matter of right, without any requirement for political service in return, and that they be supervised by men from among their ranks who were skilled in their trades, rather than by "political creatures" who obtained their positions by working for ward politicians.[7]

After it became clear to members of New York's upper class that they could retain control of elective offices without allying with professional politicians, most were prepared to acquiesce to machine government as long as the machine nominated "suitable" candidates rather than "demagogues" who pandered to such sentiments. In this sense, the patronage system administered by machine politicians was the mean between polar approaches to governing the city that had been advocated by the labor reformers and patricians who had opposed the efforts of professional politicians to become key figures in municipal politics. Patronage embodied a tacit compromise between the constituencies that these competing leaders sought to mobilize—namely, New York's working and upper classes.

The leaders of Tammany Hall were also prepared to make major concessions to New York's leading businessmen and creditors on questions of municipal fiscal policy to secure their acquiescense to machine government. Because the organizational foundations of the modern Tammany machine were laid in the wake of New York's most serious fiscal crisis of the nineteenth century—which toppled the Tweed Ring in 1871—its sources and consequences are salient at this point.

William Tweed emerged as the dominant figure in New York politics in the 1860s, after Mayor Fernando Wood was expelled from Tammany Hall for adopting the demands of the unemployed that the jobless be put to work constructing municipal housing on city-owned land and that the city sell food to the poor at wholesale prices—proposals that were anathema to the city's business elite. Tweed and his closest associates—known as the Tweed Ring—achieved their position of dominance by sponsoring and controlling the administration of an ambitious development program in upper Manhattan—the construction of new streets, water mains, sewers, parks, and streetcar lines.

Tweed's program served a number of purposes. It won him the support of those segments of the city's business community whose interests were directly or indirectly served by uptown development—real estate owners, mortgage bankers, street railway promotors, building contractors, and businessmen who sold in local markets or who benefitted from the availability of a large labor force and would therefore prosper if the city grew. This development program also enabled the Tweed Ring to provide jobs to thousands of unskilled laborers—many of them Irish—who would then have a strong incentive to vote the Tammany ticket. The money the Ring collected by demanding kickbacks from municipal contractors enabled Tweed and his associates not only to line their own pockets, but also to distribute relief to the poor. Because Tweed did not command a disciplined party organization, he also used some of the money the Ring stole to bribe other politicians and secure their support for the Ring's policies and programs.[8]

In other words, the Tweed Ring's profligate policies and corrupt

17

practices were a consequence of its members' efforts not only to make a killing in politics, but also to hold together a heterogeneous coalition of social groups in the absence of a party apparatus that could reliably produce majorities in the city's electoral arena and policymaking institutions. Some spokesmen for New York's downtown business community denounced the Ring's development program as pure and simple jobbery, but because New York's economy boomed in the 1860s and early 1870s, it appeared that the city would have no difficulty redeeming the bonds it issued to finance this program, so investors ignored these charges.

The full extent of Tweed's depredations were discovered in 1871, after the city auditor, a member of the Ring, was killed in an accident. This led to a suspension of trading in New York bonds on European exchanges and threatened the municipal government's credit and the value of New York securities in the portfolios of the city's banks and wealthy investors. To protect themselves and their city, New York's leading bankers and businessmen organized the Executive Committee of Citizens and Taxpayers for Financial Reform of the City, commonly known as the Committee of Seventy. To bring down the Tweed Ring, the Committee organized a tax strike and an investment strike. One thousand of New York's largest taxpayers announced that they would not pay their taxes until the municipal government's books were audited, and the city's major bankers indicated that they would not extend any loans to the municipal government until a man of their choosing, Andrew Haswell Green, was granted full authority over the city's finances. This brought down the Tweed Ring, and the Committee of Seventy delivered the *coup de grace* by joining with the Republicans and electing a slate of candidates pledged to "reform" in the 1871 municipal elections.[9]

The Tweed scandals threatened to discredit permanently the New York Democrats, a prospect that deeply troubled many Tammany politicians and also those elements of the city's upper class that supported the national Democratic party's low-tariff, hard-money policies. To avoid this catastrophe, a coalition of ward politicians and politically active merchants, bankers, and lawyers—known, because of their frock coats, as the "Swallowtails"—joined to elevate to Tammany's leadership "Honest John" Kelly, a professional politician who had not been implicated in the Tweed scandals. Under Kelly's leadership, Tammany sought to placate the investors, taxpayers, and voters who had been outraged by Tweed's behavior, and wanted municipal expenditures to be cut, by nominating for mayor a series of respectable merchants committed to fiscal retrenchment.

18

Building Organizational Capacity

Tammany's leaders not only discovered the terms upon which it was possible to unite a heterogeneous coalition of social forces, they also were able to secure enactment of the legislation and control over the patronage that won them the support of these diverse groups, and they constructed a highly centralized, extensively organized party apparatus that enabled them to stay in power. Because Tammany was affiliated with one of the nation's major parties, its representatives were able to join forces with fellow partisans to obtain the majorities in the state legislature and in Congress needed to enact legislation. Those who competed with Tammany for the leadership of the city's working classes (e.g., the United Labor Party in 1886) or for the leadership of the city's upper and middle classes (e.g., the Committee of Seventy in 1871) did not have such affiliations. And Tammany leaders, like machine politicians elsewhere in the nation, were able to distribute patronage to their supporters because they could extract it from the bureaucracy. It was possible for them to do this during the middle decades of the nineteenth century because their effort to build a mass-based party fueled by patronage preceded the enactment of civil service laws and the formation of political constituencies that were powerful enough to protect executive agencies from the raids of patronage seeking politicians.[10]

The first moves to centralize and strengthen the Tammany party apparatus were taken by John Kelly in the 1870s. The central leadership of Tammany established its authority to reorganize the membership of Tammany's district committees, to reject nominations made by the organization's district conventions, and to issue instructions to public officials elected on the Tammany ticket. They also established the principle that patronage would be distributed through the organization rather than being allocated to individual politicians or public officials who would then distribute it to their personal supporters. This policy enabled Kelly and his associates in Tammany's top leadership to expel from the organization those politicians who had been closely associated with Tweed and to impose some restraints on the profligacy and corruption of Tammany's officials. This placated many of the political forces that had rallied against the machine in the wake of the Tweed scandals.

Eventually, serious tensions developed between Kelly and his Swallow-tail allies. The centralization of the Tammany organization they had sponsored increased Tammany's strength relative to that of the Swallow-tails, and they were especially distressed when, for the sake of enhancing

19

Tammany's power in the city, Kelly took steps that threatened their influence in state and national politics. Consequently, a majority of Tammany's Swallowtails abandoned the organization between 1878 and 1880 and joined or founded competing factions of the Democratic party. These factions, which attracted ward politicians who resisted Kelly's centralizing policies, were able to compete on equal terms with Tammany from the late 1870s through the mid-1880s.[11]

After 1886, however, the influence of Swallowtail-dominated, anti-Tammany factions began to wane. During this period Swallowtail merchants faced increasing competition for the political leadership of the city's upper and middle classes as financiers and corporate executives became key actors in New York's economy. In addition, a Protestant revival led many wealthy New Yorkers to reject the Swallowtail doctrine of "personal liberty" and to advocate the enactment and strict enforcement of blue laws. It led others to denounce Swallowtail alliances with machine politicians and to establish organizations that evaluated candidates for public office and advocated reforming the structure of municipal government. Yet others rejected the Swallowtail policy of municipal retrenchment and advocated that the city government do more to promote the health and welfare of the poor. (This impulse was not unrelated to the United Labor Party's strong showing in the 1886 mayoral election—the city's settlement houses were all established in the wake of Henry George's campaign.) These upper-class moral, governmental, and social reformers joined with prominent business leaders in sponsoring a series of campaigns against Tammany, coordinated by a succession of nonpartisan citizens' committees and good government groups between 1890 and 1903.[12]

Tammany ultimately triumphed over this opposition and established itself as the dominant political organization in New York for a combination of reasons. The defections Tammany had suffered to the United Labor Party in 1886 encouraged its leaders to strengthen their district organizations by establishing a network of clubs that involved the machine in the social lives of Democratic voters. Also, the weakening of anti-Tammany factions within the Democratic party had greatly strengthened the capacity of the machine's top leaders to impose discipline upon their subordinates, since politicians no longer had the option of defecting to another faction whose patronage resources equalled or exceeded Tammany's. For the most part, Tammany's top leaders used this power to prevent party functionaries and public officials affiliated with the machine from engaging in blatantly corrupt and profligate behavior that could provide ammunition to their reform opponents.

Near the turn of the century, Tammany's leaders made other concessions

20

to strengthen the machine's ties to potential supporters and to win the acquiescence of potential opponents. Beginning in 1897, Tammany appealed for the support of unionized workers by pledging not to use the police and courts against striking workers in labor disputes and presented itself as a model employer by granting an eight-hour day to workers on the city's payroll. Tammany administrations carried out an ambitious program of public works—the construction of subways, bridges, and harbor facilities—that the Chamber of Commerce advocated as necessary for the continued growth of the city's economy. Finally, mayors elected with the machine's support made concessions to an important segment of the municipal reform movement by appointing men with professional training to top positions in a number of municipal agencies.[13]

In sum, the construction of a centralized, mass-based party organization enabled Tammany's leaders to compel their subordinates to make concessions to the machine's upper-class allies as well as to mobilize reliable majorities among voters lower on the class scale. This party apparatus thus contributed to the development and maintenance of the cross-class coalition upon which the machine's political hegemony rested.

The Machine/Reform Dialectic

Tammany emerged as the dominant political institution in New York because it arranged a series of accommodations acceptable to the major interests with a stake in municipal affairs—leading most of these interests to regard machine government as preferable to available alternatives. As changes occurred in the environment within which the machine operated, however, Tammany's top leaders did not always recognize the adjustments in municipal policies and practices that it would be prudent to make to retain the support of the many groups that could create problems for them. Nor were Tammany leaders always able to compel their subordinates or allies to accept such adjustments.

In these circumstances, the political forces that regarded it as imperative that the municipal government abandon its old commitments and strike out in new directions generally concluded that City Hall was failing to meet its fundamental responsibilities, and that machine government was serving "special interests"—namely, the interests of Tammany politicians, their cronies, and their allies—to the detriment of the "public interest."

Those sharing this view could be rallied against the machine in the name of "reform."

Four times between 1894 and 1933 reform coalitions managed to defeat the machine and take control of City Hall. The conditions leading to the emergence and success of each of these reform movements were by no means identical, but there were some broad similarities among them with regard to the composition of the anti-machine coalition, the reasons why these political forces turned against the machine, the structure of the organizations the reformers established to wage war on the machine, and finally, how the machine managed to regain and retain power in the wake of each reform episode.[14]

The Reform Vanguard

Since the end of the nineteenth century, anti-machine campaigns in New York have been initiated by what might be termed the city's "reform vanguard." The founders, directors, and financial backers of the organizations through which this vanguard has operated during most of the twentieth century—the City Club and the Citizens Union—were drawn from the city's upper classes, especially from among wealthy New Yorkers who financed organized charity. But the most numerous and active members of this vanguard were young practitioners of professions that produce, disseminate, and implement respectable opinion on political and social issues—social scientists, social workers, clergymen, and journalists. The first two of these professions were born at the turn of the century, and the latter two were transformed by the rise of liberal Protestantism and the muckraking tradition. As historian David Hammack has said of the new professionals, these "highly trained men—and women— . . . were seeking public outlets for their newly won expertise and . . . were ready to devote a good deal of effort to local politics."[15] New York's reform vanguard comprised a would-be leadership class whose members sought to supplant machine politicians as key actors in municipal government.

This reform vanguard was not a mere mouthpiece for New York's business elite. Its members sought to shape, not simply reflect, respectable opinion in New York. They believed that the machine's ties to groups with a stake in the status quo and its commitment to the patronage system led it to nominate candidates and appoint officials who were neither willing nor competent to deal with the city's most pressing economic and social problems. The reformers were appalled by the acquiescence of upper- and middle-class New Yorkers to machine government and sought to convince them that its moral and financial costs were intolerable.

Exposés and investigations were central to the political strategy of the reformers. The exposure of incompetence, the discovery of graft, or, best of all, the uncovering of ties between machine politicians and the underworld could destroy the legitimacy of the incumbent municipal administration. But neither the existence of corruption nor its discovery was sufficient to spark a full-scale reform crusade. On several occasions during this century there were well-grounded allegations of corruption that did not lead New York's civic elite to launch a reform campaign. And, even when the exposure of corruption destroyed the careers of guilty officials, the incumbent mayor or the machine itself at times found it possible to survive the storm.[16]

If the machine was to be overturned, the activists in the reform movement had to ally with other political forces that could provide financing, mass support, and the electoral machinery necessary to mobilize voters. Successful reform campaigns were associated with the development of opposition to the machine among important segments of the city's business community, the emergence of press and public concern about the machine's ability to preserve law and order as new immigrants flooded into the city, and changes in the cleavage and coalition patterns of national politics.

Business

Business leaders regarded machine government as intolerable when they became convinced that City Hall was failing to fulfill its fundamental obligations to manage municipal finances responsibly and promote the growth of the city's economy. As for the first of these problems, major reform movements were generally preceded by a municipal fiscal crisis. National recessions or depressions might have precipitated the crisis, but to the financial community the city's vulnerability in the face of a downturn in the national economy was a consequence of its unsound financial practices.

Bankers and businessmen sought to overturn the machine during a fiscal crisis not only because they regarded machine politicians as responsible for the city's problems, but also because fundamental policy choices had to be made in which they wanted to have a direct voice. To put its finances in order the city had to pursue some combination of the following policies: (1) raise taxes to finance existing levels of public services; (2) cut current expenditures; or (3) cut capital expenditures. It is

23

at this point that the issue of municipal finances intersected with what businessmen regarded as the other major responsibility of the municipal government—promoting the city's economic growth. Ever since the 1890s, they have wanted it to assume the responsibility for constructing the transportation infrastructure—subways and, later, arterial highways—necessary for the city's growth.

Generally, when New York has been faced with a fiscal crisis or demands for the construction of new transportation facilities, a substantial part of the downtown business community has united behind a program calling upon the municipal government to: (1) stop financing current expenditures with borrowed funds; (2) balance its budget by slashing current expenditures rather than by raising taxes; (3) use its borrowing capacity to improve the city's transportation infrastructure rather than for other purposes (such as building new schools); and (4) cover, to the greatest extent possible, the debt service and operating costs of these facilities with user-charges (fares on subways, tolls on bridges) rather than with local tax revenues. A program like this has never been popular with New York's electorate (there are more subway riders than there are property taxpayers). When it is resisted by City Hall, bankers and businessmen have concluded that the incumbent administration is fiscally irresponsible and is sacrificing the city's long-term interests for the sake of current political gains.[17]

New Immigrants

Another condition conducive to the emergence of reform movements has been the arrival of a new wave of immigrants. The crime and disorder that invariably follow such an influx have led upper- and middle-class New Yorkers to question the ability of the municipal administration to preserve law and order. Sensational episodes that revealed corrupt dealings between Jewish or Italian-American gangsters and Tammany politicians and policemen sparked the reform movements that elected John Purroy Mitchel mayor in 1913 and Fiorello LaGuardia mayor in 1933.[18]

At the same time, the arrival of new immigrants has provided reformers with the opportunity to extend their popular base. Members of the ethnic groups that control the city's party organizations generally have been reluctant to share the fruits of power with outsiders. Resentment over exclusion has been acute among members of other ethnic groups who seek to get ahead through politics. By nominating and appointing such individuals to visible offices and by promising to respond to their

24

grievances, the opponents of the machine have extended their base of support.

National Realignments

Finally, reform groups have gathered strength when national political alignments are in flux. When a national candidate opposed by the leaders of the city's party organizations has won the party's presidential nomination, the local supporters of this candidate have had reason to wage war on the party bosses. Under the best of circumstances, the cadres who staff New York's party organizations are reluctant to make room for enthusiastic amateurs who get involved in politics only because they are attracted to a particular presidential candidate, and when these amateurs believe that the regular party organization is sabotaging the national ticket, they have an additional incentive to wage war upon it. Correlatively, if a candidate opposed by the city's party organizations wins the presidency, the new national administration (or elements within it) might seek to build a political base in the city by lending support to opponents of the machine.

National political alignments and realignments also have had implications for whether the Republican party would join forces with the reformers and endorse a common slate of candidates. When the Republicans have been out of power in Washington, the GOP organizations in New York City have been most willing to make the concessions that such an alliance entails as they are especially anxious to obtain access to other levels of government. Republican participation in a "fusion" effort is important because the GOP has provided the reformers with two extremely valuable resources—the votes of party loyalists who would support any candidate having the regular Republican nomination, and a ready-made campaign apparatus for turning out voters on election day.

The Organization of Fusion Movements

Upper- and middle-class reform activists, prominent business leaders, spokesmen for minority groups, dissident Democrats, and Republicans together compose the core of an anti-machine "fusion" movement. From 1894 to 1933 fusion campaigns were organized through citizens committees composed of prominent members of New York's economic and civic elite. Beginning in 1937 reform candidates conducted their campaigns through parties affiliated with the city's labor movement—first the American Labor party and later the Liberal party. Reformers and their

25

allies in the business and financial communities often sought to turn the citizens committees or other organizations they controlled into virtual countergovernments which performed the functions of public institutions. These organizations financed and conducted investigations of the municipal government and brought charges against public officials they deemed guilty of corruption or incompetence. They also demanded, as a condition of lending the city money it needed to cope with its fiscal problems, that individuals who enjoyed their confidence be appointed to top financial positions in the city government and that city officials implement their proposals for cutting expenditures and raising revenues. By usurping the powers of public institutions in these ways, they undermined the legitimacy of incumbent officeholders and weakened the machine.

Fusion in Power

When fusion coalitions succeeded in gaining control of the city government in 1894, 1913, and 1933, they enacted substantive policies speaking to the concerns of their supporters and undertook to reorganize municipal agencies. These efforts characteristically were resisted by the interests whose influence they would diminish. Moreover, though reformers periodically were able to unite substantial numbers of voters, political activists, and businessmen in opposition to the machine, the concerns of these members of fusion coalitions were not identical, and reorganizing municipal agencies and reallocating their benefits to please one constituency often infuriated the others. Finally, efforts to alter how municipal agencies dealt with new immigrants to the city or how immigrants were mobilized politically often provided an opening for radicals from these groups to gain positions of prominence. These developments were viewed with horror by many members of the fusion coalition, creating internal strains that led the coalition to crumble.

The Machine's Return to Power

New York City's Democratic machine was able to bounce back after each episode of reform not only because fusion administrations alienated important groups in the city, but also because the machine was able to reach accommmodations with many of the political forces in the fusion coalition. It placated many of the business interests and civic associations that had rallied under the banner of reform by nominating candidates who were prepared to construct the capital projects and pursue the financial and substantive policies these groups advocated. Tammany also saw the wisdom of coming to terms with those exercising predominant influence in the national Democratic party. Most strikingly, after each episode of municipal reform the leaders of the city's regular Democratic and Republican organizations entered into collusive arrangemens that helped each maintain control over his own party, enabled them to ward off the threat of third parties, and provided the Republicans with patronage in compensation for abandoning the fusion coalition.

Other actors in New York politics had a motive to come to terms with machine politicians because as heirs to the party organizations constructed during the late nineteenth century they had an independent political base. Machine politicians did not simply live off inherited capital, however. Patronage-oriented party organizations survived because they continued to provide the groups and individuals having the most immediate stake in city politics with a way to get what they wanted out of the municipal government; that is, they continuously recreated a constituency for themselves.

Once the danger of excluding the members of new ethnic groups was brought home to the Democratic machine, ambitious politicians from those groups had a strong incentive to work through or seize control of the party's district organizations. An affiliation with the regular wing of the city's majority party was personally advantageous to these politicians— for example, it provided them with the opportunity to obtain lucrative legal fees and brokerage commissions. It was politically advantageous as well, because the affiliation provided assistance for defeating rivals for the political leadership of their ethnic or racial group.

Firms doing business with the city or regulated by the municipal government also had strong reasons to cultivate good relations with New York's regular party organizations. Especially important among these were construction firms seeking municipal contracts and real estate owners and developers, the value of whose holdings was heavily influenced by the public facilities the city constructed, the tax abatements and zoning variances it granted, and the building plans it approved. Unions in the building trades and mortgage bankers had similar interests; they, along with contractors, developers, and realtors, were the largest contributors to the city's regular Democratic organizations.

Finally, mayors found it useful to work through the regular party organizations. Because the majority of New York city councilmen and state legislators are normally party regulars, the mayor had to come to terms with the regulars if he was to govern the city and carry out the programs necessary to win the backing of other groups he relied upon for political support—be they labor unions, civic associations, business groups, or newspapers.

The cyclical pattern characterizing New York politics during the first

half of the twentieth century—the periodic election of reform administrations and their subsequent defeat by candidates who had the support
of the city's regular party organizations—can be understood, then, as a
process of "serial bargaining." This process of bargaining carried out
over time enabled machine politicians to adjust to the demands of (1)
business interests that wanted the municipal government to pursue sound
financial policies and construct projects they believed were crucial for
the city's continued prosperity; (2) new ethnic or racial groups that
wanted political recognition; and (3) middle-class professionals and the
local allies of newly powerful national forces that wanted to extend their
influence over the city government.

The regimes that came to power after the defeat of fusion administrations granted these concessions. In return, however, each of these groups
had to give up demands that other political forces in the city would not
tolerate. Thus, these regimes generally took the steps necessary to put
the city's finances on a sound basis and to construct the projects that
business interests favored. In exchange, business interests tolerated the
costs of machine government; that is, the expenditure of municipal
revenues for programs and projects they considered wasteful and the
occasional diversion of public monies into the pockets of politicians.

In a parallel fashion, after each episode of reform those ethnic groups
that had been courted by the fusionists were granted increased representation in important elective and appointive offices by the machine. The
price new ethnic groups had to pay for this recognition, however, was
to abandon leaders who were considered too radical or too closely
associated with criminals to be acceptable to other established interests
in the city. Finally, after the defeat of reform movements, middle-class
professionals were generally accorded additional influence over certain
municipal agencies, and the party's regular leadership came around to
endorsing candidates committed to the policies of newly powerful
national political movements such as Progressivism and New Deal
liberalism. These concessions were granted by the party leadership to
induce erstwhile opponents to abandon their efforts to destroy the regular
party organization and take over the entire municipal government.

But as changes in the larger political and economic system led new
national coalitions to form, new ethnic groups to arrive in the city, and
new programs for fostering the city's growth to be advocated, and as the
cost of financing both the machine's operation and the concessions it
made to other political forces came to exceed the city's revenues and
generate fiscal strains, these regimes, in turn, were successfully challenged
by new political coalitions. To regain control of City Hall, machine

politicians had an incentive to make concessions to their new opponents, thus concluding another phase of the machine/reform cycle. This serial bargaining explains how machine politicians were able to maintain their central position in New York politics for more than a century and why the most important political conflicts in the city were expressed through the machine/reform dialectic.[19]

Machine/Reform Dialectic and the Creation of the Pluralist Regime, 1945–60

Although the conflict between machine politicians and reformers in New York has followed a cyclical pattern, all phases of the cycle have not been identical. Reform episodes have differed in the importance of financial issues relative to other considerations in generating opposition to the machine. Imminent municipal bankruptcy precipitated the reform movements of 1871 and 1933, while in the periods of 1894–1901 and 1907–13, the issues of municipal expenditures, indebtedness, and taxation chiefly arose in relation to how new subway construction was to be financed. Changes have also occurred in the relative importance of various participants in fusion movements and in the organization of fusion campaigns. From 1871 through 1933, New York's civic and business elites were senior partners in reform campaigns, organized by citizens committees which they dominated. Beginning with Fiorello LaGuardia's campaign for a second term in 1937, political parties organized by labor unions became essential vehicles for fusion forces to mobilize voters against the machine.

Most important, the concessions machine politicians made to regain control of City Hall after each episode of reform altered both the balance of power among the leading political actors in the city and the structure of the political organizations and institutions through which political conflicts were conducted. In general, these concessions narrowed the domain of the patronage system and increased the strength of other organizations and institutions relative to New York's Democratic machine. Because the changes in this regard occurring in the wake of the LaGuardia administration established the context within which the most recent phase of the machine/reform cycle erupted, it is essential to analyze those changes.

The Post-LaGuardia Accommodations

By extending the political base of his administration beyond the usual confines of fusion movements, Fiorello LaGuardia in 1937 became the first reform mayor in New York's history to win reelection and, in 1941, became the first mayor of any stripe to win a third four-year term. A number of tensions tore apart the LaGuardia coalition in the mid-1940s, however, and rather than face what at best would have been a difficult campaign, LaGuardia decided against running for a fourth term. Equally important, LaGuardia's reelection prospects were bleak in 1945 because the Democrats came to terms with many of the political forces that had once united behind LaGuardia.

One of the first concessions the Democrats made in their effort to regain control of City Hall in 1945 was to make peace with Robert Moses. In 1929 Moses, who was chairman of the Long Island State Park Commission, planned an extensive and integrated network of highways, bridges, and parks for the New York metropolitan area, but because Tammany neither controlled nor needed Moses, it refused to endorse his plan. Mayor LaGuardia, however, appointed Moses to positions in the city government (Parks Commissioner and Chairman of the Triborough Bridge Authority) that enabled him to construct the projects Tammany had blocked. These projects won Moses strong support from city newspapers, construction unions, and the general public, as well as from businessmen with direct interests in their construction or who believed that a highway network that would bring New York into the automotive age was necessary if the city was to grow and prosper. William O'Dwyer, the Democratic mayoral candidate in 1945, sought to win the support of these constituencies by pledging not only to reappoint Moses to the positions he had occupied in the LaGuardia administration, but also to appoint him to a number of others (most notably, the newly created post of City Construction Coordinator). O'Dwyer's two Democratic successors (Impellitteri and Wagner) also appointed Moses to these positions, so that from 1945 to 1960 he had virtually complete control over what public facilities would be constructed in New York and where they would be located. In return, Moses channeled much of the patronage generated by his activities to business firms and individuals with ties to New York's Democratic machine politicians. This arrangement helped finance New York's regular Democratic party organization during the postwar period, and it gave the mayors elected with its support the backing of newspapers, voters, and segments of the business community that approved of Moses's development program.[20]

30

The post–World War II Democratic regime also assured former fusion supporters that, in contrast to the two previous Tammany-backed administrations, it was fiscally responsible. Municipal expenditures increased steadily during 1945–1960, but the rate of increase was kept moderate by the dominant bloc on the Board of Estimate, which was sensitive to the concerns of homeowners and small businessmen who formed the core of the Democratic machine's constituency in the outer boroughs. Moreover, City Hall did not finance current expenditures with borrowed funds. It balanced the city's budget by, among other ways, increasing the sales tax and abandoning the five-cent subway fare, a Tammany commitment for almost fifty years. And, to demonstrate to the city's business community that he was determined to increase the efficiency of the municipal government, Mayor O'Dwyer established the Mayor's Committee on Management Survey for the purpose of recommending changes in the organization and procedures of the city government. Some of these recommendations were implemented by Mayor Wagner.

Another element of the LaGuardia coalition with which New York's postwar regime came to terms was the city's elite civic associations and charitable organizations. To a greater extent than their machine-backed predecessors, Mayors O'Dwyer, Impellitteri, and Wagner appointed to health, education, and welfare agencies commissioners who enjoyed the confidence of these organizations. The commissioners, in turn, accorded these organizations substantial influence over the formulation of new policies. The tacit quid pro quo was that they abandon the direct involvement in electoral politics that had played an important role in Tammany's defeat in 1933.[21]

New York's postwar regime also accorded greater political influence to the Italians and Jews who had provided LaGuardia with much of his electoral support. In 1945, for the first time, the Democrats nominated an Italian and a Jew for citywide office, and the party continued to do so for the next twenty years. During this same period, the number of Italians and Jews appointed as commissioners in the municipal government also rose to new heights.[22]

Not unrelated were changes that occurred in the character of the linkages between the city's political system and Italian and Jewish communities. In the 1930s and 1940s, a significant proportion of the Italian and Jewish Democratic machine politicians in Manhattan (and to a lesser extent, in Brooklyn) had close ties to the city's criminal underworld. These connections emerged partly as a result of Tammany's loss of municipal patronage during the LaGuardia years and partly as a consequence of its failure to mobilize a substantial following in Italian and Jewish neighborhoods. The conjunction of these conditions meant that the manpower and money that gangsters could provide to politicians with whom they were allied were sufficient to enable these politicians to control many Democratic district leaderships in Italian and Jewish neighborhoods. The ties between Tammany politicians and the underworld, however, provided the machine's opponents with ammunition to discredit it in citywide elections. To overcome this problem, Carmine DeSapio— who in 1949 became the first Italian-American leader of Tammany— moved to replace these district leaders with other Italian and Jewish politicians who would not be such a liability to the party.

Another important linkage between New York's political system and its Jewish and Italian communities in the 1930s and 1940s was the American Labor party (ALP). The Democratic citywide ticket was endorsed by the ALP in 1945, numerous Democratic city councilmen, state legislators, and congressmen also ran on the ALP line, and in many predominantly Jewish districts and some Italian districts (most notably, Congressman Vito Marcantonio's), the votes cast on the ALP line provided the winning candidate with his margin of victory. During the mid- and late-1940s, however, the ALP fell increasingly under the influence of the Communist party, and, as the Cold War intensified, the ties between Democratic politicians and the ALP in Jewish and Italian neighborhoods became embarrassing to the Democratic party citywide. To deal with this problem, top Democratic public officials and party leaders joined with the Republicans and the Liberal party (which was organized in 1944 by the anti-Communist faction of the ALP) in a successful campaign to destroy the American Labor party. The laws governing elections were changed in ways that worked to the disadvantage of the ALP, and in some districts (one of them was Marcantonio's) the Democrats, Republicans, and Liberals nominated a common candidate to run against the candidate of the ALP.

After the ALP was destroyed, the Democrats and Liberals entered into a standing alliance. In return for the Democrats' nominating candidates and pursuing policies that the Liberals found acceptable (and also distributing patronage to that party's functionaries), the Liberals would endorse the Democrats' candidates, thereby assuring them the support of tens of thousands of Jewish voters for whom the Liberal imprimatur was significant. The terms of this alliance were negotiated and renegotiated by Tammany leader Carmine DeSapio, Alex Rose (the Liberal party's chief tactician), and Robert F. Wagner, whose political career they jointly promoted. Through the DeSapio-Rose-Wagner troika, Italians and Jews

32

gained substantial influence in New York politics, but again there was a tacit quid pro quo. The price of their inclusion was the simultaneous exclusion of those contenders for the leadership of these ethnic communities whom other participants in the city's politics found unacceptable by virtue of their criminal ties or radical ideology.[23]

During the postwar period, New York's regular Democratic party organizations also established an accommodation with another participant in the fusion coalition: the Republican party. The Democrats and Republicans joined forces not only to destroy the ALP, but also to repeal proportional representation (PR) in elections for the city council, because it had enabled the Communists to win two seats on the council and had greatly weakened the control that both parties could exercise over their respective members on the council. The repeal of PR reduced Republican representation on the city council, but the Democrats in effect compensated the GOP for these losses by endorsing some Republican candidates in elections for other offices, especially judgeships, and channeling patronage to the regular Republican organizations in the city.

The leaders of New York's postwar regime also altered their behavior with regard to another political force—municipal employees—to which Fiorello LaGuardia had made some overtures. Prior to LaGuardia's election, the dominant organization of New York City employees, the Civil Service Forum, was essentially an adjunct of the Democratic machine. One way the LaGuardia administration sought to weaken the machine was by offering assistance to municipal employee organizations that were independent of the city's regular Democratic party organizations and wanted to advance the collective interests—as opposed to the individual interests—of their members. After LaGuardia left office the Forum did not regain its dominant position, but the Democrats secured the support of city employees by tightening the rules and procedures that protected the autonomy of the civil service (limiting the authority of supervisors to reward, discipline, or redeploy their subordinates). They also increased promotion opportunities for civil servants by extending the principle of "promotion from within."[24]

Finally, the leaders of New York's postwar regime also made some overtures to blacks. During the 1940s and 1950s black politicians were selected by the county Democratic organizations or the city's mayors to serve as party district leaders, city councilmen, state legislators, judges, and, most visibly, as borough president of Manhattan. In the 1950s, the city council enacted a local law banning racial discrimination in the sale or rental of housing, and a Commission on Intergroup Relations was established to indicate the city's commitment to the goal of racial harmony. The municipal hospital system, one of the more rapidly growing city agencies, hired large numbers of blacks as orderlies and maintenance personnel.

However, blacks continued to receive less than their share of the benefits distributed by the municipal government—as had been true of Italians and, to a lesser extent, Jews, prior to the LaGuardia era. Racial minorities also had to bear a disproportionate share of the burdens generated by the policies the municipal government pursued. For example, a large number of nonwhites were evicted from their homes by Robert Moses's construction projects, and the civil service recruitment procedures so staunchly defended by municipal employee organizations awarded a very low percentage of the most desirable municipal jobs to blacks.

Blacks received less than their due from the municipal government in the 1940s and 1950s because the members of ethnic groups that arrived earlier in New York had no desire to sacrifice the rewards of power for the sake of blacks. Black officeholders and party politicians could not compel their white colleagues to make greater concessions in part because electoral turnout rates were low among blacks, and because white politicians feared that making substantially greater concessions might alienate white voters. And, to complete the circle, the low black turnout rates were due in part to Democratic machine politicians' hesitation to mobilize more blacks into the electorate lest it result in increased pressures for a more equitable distribution of municipal benefits to blacks, and therefore to greater dangers of alienating white voters.[25]

The circumspection with which white politicians dealt with policies of concern to minorities left blacks open for mobilization by leaders who did not have strong ties to the regular party organizations. The most prominent of these politicians in the 1940s and 1950s was Adam Clayton Powell, who played a role as chief spokesman for New York's black community similar to the one that Fiorello LaGuardia had earlier played for Italian-American New Yorkers. Racial minorities were also left open to the appeals of protest leaders who mobilized followers outside electoral channels. This, as we shall see, contributed to the overthrow of the regime that governed New York after LaGuardia retired from office.[26]

The Structure of the Pluralist Regime

The concessions Democratic politicians and public officials made to regain and retain control of City Hall following LaGuardia's mayoralty had profound consequences not only for the relative power of various political forces in New York, but also for the structure of the regime that governed the city. After Mayor LaGuardia left office, the machine was no longer the central institution through which disparate interests were articulated and aggregated. Rather, for the reasons elaborated in the following pages, New York's political system during this period can aptly be termed a "pluralist" regime.[27]

First, a large number of social forces organized as genuinely independent interest groups. The Liberal party stands out as an example of this point. Prior to the LaGuardia administration, the chief channel of influence for liberals in New York was the access they had to Al Smith and his kitchen cabinet. Consequently, after a faction that was led by Tammany boss John Curry and was hostile to Smith gained control of the machine in 1929, liberals had no direct means of influencing the municipal government. In the post-LaGuardia period, however, the Liberal party provided the moderate left with a major (though not their only) means of influencing municipal affairs. If the Democrats nominated a candidate the Liberals found unacceptable, they could threaten to defeat, or at least endanger, the Democratic nominee by fielding a candidate of their own. This prospect induced Democratic leaders to enter into negotiations with leaders of the Liberal party to find a candidate whom both parties would be prepared to support. In other words, by organizing an independent party, liberals gained considerable tactical flexibility and an institutionalized means of influencing the city government.

Second, the independent interest groups that organized after LaGuardia's mayoralty gained access to the municipal government through a variety of political channels and governmental institutions—most importantly, the mayoralty and the Board of Estimate. When William O'Dwyer and Robert Wagner occupied the city's highest office, the mayor was the municipal official most inclined to pick up the proposals of civic associations, newspapers, or liberal political forces that wanted the city to enact new policies, increase expenditures on existing programs, or reorganize various municipal agencies. The dominant bloc on the Board of Estimate, however, was composed of officials (the city comptroller and the five borough presidents) who owed their nomination and election almost entirely to the city's regular Democratic organizations and therefore were especially responsive to the concerns of homeowners and small businessmen, the core constituency of those party organizations. This led the Board to resist proposals to greatly increase expenditures on municipal programs or enact new programs that might prove costly. Also, the Board of Estimate listened sympathetically when organizations of municipal employees complained that some proposal to enact a new policy or reorganize a municipal agency would disrupt current bureaucratic routines or threaten the promotion opportunities of their members.[28]

Finally, because the mayor, the Board of Estimate, the Moses empire, and many agencies in the executive branch of the municipal government all enjoyed a substantial measure of political independence (that is, none totally controlled any of the others, nor were they subject to the control of a common master), the interests that were articulated through these different institutions were aggregated not through a centralized process over which a party boss presided, but rather through a process of pulling and hauling, conflict and bargaining, among these separate institutions. A good deal of diversity existed in the ways in which the municipal government handled proposals for new policies in postwar New York, but one pattern of policy formation predominated. Proposals for new policies were usually initiated by the city's civic associations (such as the Citizens Committee for Children, the Citizens Housing and Planning Council, and the Community Council) and then picked up by the mayor. When presented to the Board of Estimate for enactment or funding, these proposals were commonly watered down so as not to violate vested bureaucratic interests or alienate the city's taxpayers. This was at once acceptable and frustrating to major interests in the city. The mere enactment of a policy proposal, in whatever form, permitted executives of civic associations to report to members that their organization was influential and effective. It also enabled the mayor to establish a record he could point to when seeking support within the city's liberal community. At the same time, the watering down of policy proposals by the Board of Estimate—often to the point of evisceration—though frustrating to liberal political forces, enabled taxpayers to avoid having to bear substantial new burdens and enabled bureaucrats to avoid disruption of their established work routines.

Although these political forces had access to New York's postwar regime, they were less than completely satisfied with how the municipal government operated and with the policies it pursued. Civic leaders and members of the liberal community almost certainly preferred half a loaf to nothing, but obviously would have preferred making fewer concessions to their political opponents. Taxpayers did not face monumental tax increases each year, but did have to bear the burden of financing creeping budgetary inflation. And while city employees did not face major threats to the integrity of established procedures governing the recruitment, supervision, and promotion of civil servants, they did bear the burden— in the form of low salaries—of the Board of Estimate's efforts to moderate the pace of budgetary inflation.

Because most of the city's interest groups were independently organized, they were in a position to express their dissatisfaction through independent action in the city's electoral arena. Their doing so in 1961 upset the delicate structure of compromises upon which New York's postwar regime had rested. And when some of these groups joined forces in the mid-1960s with the racial minorities who had occupied a subordinate position in New York's postwar regime, that regime was overthrown—initiating the chain of events that culminated in the 1975 fiscal crisis.

PART II

THE POLITICAL
SOURCES OF
NEW YORK CITY'S
FISCAL CRISIS

3

The Reform Attack on
the Pluralist Regime

THE ORIGINS of New York's current fiscal crisis lie in the 1960s, a decade that witnessed the triumph of one of the city's periodic reform movements. As in previous episodes of reform, an important impulse behind this movement was opposition to the municipal government's fiscal policies and practices. There were other similarities between the reform movement of the 1960s and earlier anti-machine crusades: the attack upon the incumbent regime was initiated by young professionals who wanted to displace machine politicians as the key actors in municipal government; the movement was backed by businessmen who were unhappy with the city's development policies as well as its fiscal practices; the relationship between the municipal government and the most recent migrants to the city—blacks and Puerto Ricans—was a major concern of the reformers, and members of these minority groups provided crucial political support to the reform administration. Finally, the reformers were closely allied with key figures in the national government who sought to alter the policies of the municipal government and the balance of power in the city.

There were, however, some important differences between the reform movement of the 1960s and previous campaigns against machine government. For example, the young professionals attacked the prevailing regime on a number of fronts, rather than directing their fire exclusively against Democratic machine politicians. The conflicts between reformers and their opponents were conducted over an extended period of time and involved kaleidoscopic shifts in alliance patterns among political leaders in the city. And, of special concern to us here, the objections raised about the municipal government's fiscal policies in the 1960s were more varied than those raised during previous reform movements, when the central goal of members of fusion coalitions was to reduce the city's operating expenditures and cut municipal taxes.

These and other differences between the reform movements of the 1960s and of earlier decades were largely a consequence of the changes that occurred in the structure and relative power of the major political organizations and institutions in New York City during the post-LaGuardia years. These differences help explain why the reform movement of the 1960s, in contrast to earlier ones, ultimately contributed to the intensification, rather than the resolution, of the fiscal problems that had played a role in the reformers' initially gaining power.

An Overview of New York City Politics, 1961–65

The attack upon New York's postwar regime was initiated by young men and women who regarded themselves as reformers and who directed their fire against three of the pillars supporting that regime—the city's regular Democratic party organizations, the public works empire of Robert Moses, and the municipal government's welfare bureaucracies. These attacks contributed to the defeat of a number of incumbent party leaders and office holders. To avoid that fate, Mayor Robert Wagner in 1961 turned against his political mentor, Carmine DeSapio, and ran for a third term against a candidate, Arthur Levitt, backed by New York City's five Democratic county leaders. Wagner's candidacy was supported by reform Democrats, the majority of New York's labor unions, and most of the city's newspapers. Wagner trounced his opponent in the Democratic primary and won a solid victory in the general election, where he ran as the nominee of both the Liberal and Democratic parties.

Wagner's third term was marked by political and social upheaval. Civil rights leaders demanded that the city schools be integrated, and sponsored student boycotts to back up their demands, while opponents responded with demonstrations in support of "the neighborhood school." In 1964, the first in the national wave of ghetto riots erupted in Harlem. On numerous occasions, public employee unions threatened strikes. Some carried out their threats, though in most instances strikes were averted at the last moment, when the mayor intervened to arrange a settlement. Finally, new municipal taxes were enacted each year of Wagner's third term to cover the city's steadily rising expenditures, but even so, the budget was balanced only by various fiscal "gimmicks," which business groups such as the Citizens Budget Commission labeled as thoroughly unsound. Their denunciations reached a crescendo in 1965 when the administration closed its budget gap by borrowing against the revenues of a tax it proposed to levy in the future but did not yet have even the constitutional authority to enact.

For these reasons several groups in the Wagner camp in 1961 abandoned it in 1965. The mayor did not stand for reelection that year, but sponsored the candidacy of City Council President Paul Screvane. Screvane was opposed in the Democratic primary by Comptroller Abe Beame (who, like Screvane, had run on Wagner's slate in the 1961 primary) and by Congressman William Fitts Ryan, a leading figure in the Democratic reform movement. Beame, backed by the most powerful Democratic county machines, won the primary.

In the general election Beame was opposed by a fusion candidate, John V. Lindsay, the nominee of the Republican and Liberal parties, and by William F. Buckley, the nominee of the newly formed Conservative party. In his campaign Lindsay repeatedly attacked the "power brokers" (by which he meant civil service union leaders, Democratic party politicians, and Robert Moses), whom he asserted were the dominant forces in the Wagner administration and were responsible for the administration's failure to come to grips with the city's racial, financial, transportation, and other problems. The support Lindsay received from regular Republicans, from Liberals, and from reform Democrats who defected to him after the machine-backed Beame won their party's primary, along with the division of the opposition vote between Buckley and Beame, enabled Lindsay to win the general election with less than 44 percent of the total vote.

The Reform Vanguards

Each of the institutions the young reformers attacked was headed by a leader admired by their elders for having arranged an acceptable compromise between the old politics and the new, but who the reformers felt personified a set of morally indefensible compromises. The reformers' sense that they were fighting a great evil enabled them to carry on against staggering odds. Their attacks placed their targets on the defensive, providing more established political forces with an opportunity to attempt to readjust the accommodations underlying the pluralist regime in ways that would work to their own advantage or would further their principles. These efforts split the coalition that had supported the postwar regime and ultimately contributed to its collapse.

The Democratic Reform Movement

A major compromise underlying New York's postwar regime was one involving New Deal liberals and Democratic machine politicians. The reform movement that emerged within the Democratic party in the 1950s was founded by young, well-educated professionals who sought to replace these machine politicians with leaders drawn from their own numbers and to increase their own influence in municipal affairs at the expense of other members of New York's governing coalition.

Carmine DeSapio was a machine politician who publicly endorsed liberal legislation, secured the Democratic nomination for liberal candidates, and forged an alliance with the Liberal party. DeSapio also democratized the party organization—by requiring that district leaders be directly elected by the party's members—and sought to get local Democratic clubs to welcome newcomers who wished to participate in politics at the grassroots. None of this, however, impressed the reform Democrats. Although their differences with DeSapio on issues of public policy and even party procedures were not great, to the reformers he symbolized not a happy reconciliation between the old politics and the new but an evil form of Tammany politics that it was their mission to destroy.

New York's Democratic reform movement turned against Tammany for two reasons. Many of its members were drawn into politics by Adlai Stevenson's presidential campaigns and blamed Democratic machine

44

politicians for Stevenson's failure to carry New York. Jewish professionals, the predominant group in the reform movement, were fiercely devoted to Stevenson because he embodied the virtues of intelligence and urbanity they most admired. With considerable justification, they believed that Carmine DeSapio and his associates were more interested in the outcome of local elections than in sending Stevenson to the White House.[1]

Second, the reformers were repelled by the precinct workers and leaders of the city's regular Democratic clubs. They were far more likely than machine politicians to be well-educated, to be employed in the professions, and to have acquired the cosmopolitan demeanor and views of the social stratum they had entered. Many machine politicians were as wealthy, and their forebears may have lived in America as long or longer than those of the reformers, but they tended to be more parochial. They had moved a shorter distance—both literally and in terms of their outlooks and ways of life—from their parents or grandparents than had the reformers. The repulsion with which the reformers viewed the "hacks" who staffed the machine reflected their contempt for those beneath them on the social scale.[2]

How did a movement with such a narrow social base come to exercise influence in New York City's politics? Largely it did because, as in earlier reform campaigns, prominent figures joined forces with it and were able to bring with them substantial public support. The most important of these figures were former Governor Herbert Lehman and Eleanor Roosevelt, the two living New Yorkers most closely associated in the public's eyes with the New Deal. From its earliest days, the New Deal coalition had been composed of machine politicians as well as labor leaders and liberal ideologues. President Roosevelt had found it useful to ally with such politicians because they brought independent strength to the Democratic ticket. By the late 1950s, however, the Democratic electorate was so firmly committed to programs and policies of the New Deal, and New York's Democratic machine was so weakened by the concessions made to regain power after the LaGuardia administration, that liberal Democrats were prepared to dispense with these allies. After Thomas Finletter, the candidate supported by Governor Lehman and Eleanor Roosevelt for the Democratic nomination to the United States Senate at the party's 1958 state convention, was defeated by DeSapio's candidate, Frank Hogan (who had been regarded as a paragon of good government during the twenty years he served as District Attorney of Manhattan), Lehman and Eleanor Roosevelt extended their support to the reformers and established the Committee for Democratic Voters (CDV) to serve as the umbrella organization for the city's reform clubs.[3]

After Governor Lehman and Eleanor Roosevelt threw their enormous prestige behind the crusade against "bossism," the reform Democrats enjoyed greater success than ever before and were able to defeat an incumbent congressman and several incumbent state legislators. This was what convinced Mayor Wagner that Carmine DeSapio had become a liability. Wagner campaigned for a third term in 1961 as an opponent of "bossism," receiving the support of the CDV.

Measured by the votes they directly comanded, the contribution of reform activists to Wagner's victory in the 1961 Democratic primary was not large. Whereas reform clubs were strong in only a few neighborhoods in Manhattan, Wagner won substantial majorities in all five boroughs. However, this reform vanguard did provide Wagner with an issue he could use to advantage. Four years later, John Lindsay picked up and expanded upon the issue of "bossism" when he campaigned against the city's "power brokers."

The Anti-Moses Crusade

The public works empire headed by Robert Moses was the target for an attack launched in the late 1950s by a second group of reformers—in this case, a group of young journalists. Their crusade was not the first opposition Moses had confronted during his long career in New York politics. Many of his projects were vehemently opposed by the people whose homes were ultimately destroyed by them. Also, New York's elite civic associations fought Moses on many occasions because he resisted their efforts to implement comprehensive land-use planning. Yet until 1956 this opposition had virtually no effect. A major reason was that the city's newspapers gave little coverage to Moses's critics.[4]

In the mid-1950s two controversies erupted that tarnished Moses's image. The first involved his attempt to construct a parking lot in Central Park, adjacent to an expensive restaurant, the Tavern on the Green. The second involved an effort to end a series of free performances of Shakespeare's plays in Central Park, supposedly because the audience at these performances trampled on the grass. These controversies damaged the reputation Moses had propagated through the press for thirty years—that of a public servant whose imperious methods enabled him to get things done that served the public good—and made him vulnerable to more serious attack.

The Title I scandals of the late 1950s posed a significant threat to

Moses and his political allies. ("Title I" refers to the section of the 1949 Housing Act authorizing the federal urban renewal program.) Questionable practices in New York's urban renewal program were first uncovered in an investigation conducted by a committee of the United States Senate in 1954. The committee's investigations revealed that the developers of the Manhattantown urban renewal project, who had owned the renewal site for two years, had yet to begin construction of a single building. Rather, they were continuing to collect rents from the slum buildings on the site, while providing few services and allowing the tenements to deteriorate further. New York's newspapers reported the committee's findings, but then dropped the story after the hearings ended.

In 1956, after the Tavern on the Green episode, a reporter on the *New York World-Telegram*, Gene Gleason, began a follow-up investigation of the city's urban renewal program and his findings were written up by another reporter, Fred Cook. In a series of articles published between 1956 and 1958, Gleason and Cook reported many irregularities in this program, which they attributed to ties between a number of developers of renewal projects and Tammany and the Bronx Democratic machine. Other New York newspapers picked up the Title I story, but by 1959 all of the city's newspapers, including the *World-Telegram*, were losing interest in the scandal.

To compel his own paper to continue printing Title I stories, Gleason gave some of his information to a reporter at the *New York Post*, the one city newspaper that was hostile to Moses. With the competition giving headline treatment to the scandal, the *World-Telegram* found it necessary to do the same, as did the city's other newspapers. To keep up the pressure on their editors, a number of reporters who covered the Title I story for different newspapers met regularly and parceled out information that each paper's editor, in turn, would give headline treatment as an exclusive.

Robert Caro has offered a perceptive analysis of the motives of the reporters who played a key role in undermining one of the pillars of New York City's postwar regime:

In any assessment of their motivations, their age is important. Everyone in the circle was in his late twenties or early thirties. Recalling those days . . . [one of them said] "Our motives? It was us against the world, us against them—the city, corruption, unmovable forces. We were young enough to breathe that kind of air then." Moreover, these young idealists hadn't even been born when Robert Moses had been on the front pages battling the robber barons to open Long Island to the masses. . . . The Robert Moses they knew was not the Robert Moses of the beautiful parks and the beautiful parkways—the parkways that were going

47

to solve traffic problems. The Robert Moses they knew was the Robert Moses of the Tavern-on-the-Green and Manhattantown and those damned expressways he insisted on building even though everybody knew the city should be building subways instead, and for which he evicted thousands of helpless families. . . . [Another said] "I felt he *had* to be stopped. And there wasn't anyone else to stop him but us."[5]

With their youth, esprit, and conviction that it was their special mission to put an end to evils their elders had tolerated too long, the group of crusading reporters resembled their contemporaries in the Democratic reform movement, as well as members of previous reform vanguards. In addition, there were some direct connections between the reporters who led the attack upon Moses and the reformers who were seeking to take control of the Democratic party. In a special issue of *The Nation*, Fred Cook and Gene Gleason published a lengthy analysis of New York politics in general, and the Title I scandals in particular. Borrowing from Lincoln Steffens, the article was entitled "The Shame of New York," and its peroration was that the Democratic reform movement was the last, best hope for the city. The Manhattantown renewal site was located in a strong reform assembly district and the scandal surrounding the site was a central theme in the successful campaign of the reformers to gain control of the Democratic leadership of that district. Ultimately, two of the five reporters who met regularly to exchange information about Moses became personally involved in reform politics. William Haddad ran as the reform candidate against an incumbent congressman affiliated with the regular party organization, and Woody Klein served as press secretary in John Lindsay's 1965 mayoral campaign.[6]

The attack upon Moses launched by these reporters had two important and interrelated consequences. First, it undermined the legitimacy of an alliance central to sustaining New York's postwar regime—that between Moses, the press, Democratic machine politicians, and the mayor. After 1959, being publicly associated with Moses was no longer as beneficial to Mayor Wagner as it formerly had been, and because Tammany was implicated in the Title I scandals, his association with Carmine DeSapio was no longer without cost. Second, the Title I scandals drove Wagner into the arms of another element of his political support coalition, New York's elite civic associations. To avoid being sullied by the scandal, the mayor placed—at least in public—some distance between himself and Moses and identified more closely with Moses's long-time critics in those associations, particularly the Citizens Housing and Planning Council (CHPC). Wagner appointed a special consultant to devise a plan for reorganizing the city's housing programs; in turn, the consultant was advised by CHPC and his reorganization plans were endorsed by that organization.[7]

These maneuvers enabled Wagner to run as a reformer in 1961, despite the fact that the Title I scandals erupted while he was mayor. They did not, however, put an end either to Moses's political influence or to the political problems he created for the mayor. On the one hand, because he was able to retain control of his most important power base, the Triborough Bridge and Tunnel Authority, Moses remained a power with whom the mayor had to contend. He also had an unmatched record for getting things done. For these reasons, Wagner found it useful to put Moses in charge of the 1964 World's Fair. On the other hand, the city's newspapers, now on the lookout for patronage and profiteering in Moses's operations, found that the World's Fair provided them with plenty of grist for their mills.

Wagner was unable to do anything about Moses, patronage, or profiteering. This inability contributed to the image of ineffectuality that his opponents asserted characterized his entire stewardship of the city. In campaigning for mayor in 1965, John Lindsay cited Moses as one of the power brokers who really ran New York. Even more telling than Lindsay's running against Moses, however, was that *every* mayoral candidate in the 1965 primary and general elections sought to dissociate himself from Robert Moses, who had once been lauded as New York's "masterbuilder." This was an ironic reversal of what happened during the campaign to succeed Fiorello LaGuardia twenty years earlier, when every candidate for mayor pledged to keep Moses in his administration. It indicated the extent to which the journalistic wing of New York's reform vanguard contributed to the fall of one of the pillars of the city's postwar regime.

The "Advocacy Professionals"

The final attack that reformers launched against New York's postwar regime was in the realm of social welfare policy. It was spearheaded by a group of Young Turks in social work who wanted to change the ways in which the city government dealt with the poor. These "advocacy professionals," as they came to be called, were able to influence events because other political forces found they were useful allies in their own efforts to alter municipal welfare policy. However, the resistance that these reformers encountered convinced them that there were fundamental differences between the interests of the poor and the political alliances underlying the welfare policies and practices of New York's postwar regime. Their determination to fight on behalf of what they regarded as

49

the interests of the poor generated conflicts, contributing to the fragmentation of the city's governing coalition.

During the postwar period, a fairly stable pattern of alignments and cleavages had characterized the politics of welfare in New York. Efforts to get the municipal government to increase the range of services it directly provided to the poor were pressed by "secular" (though Protestant-dominated) charitable organizations, civic associations concerned with social welfare policies, good government groups, liberals, and the newspapers that expressed the views of these political forces. Such proposals were generally opposed by spokesmen for tax-conscious homeowners, the conservative newspapers, and the two major "sectarian" welfare federations—Catholic Charities and the Federation of Jewish Philanthropies. The sectarian federations commanded an extensive network of charitable institutions and wanted the municipal government to give cash relief to the poor and grant subsidies to private charitable institutions that would provide other social services to the recipients of such relief. Finally, the employees of public agencies that dealt with the poor characteristically favored expanding the functions of those agencies, but opposed any proposals that threatened what they regarded as their prerogatives as professionals—especially any that might undermine their ability to control unruly clients. Welfare policymaking during the postwar period involved a jockeying for marginal advantage among these groups. At the same time, each participant in the formulation of welfare policy recognized that public officials could not completely ignore the concerns of any of the other important political forces interested in these policies. This set of alliances, it should be noted, did not include the poor themselves.[8]

It was precisely these alliances that the Young Turks rejected. The intellectual center of their movement was Columbia University's School of Social Work, and the initial statement of its point of view was formulated by Columbia professors Richard Cloward and Lloyd Ohlin in their 1960 book, *Delinquency and Opportunity*. The authors argued that adolescents became delinquents not because they were socialized into deviant values, which was the prevailing view at the time, but because they were denied the opportunity to pursue the American value of material success through legitimate channels, which included institutions, such as public schools, that purportedly sought to help the poor. The implication of this analysis was that solving the problem of delinquency required changing how public agencies dealt with the poor.[9]

Advocacy professionals were able to influence public events for two reasons. First, in the late 1950s and early 1960s there was widespread

50

concern among New Yorkers about gang violence and delinquency on the part of black and Puerto Rican youths. This was a familiar pattern: in the late nineteenth and early twentieth centuries the city's middle and upper classes had been concerned about the problem of crime among the children of Irish, Jewish, and Italian immigrants. This concern made it politically feasible in the 1960s to secure the support of elected officials for new programs to combat juvenile delinquency.[10]

The second reason for the Columbia social workers' success was that other groups attempting to influence municipal welfare policy and having some leverage against City Hall found it useful to join forces with them. Especially important in this regard were institutions belonging to (and political forces allied with) the secular wing of the city's welfare establishment, elements of the national administration, the Ford Foundation, and, somewhat later, community activists who sought to assume leadership of the city's racial communities. These political forces first joined to establish Mobilization for Youth (MFY), a program designed to combat juvenile delinquency on Manhattan's Lower East Side.

The idea of establishing a program to deal with the problem of delinquency on the Lower East Side originated at the Henry Street Settlement House, a cornerstone of the New York secular welfare establishment. To get some of the money needed for this project, the settlement house's directors turned to the National Institute of Mental Health, the President's Committee on Juvenile Delinquency, and the Ford Foundation. These institutions insisted that MFY's programs be theoretically informed and carefully evaluated, so that those proving successful could be replicated elsewhere. They also insisted that MFY conduct its activities in collaboration with the city government, so that its programs would become part of the regular routines of municipal agencies.[11]

The Henry Street Settlement House met the first of these requirements by turning to Columbia's School of Social Work for assistance in designing, staffing, and evaluating MFY's programs. It was able to meet the second requirement because the secular welfare establishment had ties to individuals and institutions supporting the Democratic reform movement. To win reform support in the 1961 primary election, Mayor Wagner pledged to vest supervisory authority over municipal agencies performing youth services in the Office of City Administrator—"a traditional Protestant baliwick"—that sought to encourage neighborhood-based delinquency programs such as MFY.[12]

MFY, then, was founded by a coalition of political forces that became allies for a number of reasons, and once it began operations the tensions among their disparate aims became evident. MFY's community organization program was especially controversial. MFY organized or provided its staff and facilities to others who organized rent strikes, a school boycott for racial integration, demonstrations at construction sites demanding that more blacks and Puerto Ricans be hired in the building trades, and a campaign to establish a civilian review board to hear complaints of police brutality.

The actions of MFY's community organization program aroused furious opposition. In January 1964, after a group of Puerto Rican mothers organized by MFY called for the removal of a school principal who had adamantly rejected some modest requests they had made earlier, the principals of twenty-six schools on the Lower East Side counterattacked with a public statement accusing MFY of waging "a war against individual schools and their leaders," and of employing "full-time paid agitators and organizers for extremist groups." In August 1964, the *New York Daily News*—a tabloid with the largest circulation of any newspaper in the city—launched a crusade against MFY, beginning with a story claiming that the program was "under intensive Federal and city investigation as a suspected Red honeycomb for leftists who have used its facilities—and juveniles—to foment rent strikes and racial disorders."[13]

It is not surprising that MFY was viewed by its opponents as seditious because it violated a number of tacit compromises among members of New York's postwar coalition. In the first place, a few members of MFY's staff indeed were, or formerly had been, Communists. An FBI loyalty check of MFY employees requested by the city after the publication of the *Daily News* story revealed that two currently belonged to the Communist party itself, one was a member of the Maoist Progressive Labor Movement, and one belonged to the Trotskyite Socialist Workers party. In addition, approximately fifteen MFY employees (the precise number was a matter of sharp dispute) had, during the 1930s and 1940s, engaged in precisely those sorts of activities for which civil servants had gotten into trouble or had been fired during the height of the McCarthy era, such as attending festivals sponsored by Communist youth organizations, or sending May Day greetings to the *Daily Worker*.[14]

The critics of MFY also regarded its community organizers as troublemakers because they mobilized poor blacks and Puerto Ricans, who occupied a peripheral position in New York's postwar regime, against the social welfare agencies that had supplanted the machine as the chief institution linking the poor to the city's political system. To the bureaucrats who staffed these agencies, the efforts of advocacy professionals to alter how city agencies dealt with their clients were intolerable. The reformers threatened to undermine the rather fragile authority the bureaucrats exercised over their clients, an authority they regarded as a prerequisite for doing their jobs. It was small wonder, then, that the twenty-six school principals who denounced MFY regarded its community organizers as, in their words, "agitators" who were "warring" on the schools.

The crusade against MFY for harboring subversives and stirring up trouble terrified the Wagner administration. It was precisely the sort of attack that liberal politicians in New York had attempted to defend themselves against ever since the 1940s by instituting loyalty-security programs of their own.[15] Within hours of the publication of the *Daily News*'s exposé, City Council President Paul Screvane, the chairman of New York's Anti-Poverty Operations Board, announced that the city was conducting an investigation of its own and that he "would have to consider very carefully the continuance of this kind of program if it is infiltrated with people of leftist leanings."[16]

A split developed within MFY over how it should respond to this attack. Its board of directors, dominated by members of the private and public welfare establishment, saw the attack as a threat to the agency's existence. They were prepared to conduct an inquiry of their own into the charges and to cooperate with investigations being conducted by the city and a state legislative committee. MFY's staff, on the other hand, regarded the charge that the agency employed subversives and agitators as a transparent effort to destroy its most innovative program—community organizing. Any concessions to the agency's critics that involved scuttling the community organization program or firing personnel who sympathized with the cause of the downtrodden were considered by staff members as totally inconsistent with MFY's mission and therefore totally unacceptable.[17]

The controversy generated by MFY, then, divided the coalition that had established the organization and led its staff to conclude that there were fundamental conflicts of interest between the poor and the social welfare bureaucracies, the private welfare establishment, and elected officials. Of course, the 350 members of MFY's staff did not carry much weight in New York City politics. Nonetheless, the controversy surrounding the organization was significant. One reason was that it was covered extensively in the press and created quite a stir in New York's liberal community. The defense of civil liberties is probably the cause closest to the hearts of liberal intellectuals—and political activists who regard themselves as intellectuals—so Wagner's and Screvane's efforts to placate conservatives who claimed that civil rights demonstrations and rent strikes were fomented by MFY agitators led liberal and reform Democrats

53

to turn against them. The reform Democrats, who had reluctantly supported Wagner in 1961, strongly opposed his designated heir, Screvane. In the 1965 Democratic mayoral primary, reform candidate William Fitts Ryan made a major issue of Screvane's participation in the attack on MFY. John Lindsay, the fusion mayoral candidate in the 1965 general election, warmly endorsed MFY's community action program and this contributed to his support in reform quarters after Ryan lost in the Democratic primary.[18]

Another factor that made the controversy surrounding MFY significant was that it did not represent an isolated incident. After the enactment of the federal anti-poverty program in 1964, the major points at issue in the MFY episode arose on a broader scale. The extent to which local community action agencies should be subject to control by City Hall was a major source of controversy, as was the question of whether they should confine their activities to delivering social services to the poor or pursue a strategy of community mobilization, organization, and protest. Conflicts surrounding these issues roughly followed the sequence that had occurred earlier in the case of MFY. Initially, organizations belonging to the secular wing of the welfare establishment joined with activist social workers, black community organizers, and the staff of the federal Office of Economic Opportunity to advocate that neighborhood community action agencies be granted substantial autonomy to appoint personnel and engage in activities of their own choosing. This was done because decentralization and the support of these neighborhood allies provided the secular charitable organizations with a means to circumvent the substantial influence that their sectarian opponents exercised at the center of the city's political system. Wagner and Screvane, however, resisted decentralization and its likely corollary, community organization. They recognized—presciently—that the political mobilization of poor blacks could generate intense conflicts that their political coalition would be unable to contain, thereby threatening the very survival of the pluralist system.[19]

Activist social workers were more than willing to threaten the survival of the pluralist system, because the resistance encountered by MFY in its efforts to advocate the cause of the poor had convinced them that the agreements underlying Wagner's social welfare policies were struck at the expense of those at the bottom of the city's social structure. As with the MFY controversy, the stance taken by the advocacy professionals was not in itself of great consequence in the city's politics. The professionals did, however, establish an organization of black and Puerto Rican community activists who demanded that control of the city's poverty programs be turned over to representatives of the poor, and the issues they raised led other, more powerful, interests to turn against the Wagner administration.

The reform Democrats were the first major political group to share the advocacy professionals' view of the controversy over the poverty program. The reform Committee for Democratic Voters issued a statement in 1965 asserting that welfare agencies "perpetuate poverty" and that the anti-poverty program should be run by people at the grassroots level. The reformers regarded City Hall's efforts to retain control over the poverty program as an indication of Wagner's and Screvane's commitment to the status quo. By 1965 this issue had supplanted "bossism" as the chief concern of the city's Democratic reform movement.[20]

More significant, the organizations and the publications that expressed elite opinion in New York joined with their traditional allies in the secular wing of the city's welfare establishment to call for greater "community participation" in the poverty program. Wagner and Screvane sought to placate these forces by increasing the representation of secular welfare agencies on the committee that nominally supervised the city's poverty program. The powers of this committee were rather limited, however, and hence this concession was not satisfactory to these political forces. In response, the administration found it necessary to make a number of additional concessions, which ultimately gave the secular welfare establishment a substantial role in the administration of the city's poverty program. This suggested that the Wagner administration was no longer in command of events. Moreover, concessions to secular charitable organizations did not placate the advocacy professionals and black activists who wanted control of the poverty program placed in their own hands, not simply in those of another wing of the city's welfare establishment. Therefore, these concessions did not end the vehement protests against the Wagner administration's policies.[21]

The continuation and escalation of this turmoil ultimately drove a wedge between the secular welfare establishment and many of their traditional allies among New York's civic and business elites. Making marginal adjustments in the policies that had characterized municipal welfare policy during the postwar period was no longer very successful in linking poor blacks and Puerto Ricans to the city's political system. This, in turn, suggested that it might be advisable to completely refashion the city's welfare policies and, correlatively, put together a new coalition of political forces in this field. Mayor Wagner's commitment to—and his reluctance to make more than marginal adjustments in—the city's then current policies for dealing with the poor prevented him from taking the lead in such an endeavor. By contrast, John Lindsay, as his political ads announced, appeared "fresh, while everyone else is tired." Lindsay's promise to forge new links between the municipal government and the nonwhite poor contributed to the willingness of many members of New York's civic and business elite to abandon the political forces with which they formerly had been allied and to put their money (in some instances, quite literally) on the policy experiments and the political experiments Lindsay proposed to conduct.

There were a number of similarities between the attacks upon New York's social welfare establishment in the early and mid-1960s and the attacks against the city's regular Democratic party organizations and the empire of Robert Moses, which reached a peak at roughly the same time. Each attack was initiated by young men and women who regarded the compromises underlying New York's pluralist regime as morally indefensible, and whose youth and ardor made them willing to fight in the face of apparently great odds. Their attacks in themselves were not all that dangerous to the dominant political actors and institutions of New York's postwar regime. These reform vanguards became dangerous, however, when they were able to convince important elements of New York's civic elite that it was feasible to dispense with many of the compromises they had made with politicians and organizations representing other social strata. Their rejection of these compromises expressed itself in the civic elites' view that Mayor Wagner, though well-meaning, was indecisive and a vacillator. Thus the very techniques of delay and compromise that had enabled Mayor Wagner to hold together a heterogeneous political coalition for twelve years came to be regarded by some of his former supporters as grounds for opposing him.

Business Elites

During the 1960s, members of New York's business elite also became unhappy with the policies and practices of the municipal government. This occurred for reasons resembling those of businessmen who had joined earlier reform crusades. They were concerned about the incumbent administration's capacity to pursue policies regarded by the business elite as necessary if the city's economy were to prosper, and they were appalled at what they considered to be the mayor's mismanagement of municipal finances. These problems were exacerbated by the changes in the structure of the city's politics brought about by Mayor Wagner's successful bid for a third term. Consequently, many members of New York's business elite came to regard the installation of a new administration backed by a new political coalition to be a prerequisite for setting the city's house in order.

The early 1960s were years of both hope and fear for those with the largest stake in the health of New York's central business district. This was a period of unprecedented prosperity in the United States (and in the Western world as a whole) and of sustained growth for America's great national and multinational corporations. The question was whether New York would reap the benefits of this prosperity.[22]

The sense that New York was at a crossroads and that steps would have to be taken to ensure that it would proceed down the correct path was most acute among the executives of firms that for one reason or another could not readily leave New York, and whose fortunes varied with the health of the city's economy. Chief among them were the owners and developers of real estate and office buildings in the central business district and firms whose customers were national corporations. These firms—namely, commercial and investment banks, law firms, advertising agencies, accounting firms, and so forth—depended upon face-to-face communications with their customers and with one another. In addition, they were not indifferent to the health of the city's manu-facturing sector because they depended upon a large clerical workforce, recruited primarily from among the daughters of the city's working and middle classes. Finally, newspapers, public utilities, and retailers also had a stake in the prosperity of the city's economy because the volume of their business was dependent upon the middle class remaining in New York.[23]

There were a variety of policies that the business community wanted the municipal government to pursue or abandon to make it profitable for national corporations to locate in New York and for manufacturing firms to remain in the city. Despite these imperatives, in their view the Wagner administration was either mired in inaction or committed to practices that were counterproductive.

Capital Infrastructure

If New York's office district were to grow, transportation facilities had to be improved so that it would be possible for more people to commute from their homes, land had to be available for the construction of new office buildings, and housing had to be available for the employees of firms located in the business district. Prominent leaders of the Wall Street business community advocated the construction of a number of projects designed to accomplish these purposes.

The two most important transportation projects business leaders endorsed were a new subway line on Manhattan's Upper East Side and the Lower Manhattan Expressway. The subway would provide a link between an area of the city experiencing a boom in the construction of luxury housing and the downtown office district. Mayor Wagner recognized the benefits of such a project, and in 1955 the city floated $500 million in bonds to construct a new Second Avenue subway line. But his administration spent the money for other purposes—just as the Tammany administrations of the 1920s had done with money they had borrowed to build a tunnel between Brooklyn and Staten Island and a bridge between the northern tip of Manhattan and the Bronx.

In 1965, the Downtown-Lower Manhattan Association (DLMA)—an organization of banks and other financial institutions, real estate firms, and corporations located in the Wall Street area—projected that over the next ten years the number of persons working in Lower Manhattan would increase by 50,000 to 75,000. Desperate to find some way of getting those people to work, it commissioned a study of the feasibility of extending the Lexington Avenue subway line to the Battery. This was a second-best solution, however, and Mayor Wagner's frittering away of a half-billion dollars earmarked for the Second Avenue subway led them to conclude that the municipal government under his stewardship was drifting, rather than rising to the challenges that confronted it.[24]

The other major transportation project the DLMA advocated—the Lower Manhattan Expressway—would serve a number of purposes. Most important, by providing a direct link between the Holland Tunnel (which crosses the Hudson river) and the bridges spanning the East river, it would enable trucks and automobiles to travel between New Jersey, on the one side, and Brooklyn, Queens, and Long Island, on the other, without congesting the streets of Lower Manhattan. It also would remove from the streets trucks that moved goods to and from the loft district north of the proposed expressway and serve as a barrier to the movement of manufacturing firms downtown. Finally, the expressway would make it easier for office workers to commute by automobile to the downtown financial district.[25]

Although the expressway had been incorporated into the city's highway map in 1945, it was not until 1959 that a complete set of plans was submitted to the Board of Estimate, and it was only in 1962 that a request to begin acquisition of property for the highway was submitted to the Board. By this time, the residents and small businessmen who would be displaced by the project had mobilized against it. They were joined by a number of civic associations that argued that the proposed elevated highway would ruin the surrounding neighborhood and should be built below ground. In December 1962, the Board of Estimate gave in to the opposition. In May 1965, however, Mayor Wagner—under strong pressure from Robert Moses, the leader of the Central Trades and Labor Council, and the DLMA—reversed himself and announced that work on the elevated highway would begin immediately. Five months later, in the face of pressure from the civic associations, the mayor changed his position once again and proposed that the highway be built under ground. This vacillation convinced both proponents and opponents of an elevated highway that the Wagner administration was incapable of pursuing policies that served the public at-large in the face of opposition from what, in their respective views, were self-interested political forces.[26]

The DLMA initiated or supported a number of other projects—among them the World Trade Center and several urban renewal projects—that would use the authority and resources of the government to increase office space downtown and build housing and other amenities for people who worked in the downtown office district. The history of the projects undertaken by the city, however, was similar to that of the Lower Manhattan Expressway. The Wagner administration announced its intention of proceeding with them, but for various reasons—among them its tendency to cave in to opposition—the projects were modified and delayed time and again. (For example, in 1961 the city announced plans to build a new wholesale food market at the Bronx's Hunts Point and to construct luxury housing on the site of the old Washington market, adjacent to the financial district. Four years later, not a single building had yet been erected on the old market site and 38.5 acres of prime real estate lay barren.) By contrast, John Lindsay promised to centralize all housing and redevelopment functions in a single superagency, headed by a housing "czar," and thereby overcome such delays.[27]

Although many executives in the downtown office district wanted to exclude manufacturers and other small businesses from land that was attractive to firms in their own sector of New York's economy, they did not necessarily wish to drive these businesses from the city entirely. They were well aware that these firms were a major source of employment for the city's working and lower-middle-class population. If these businesses left New York many of these families would leave as well—and with them would go the pool of young women from which they recruited their office personnel. Those who were less able to leave the city—chiefly nonwhites—would be left jobless, creating all the social problems that accompanied unemployment.

To keep businesses in New York, the Wagner administration established a Department of Commerce and Industrial Development in 1962, whose stated mission was to "foster, retain, attract, and expand business, industry, and commerce in the city."[28] Three industrial parks were planned in addition to a revolving fund which would have provided small businesses with the financing they needed to modernize their equipment and expand their facilities. By 1965, however, little had come of these efforts: the industrial parks had not progressed beyond the planning stage, and loans had been extended to fewer than a dozen businesses.

Despairing of the Wagner administration's ability to solve this problem, in March 1965 the presidents of the DLMA, the Chamber of Commerce, and the Commerce and Industry Association appointed a committee of fourteen leading businessmen—among them the presidents of Chase Manhattan Bank, New York Life Insurance Company, Standard Oil of New Jersey, and Consolidated Edison—to establish a privately financed and operated business development corporation. The creation by business leaders of a private organization to perform public functions indicated their belief that the incumbent administration was not meeting one of its fundamental responsibilities. Historically, such endeavors were preludes to reform campaigns.[29]

Anatomy of a Fiscal Crisis

During Mayor Wagner's third term, organizations representing New York's business elite became increasingly unhappy with the city's fiscal practices, as well as with its development policies. The view of these organizations was that the Wagner administration's fiscal sins grew increasingly egregious during the mayor's third term, but were not without precedent in his first two terms. In an apparent effort to raise the issue of municipal finances in the 1961 mayoral election, the Chamber of Commerce in December 1960 and the Citizens Budget Commission in February 1961 published detailed analyses of budget trends demonstrating that local expenditures and taxes were increasing more rapidly than the ability of the city's residents to bear these burdens. The publication of these analyses did not, however, spark a taxpayers' rebellion. To the contrary, the political upheaval of 1961 loosened a number of previous restraints on municipal budgetary inflation.[30]

Mayor Wagner's break with the leaders of New York's county Democratic organizations on the eve of his campaign for a third term increased his dependence upon expenditure-demanding political forces—most notably, the Liberal party, civil service unions, and civic associations such as the United Parents Association—and greatly weakened his administration's ties to the homeowners and small business interests whose sensitivity to taxation had placed some limits on the pace of expenditure increases during the mayor's first two terms. This helps explain why locally financed municipal expenditures rose twice as rapidly during Wagner's third term as during his first and second terms (see figure 5.1, page 114). To finance these expenditures, the Wagner administration was compelled to raise municipal taxes. In 1963 the sales tax was raised from 3 to 4 percent—the first such increase in twelve years—and the base of the city tax on commercial rents was broadened and rates increased so that its yield went up by 800 percent.

During its third term, the Wagner administration also relied increasingly on accounting "gimmicks" to balance the city's budget. For example, the city advanced the collection dates of some taxes that were due on July 1, 1965 (the first day of the 1965–66 fiscal year), to June 30, 1965 (the last day of the previous fiscal year), gaining $45 million in tax revenues to balance its 1964–65 budget. This seemingly painless way of balancing the budget came at a price, however. First, the additional revenues would not be available to balance the 1965–66 budget, and second, in order to use revenues that would not be received until June 30, 1965, to cover expenses occurring before that date, the city would have to borrow money (by issuing tax anticipation notes) and pay interest on the money it borrowed. The other fiscal gimmicks that the Wagner administration relied on further compounded the problem of balancing the budget in future years and required that the city borrow additional funds.[31]

This record of fiscal legerdemain culminated in the procedure the Wagner administration devised to raise the $250 million it needed to close its 1965–66 budget gap. The mayor sought to generate the necessary revenues by increasing real estate taxes; to do so, however, required amending the provision in the state constitution that placed a limit on the city's property tax rate. This created a problem because constitutional amendments had to be approved by the state assembly and senate in two successive legislative sessions, and then had to receive the support of the voters in a referendum. Even if Wagner's proposed constitutional amendment survived each of these tests, it would be two years before the city could collect the additional real estate taxes the mayor wanted. Therefore, to balance the 1965–66 budget, the administration proposed selling municipal securities that would be redeemed with the tax revenues the city would collect two years hence. This proposal was considered

61

unsound in financial circles not only because it involved financing current expenditures with future revenues, but also because there was no assurance that the state legislature and the electorate would approve the administration's proposed constitutional amendment. It was by no means certain that the city would have the tax revenues in 1967 necessary to redeem the notes it issued in 1965.

The fiscal policies and practices of Mayor Wagner's third administration generated a firestorm of opposition within the city's business community. The *New York Times* described the controversy over the tax increases the mayor had proposed in 1963 as an "uproar lasting two months."[32] The city's increasing reliance on accounting gimmicks and short-term borrowing aroused an equally shrill response: the Citizens Budget Commission (CBC) entitled its 1963 annual report "New York at the Crossroads," and its 1964 report "Hurricane Watch." By November 1964, the CBC was prepared to declare that the city was in the midst of a full-scale fiscal crisis.[33]

Why did spokesmen for New York's business community react so strongly to the Wagner administration's fiscal practices? One reason was that borrowing to finance current expenditures added the cost of interest to the goods and services the city purchased, and when the city began redeeming its notes by borrowing additional funds, it found itself in the position of paying interest on interest. Another reason was that New York's unorthodox financial practices led the bond rating agencies to lower the city's credit rating, which increased the interest rates the city had to pay to sell its securities and lowered the price of its outstanding bonds. This was of great concern to New York's major banks because, in the early 1960s, Comptroller Abe Beame had implemented a change in the city's debt management policies that involved purchasing corporate securities rather than New York City bonds for the city's pension funds. The pension funds' holdings of New York City bonds were sold largely to the major Wall Street banks. This greatly increased the stake of New York's financial community in the value of the city's outstanding securities and their distress over policies that lowered the price of city bonds.[34]

New York's business community was also appalled at the city's deficit financing because it involved an effort to evade any limitations whatever upon the growth of municipal expenditures. As long as the city was compelled to balance its budget, the rate of expenditure growth was limited by its political capacity to raise taxes. Although Mayor Wagner secured enactment of the tax increases he proposed in 1963, his victory was not costless. One hundred twenty-five witnesses testified against the mayor's proposals at hearings before the City Council, whereas only two were prepared to testify on behalf of the proposals. Comptroller Beame, seeing an opportunity to profit politically from this dissatisfaction, broke ranks with the mayor and proposed his own package of tax increases and expenditure reductions to balance the budget. These were the sort of costs politicians do not happily incur, and Wagner's borrowing schemes were an effort to reap the benefits of higher municipal expenditures without having to bear them. Even more serious, if the mayor's 1965 plan to borrow against a future increase in real estate taxes were enacted, business groups would be placed in an impossible situation. If they fought against the tax increase, the city might not be able to pay back the money it borrowed and could be driven into bankruptcy. It was not surprising, then, that the CBC denounced Mayor Wagner's proposal as "financial blackmail."[35]

The business community considered the city's finances to be in a state of crisis not only because its problems were severe, but also because their source was very deep. In a statement explaining why it lowered New York's credit rating Moody's Investors' Service asserted, "There is increasing evidence that over the years the city government has tended to succumb to the pressure of special interests and minority groups thus permitting spending to get out of hand."[36] The most detailed analysis from a business point of view of the source of the city's financial problems, however, was issued by the Citizens Budget Commission in November 1964 in a publication entitled "Anatomy of a Fiscal Crisis."[37]

The CBC argued that there were four major sources of the city's fiscal crisis. The first, a steady growth in the number of municipal employees, reflected the administration's failure to allocate resources rationally—by balancing payroll increases in high priority programs, such as education or police patrol, with reductions in low priority programs. The second problem was the administration's increasing tendency to overestimate its revenues and underestimate its expenditures when making up its budget; revenue shortfalls and expenditure overruns, in turn, led the government to rely on borrowed funds to get through the fiscal year. A third source was the administration's failure to take into account the economic consequences of the taxes it levied; the CBC pointed to recent increases in the commercial occupancy and sales taxes in the face of warnings that these would drive businesses from the city. Finally, the report asserted that there was a breakdown in the city's economic machinery. In particular, the City Administrator's office, which had been created to upgrade municipal management and rationalize municipal administration—by establishing programmatic priorities, eliminating waste and duplication, and introducing long-range financial planning—found itself powerless to do the job for which it had been established.

The sources of fiscal imprudence cited by Moody's and the CBC reflected the political coalition underlying the Wagner administration. The municipal government was vulnerable to the pressure of "special interests and minority groups" and levied taxes that the CBC regarded as dangerous, because Mayor Wagner depended upon the political support of a broad array of service-demanding interests. The mayor did not cut the payroll of agencies administering low priority programs or provide the City Administrator with the political backing he would need to change established bureaucratic routines because city employees were a key element in his political coalition. Finally, many of the budgetary powers that the CBC believed the mayor used unwisely—such as the power to estimate general fund revenues—had been granted by the 1961 city charter, the enactment of which was linked to the reorganization of Wagner's political coalition that year.

Because New York City's financial problems were so deeply grounded, only thorough-going remedies would suffice to deal with them. The CBC argued that the municipal government could no longer muddle through as it had in the past because local taxes were increasing considerably faster than the ability of the city's residents to pay them. The CBC and other spokesmen for the downtown business community called for substantial changes in municipal financial policy, some of which were reminiscent of steps taken to cope with the New York City fiscal crisis of 1932–34. To deal with the city's immediate problems in 1964–65, the CBC urged that the current budget be reopened and expenditures be cut enough to bring it genuinely into balance—something that had not been done since the reopening of the 1933–34 budget. To deal with longer-range problems, the CBC and other business organizations advocated a revision in the city's expenditure patterns and revenue structure. Programs designed to attract firms to the city should be given top priority, the CBC argued, and it and the Chamber of Commerce urged that steps be taken to generate continuing economies, especially in personnel costs. As for municipal revenues, the CBC and the Chamber called for a reduction in the city's general business tax (the gross receipts tax), or better still, its replacement with a tax that was less likely to drive firms from the city. Lastly, the CBC and Moody's called for an end to using municipal tax revenues to subsidize the fifteen-cent subway fare, which had become as much of a sacred cow, Moody's noted, as the five-cent fare had been in the 1920s and 1930s.[38]

To bring about these changes, New York's leading business organizations took action that again was reminiscent of behavior during the fiscal crisis of the 1930s. For one, they sought to work out a common position and present a united front on questions of municipal financial policy. This endeavor was not institutionalized in a new umbrella association— as had been the case when the Chamber of Commerce, Merchants Association, and Real Estate Board had founded the Citizens Budget Commission in 1932—but the Chamber and CBC did jointly sponsor studies of the economic effects of municipal taxes and issued a series of reports urging changes in the city's budgetary procedures and financial policies. And in an effort to gain some official or quasi-official stature for their warnings about the dangers of the city's current policies and their proposals to alter them, the CBC, Real Estate Board, and twelve other business and civic groups called upon Mayor Wagner to establish a nonpartisan commission of distinguished citizens to study the city's finances. After the storm of opposition that had been aroused by his increases in the sales and commercial occupancy taxes, Mayor Wagner saw this proposal as an opportunity to share some of the responsibility for making unpopular choices between tax increases and expenditure reductions, and therefore established the Temporary Commission on City Finances (TCCF). The composition and mission of the TCCF, along with the impetus for its creation, were similar to the Municipal Economic Commission established by Mayor John P. O'Brien in 1933.[39]

To the extent that the Wagner administration's financial policies were constrained by the composition of its political base, there were sharp limits to how far it could go in responding to the proposals of the city's business leaders. For this reason they had an interest in seeing Wagner replaced by a mayor who would find it politically possible to implement the economies they believed were imperative. The newspapers most closely associated with the city's business elite—the *Times, Herald Tribune,* and *Wall Street Journal*—were quite clear on this score. The *Times,* for example, asserted in its editorials that municipal finance was the most important issue in the 1965 mayoral election, and that the history of fiscal mismanagement over the preceeding decade was the most important reason for putting an end to the one-party Democratic rule that had brought the city to the verge of bankruptcy.[40]

John Lindsay appealed to this sentiment in several ways. He repeatedly criticized the Wagner administration's reliance upon borrowing to balance its expense budget; he promised to squeeze $300 to $400 million in "fat" from the city budget; and he claimed that by thoroughly reorganizing the municipal government and engaging in long-range financial planning rather than "crisis budgeting," continuing budgetary savings could be achieved. Lindsay never explained exactly where he would cut the budget, but his repeated attacks upon the "power brokers" made it clear that he intended to adopt the sort of economy measures the CBC and Chamber had advocated—namely, eliminating redundant municipal programs, reducing expenditures on low priority programs, and implementing managerial reforms, even if this meant cutting the number of employees in some city agencies and altering the bureaucracy's cherished work routines. Although the CBC remained officially neutral during the 1965 mayoral campaign, it made little effort to conceal its jubilation after Lindsay's victory. Whereas the annual report it had issued ten months before the election had been titled "Hurricane Watch," the one it published two months after Lindsay's victory was called "The New in New York." In it, a cartoon showed a fresh Mayor Lindsay going off to City Hall where he would face a gang of thugs carrying clubs labeled "debt," "taxes," "slums," and the like. While business organizations did not endorse candidates in 1965, it is likely that Lindsay's promise to reform the city's finances goes a good deal of the way toward explaining the support he received from prominent individuals in the business community.[41]

Although Lindsay promised to balance the city's budget, he never stated that he would reduce its total size. To the contrary, he proposed many new and costly programs during his campaign, and his opponents attacked him for failing to explain how he intended to finance these expenditures. (Even the *Times*, which strongly endorsed Lindsay, chided him on this score.) However, organizations such as the CBC and the Chamber of Commerce—to say nothing of the *Times*—did not object to increasing expenditures on "high priority" programs such as education, nor did they insist that the city stop levying new taxes. Rather, they argued that sound budgetary practice involved covering some of the costs of new programs with cuts elsewhere in the budget and covering the remainder by levying taxes that would do the least damage to the economy. Lindsay's failure to acknowledge during his campaign that new taxes almost certainly would have to be levied to balance the city's budget was rather similar to LaGuardia's silence on this score during his 1933 campaign. The LaGuardia precedent, however, was a promising one—within months of taking office LaGuardia's administration had restored New York's credit by cutting the salaries of municipal employees, financing relief with the proceeds of new taxes rather than with borrowed funds, and thereby balancing the city's budget.[42]

There were nonetheless significant differences between the 1965 and earlier fusion campaigns in the role played by fiscal crises and business elites. The 1965 fiscal crisis was less severe than the crises of 1871 and

1932–33. Although the city had to pay higher interest rates to sell its bonds, it was not frozen out of the capital market. Because New York retained its access to the market, the city's bankers were not in a position to compel the municipal government to balance its budget by taking a series of politically disastrous steps. Finally, businessmen did not play as large a role in the 1965 fusion movement as they had in earlier reform campaigns. A citizens committee of prominent businessmen was not organized in 1965 to lead a crusade against the machine and to select a slate of candidates. Rather than providing the occasion for a full-scale "insurrection of the capitalists," the 1965 fiscal crisis simply detached one more group from the coalition that previously had supported (or tolerated) New York's postwar regime, and decreased the Wagner administration's legitimacy by making it appear to be incapable of fully meeting its obligations in one more area of policy.

Blacks

As the 1960s progressed, racial issues came to play an increasingly prominent role in New York politics. As late as 1961 these issues had yet to penetrate the municipal electoral arena. By 1965, however, three issues involving blacks evoked controversy in the municipal campaign: the demand that students be bused to reduce school segregation, that a civilian review board be created to hear charges of police brutality, and that neighborhood groups in black ghettos be given greater control over the city's poverty program. These issues sharply divided the political coalition sustaining New York's postwar regime, just as issues pertaining to the municipal government's relations to recently arrived European immigrant groups had played an important role in earlier reform campaigns.

School desegregation was the first issue to emerge. In the late 1950s and early 1960s, civil rights groups in black neighborhoods pressed the Board of Education to zone new schools to foster integration, but it was not until 1963–64 that large numbers of people throughout the city became involved in the controversy over school desegregation and that conflicts over this issue became bitter. In May 1963, the state commissioner of education instructed the Board of Education to submit a plan for integrating all schools in the city in which the student body was more than 50 percent black. Civil rights groups pressed the Board to implement such a plan. Later that year, opponents of school busing established a new organization, Parents and Taxpayers (PAT), and chapters sprang up all over the city. Proponents of school integration conducted a one-day, citywide school boycott in February 1964 and more selective boycotts during the remainder of the school year. Not to be outdone, their opponents sponsored a large rally at City Hall in March 1964 and a school boycott of their own in September 1964.[43]

The controversy over school desegregation split New York's governing coalition three ways. On one side were civil rights groups and most organizations within the city's liberal community, among them the Jewish community relations agencies, the Protestant Council, and the Citizens Committee for Children. At the other pole were defenders of the neighborhood school; the leading organization in this camp was PAT. The middle ground was occupied by the United Parents Association, the Public Education Association, and the United Federation of Teachers (UFT). These organizations had a very substantial stake in the city's school system, and though they advocated racial integration (the UFT even encouraged its members to honor the picket lines during the school boycott of March 1964), they counseled against precipitate action that might lead white parents to withdraw their children from the schools. They also opposed those demands of civil rights groups that threatened the prerogatives of their members or the gains they had achieved through their privileged access to the Board of Education.[44]

The controversy over the proposal to create a civilian review board (CRB) to deal with charges of police brutality emerged later than the dispute over school integration. The charge that the police used undue force in their contacts with blacks was first raised by civil rights groups in 1964, and in April of that year a city councilman belonging to the Democratic reform movement, Theodore Weiss, introduced a bill to establish an independent review board—in contrast to the existing panel, all of whose members were employees of the police department—to hear such complaints. This proposal immediately became a central focus of civil rights agitation in the city and was supported in varying degrees by elite civic associations and liberal organizations, including the City Club, the New York Bar Association's Committee on Administrative Law, the Civil Rights Committee of the New York County Lawyers Association, the American Civil Liberties Union, the Liberal party, and the Protestant Council's Office of Church and Race. Opposition to the proposal was spearheaded by the Patrolman's Benevolent Association. Police Commissioner Michael Murphy also spoke out in defense of the department's existing procedures, and his position was backed by the Conservative party and by the Chamber of Commerce and the Commerce and Industry Association.[45]

The major difference between the rifts generated by the demands of civil rights activists for school integration and for a civilian review board was that there was less substantial organized backing for a compromise position on the latter issue. The employees of the police department were more adamant in their opposition to the CRB than were the employees of the school system to proposals for racial integration. Also, the police department had no organized clientele groups akin to the United Parents Association or the Public Education Association that had ties both to the department and to New York's civic elite. Consequently, Commissioner Murphy faced intolerable cross-pressures. On the one side, the mayor and city council, anxious to preserve civil harmony and the Democratic electoral coalition, wanted to make at least some token concessions to the proponents of a CRB; on the other, the PBA would not countenance even verbal concessions—it demanded that the commissioner "support" its members, who put their lives on the line every day. Unable to reconcile the two sets of demands, Commissioner Murphy resigned. His successor, Vincent Broderick, proposed some minor changes in the department's procedures for handling complaints, but these satisfied neither side and the issue remained alive through the 1965 mayoral campaign.[46]

Conflicts over the structure of the city's poverty program were also quite divisive. As noted earlier, the groups pressing the Wagner administration for greater decentralization of the poverty program initially included the secular wing of the city's welfare establishment and its allies in the press, advocacy professionals, black community activists, and the reform Democrats. In addition, some powerful figures in Washington—namely, Sargent Shriver, director of the Office of Economic Opportunity, and Congressman Adam Clayton Powell, chairman of the House Education and Labor Committee, which had jurisdiction over the poverty program—pressed the Wagner administration to grant substantial autonomy to neighborhood community action agencies, as did leading Republicans in the city and state who wanted to keep the patronage generated by the poverty program out of the hands of Democratic politicians in City Hall. Support for the administration's position came from sectarian welfare agencies and white politicians in racially mixed neighborhoods who did not relish community action agencies' conducting drives to register black and Puerto Rican voters in their districts. Although this issue aroused considerable passion in those quarters, there is little evidence that rank-and-file voters who vehemently opposed school busing or the creation of a civilian review board were particularly concerned about the structure of the city's poverty program.[47]

It was precisely because racial issues had the potential for dividing the coalition of forces that sustained New York's postwar regime that public officials and party politicians sought to prevent them from becoming matters of political contention. Mayor Wagner attempted to continue this approach throughout his third term. On the most contentious issue of all, school integration and busing, he simply remained silent, maintaining that the Board of Education was an independent agency over which he had no jurisdiction. Wagner sought to defuse the controversy over the civilian review board through a strategy of delegation, delay, and marginal concessions. When the issue was first raised in 1964, he commissioned Deputy Mayor James Cavanaugh to review how satisfactorily the police department had handled recent allegations of brutality. After Cavanaugh issued his report, Wagner commissioned yet another study—this time, he appointed a committee to review the deputy mayor's findings! From that date in the summer of 1964 to the end of his term, the mayor steered clear of the police brutality controversy.[48]

Wagner's—and Screvane's—behavior on the antipoverty issue appears to be an exception to this pattern, but it is an exception that proves the rule. The mayor and city council president played leading roles in establishing an antipoverty apparatus dominated by municipal officials, and for a considerable period they refused to modify this set-up, publicly defending it against attacks by critics who claimed that it failed to provide for sufficient participation by the poor. Indeed, for a time Screvane maintained this stance even after it was clearly costing him support among the reform Democrats whose votes he needed to win the 1965 mayoral primary. However, Wagner's and Screvane's very commitment to a set of political arrangements that were structured to prevent the emergence of racially divisive issues is what led them to confront this particular issue head on.

During Mayor Wagner's third term, the techniques that had formerly succeeded in placating blacks and avoiding racial confrontations no longer worked. The battles over school desegregation and the civilian review board raged without the mayor's participation, and at least some elements of the city's black community attacked Wagner for his very failure to involve himself in these issues. In particular, all sixteen chapters of the Congress of Racial Equality (CORE) in New York issued a statement in the spring of 1965 announcing their unalterable opposition to the mayor's reelection. Their chief complaint against him was precisely that he sought to avoid involving himself in racial controversies. CORE denounced this as "apathy," and as indicative of his "disregard for the Negro and Puerto Rican communities." As for disputes surrounding the poverty program, Wagner and Screvane made a succession of concessions to the advocates of greater community control, but these were regarded as too little and too late by the administration's critics.[49]

What accounts for the failure during the 1960s of the mechanisms that previously had worked to contain racially divisive issues and for the subsequent mobilization of blacks (and of other groups as well) against the Wagner administration? Political developments occurring outside New York's borders contributed to this. In particular, the eruption of the civil rights movement in the South brought about the emergence and radicalization of a new generation of black leaders who, like their counterparts among previous ethnic groups, regarded the terms upon which their group had been integrated into the city's political system (or, to use their vocabulary, the "white power structure") as unacceptable. Significantly, the three major racial issues of the early 1960s—school integration, the civilian review board, and decentralization of the poverty program—were *not* raised by black elected officials. With only one exception, such officials did not play a central role in these controversies even after they erupted. (The exception was Adam Clayton Powell, who was a major actor in the dispute over the poverty program, but Powell was important less by virtue of his local standing than because he was chairman of the House committee that had jurisdiction over the program.)

The spectacle of their brothers and sisters rising up against segregation in the South galvanized black citizens in New York, as in other northern cities, by suggesting that the problems they faced were not beyond challenge or change. In conjunction with the weakness of the links between blacks and the city's political system, it made them available for mobilization by this newly emerged leadership group. Also, black activists in New York were able to draw upon the support of state and national officials—such as the state commissioner of education and the director of the federal Office of Economic Opportunity—in their efforts to influence the municipal government.

The most dramatic manifestation of the mobilization of blacks and the intensification of conflicts over racial issues in New York were riots that erupted in the black ghettos of Manhattan and Brooklyn in the summer of 1964 after a white policeman shot and killed a black youth. Riots among members of the city's newest immigrant groups also had erupted prior to the reform episodes of 1871 and 1901, and fears of popular turbulence were not absent in the 1890s, 1910s, and 1930s as well. Like

71

these earlier cases, the 1964 riot led many New Yorkers to question the capacity of the incumbent administration to meet one of its most fundamental responsibilities—the preservation of civil order.

This concern cut in two directions. Liberals argued that the very mode of governance that characterized the Wagner administration—especially its refusal or inability to overcome entrenched bureaucratic interests that blocked the reforms demanded by blacks—were responsible for the intensification of racial conflict in New York, and that the municipal government had to establish a new relationship with the city's black community if racial harmony was to be restored. Conservatives argued that only a thin blue line stood between the city and criminal anarchy, and that to ward off this threat the police required more unequivocal support from City Hall than the Wagner administration had given to them.

Conflicts over racial issues had important consequences for the mayoral election of 1965. Paul Screvane and Abe Beame, the two candidates who had served in Wagner's City Hall, recognized how deeply the issues of school desegregation and the civilian review board divided the Democratic coalition. Consequently they sought to remove them from the arena of electoral politics. On the desegregation issue they adopted Mayor Wagner's approach and simply remained silent; on the review board issue they searched for a compromise that would defuse the conflict. Screvane proposed that the existing review board, composed entirely of police officials, be retained, but that a civilian board be created to which those dissatisfied with its decisions could appeal. The decisions of this appeals board would only be advisory, however, and the final determination of whether a policeman should be punished for brutality would remain in the hands of the police commissioner. Beame's proposal was both simpler and more explicit in its intent. He suggested that all the mayoral candidates get together to arrive at a common position on the review board, so as to remove this issue from the campaign.[50]

Silence and compromise were equally unacceptable to both the most ardent opponents and supporters of school busing and the CRB, however, and the other mayoral candidates appealed more to such voters. The Conservative party nominated the most prominent leader of the anti-busing forces, Rosemary Gunning, for president of the city council, and the party's mayoral candidate, William F. Buckley, opposed any civilian involvement in the hearing of charges of police brutality. At the other pole, Democratic reform candidate William Fitts Ryan called for the creation of a review board composed entirely of civilians, and on the school integration issue he supported the creation of intermediate schools, as a way of fostering the racial balance in the fifth through eighth grades. John Lindsay proposed adding four civilians to the police department's current three-man review board, and supported the concept of intermediate schools—the position to which the advocates of school integration had retreated.[51]

The question of how the poverty program should be structured was not of concern to as many voters as the busing and review board issues, but it was highly salient to a large number of political activists—namely, members of the Democratic reform movement. On this issue both Abe Beame and William F. Buckley came out for centralized control over the program. As mentioned, Paul Screvane initially took this position, but he eventually retreated from it in an effort to prevent members of the reform movement from defecting to Ryan, who from the very beginning of the campaign had advocated that control over the program be decentralized. Lindsay's position was substantially identical to Ryan's.

These cleavages on racial issues led many of the reformers who had supported Mayor Wagner in 1961 to abandon his heir apparent, Paul Screvane, in the 1965 Democratic primary, thus contributing to the victory of Abe Beame. In the general election, however, Beame suffered defections among conservative voters to William F. Buckley, while liberals, reformers, and some black voters defected to John Lindsay. This fragmentation of the coalition that had supported Wagner enabled Lindsay to win the general election, although he received less than 44 percent of the total vote cast.

Municipal Employee Unions

During the 1960s, municipal employee unions came to play an ever more important role in the government and politics of New York City— a development not entirely unrelated to the growing prominence of racial issues in that decade. There were two sides to this phenomenon: civil service unions became more powerful, and their increasing power became an issue in the 1965 mayoral election.

In and of itself the involvement of municipal employees in New York politics was anything but novel in the 1960s. During the nineteenth century, Tammany had used the public payroll to reward party workers, and city employees contributed to the machine and worked for its candidates in order to hold on to their jobs and obtain promotions. As long as city employees were organized through the machine, they had no capacity to act independently of it. Beginning with the organization of the Civil Service Forum in 1917, city employees established a number of organizations that were nominally independent of the machine. But most of their leaders relied upon their ties to politicians to secure benefits for their members, sharply limiting the ability of these organizations to act as independent forces in the electoral arena.[52]

During his second and third terms, Mayor Wagner helped create a new type of city employee union that enjoyed many of the legal prerogatives of private sector labor unions—exclusive recognition, dues check-offs, and the right to engage in collective bargaining. These unions competed with the party organizations and with civil service groups that had ties to the party organizations for the loyalty of municipal employees. The municipal labor relations procedures promulgated by Mayor Wagner, and the way Wagner administered the rules he had drafted, helped the new city employee unions prevail over their rivals. In turn, the unions were prepared to help Wagner when he ran in opposition to the county Democratic machines in 1961.

Municipal employee unions played a major role in Wagner's victory that year. Indeed, as political scientist Theodore Lowi has noted, in putting together his slate of running mates and his campaign organization in 1961, Wagner sought to balance them not only ethnically and geographically, as had become customary in New York campaigns, but also bureaucratically. The candidate for president of the City Council on his slate had risen through the ranks of the Sanitation Department, his candidate for Comptroller had served in the city's Budget Bureau, and his campaign manager was the Fire Commissioner.[53]

In the 1965 Democratic primary, Paul Screvane inherited this support from Wagner. Screvane was endorsed by twenty-four municipal employee unions and his campaign organization had a "civil service coordinator," a position occupied by Mayor Wagner's chief liaison with the municipal employee unions. When Screvane lost the primary, the civil service unions switched *en bloc* to Abe Beame.[54]

One of the central themes in the campaign of Beame's chief opponent in the general elections, John Lindsay, was an attack upon the civil service union leaders who, Lindsay alleged, dominated the municipal government during the Wagner years and to a considerable degree were responsible for its problems. Lindsay argued that the close ties between the civil service unions and Mayor Wagner inflated the costs of municipal labor settlements and made it impossible for his administration to increase the efficiency of municipal agencies. In addition, the civil service unions opposed reforms in personnel procedures that would enable blacks and Puerto Ricans to obtain city jobs. Lindsay's harping upon this theme in his first campaign contributed to the rancor that characterized municipal labor relations after he entered City Hall.

Republicans

Changes in the balance of power in national politics led the Republicans, who in the 1950s and early 1960s had come to terms with New York City's postwar regime, to join other political forces in attacking Democratic control of City Hall in 1965. Although there was much talk of "reform" in New York throughout the 1960s, there was little talk of "fusion" prior to 1965. The explanation for this is to be found as much in Albany and Washington as in New York City.

Nelson Rockefeller had become the dominant figure in the Republican party in New York State when he was elected governor in 1958. As the 1961 New York City mayoral election approached, he was more interested in bolstering his own chances for winning a second term—by exacerbating the cleavage between reform and machine Democrats that had helped him during his first campaign—than he was in securing the election of a Republican mayor. Since the odds of the Republicans' winning control of City Hall were small, and the patronage that came with control of the state government was extensive, the priorities of Republican politicians in New York City did not differ substantially from the governor's. In pursuit of this goal, the Republican-controlled state legislature established a commission to investigate New York City's government and to propose revisions in the city's charter that would remedy the problems uncovered. Predictably, the commission found many examples of mismanagement and corruption, which it proposed to remedy by strengthening the mayoralty and diminishing the authority of the Board of Estimate and the borough presidents. Just as predictably, the leaders of the Democratic county machines—and the great majority of the Democrats in the city council, Board of Estimate, and state legislature, who were beholden to them—opposed these proposals; they would reduce the powers and patronage of public officials with close ties to the city's party organizations.

Mayor Wagner responded to these events by seeking to disassociate himself from the investigating commission's findings of misgovernment and by embracing its proposals for charter revision. Significantly, New

York's Republicans and the city's civic associations did *not* use these findings of corruption as an occasion for organizing a fusion campaign in the 1961 municipal election. Rather, they permitted Mayor Wagner to seize the banner of reform. The governor proposed and the legislature passed a bill authorizing the mayor to appoint a charter revision commission and barring the council from creating a commission of its own (as it was threatening to do). Remarkably, the bill empowered the mayor to appropriate funds on his own authority to finance his charter revision commission if the city council and Board of Estimate refused to do so. Moreover, contrary to the spirit of the state constitution's Home Rule amendment, the legislature passed this bill without receiving a "home rule message" from the city council requesting that it enact such a bill. (When the statute was challenged in the courts on these grounds, the Citizens Union, despite its professed commitment to the principle of home rule, filed a brief arguing that it was constitutional for the legislature to proceed as it did.)[55]

The issue of charter revision contributed to the break between Mayor Wagner and the Democratic county leaders, and by the grace of the Republicans it enabled the mayor to present himself successfully to the electorate as a reformer, despite his close association with the machine during his first seven years in office. Wagner reciprocated when Governor Rockefeller stood for reelection the following year by doing little more than offering a perfunctory endorsement of Rockefeller's Democratic opponent, and during the mayor's third term this pattern continued as each helped the other secure enactment of the tax legislation necessary to balance their respective budgets.

These examples of bipartisan collusion indicate that the mere revelation of municipal corruption is not sufficient to spark a fusion crusade. This will occur only if the Republicans have additional reasons to join forces with the other traditional participants in fusion coalitions. In 1961 they did not, but four years later they did.

The incentives for the GOP to conduct a serious campaign in New York City were considerably greater in 1965 than they had been four years earlier. Lyndon Johnson's landslide victory in the 1964 presidential election, and his subsequent efforts to institutionalize the coalition that had elected him through the legislative program of the Great Society, threatened (or so it appeared at the time) to reduce the Republicans to a permanent minority party. The chairman of the Republican National Committee, Ray Bliss, thought that a victory, or even a strong showing, by the GOP's candidate in the Democratic stronghold of New York would revive Republican morale and assist his efforts to rebuild the party. For this reason he urged GOP Congressman John Lindsay to run for mayor and, more concretely, promised to help him raise the $1.5 million that Lindsay insisted was necessary to conduct a serious campaign.[56]

Among Republicans, members of the party's moderate wing had an especially strong incentive to encourage a candidate such as Lindsay to run for mayor of New York City. In 1964 the moderates had lost control of the GOP to the conservatives, whose standard-bearer, Barry Goldwater, had argued that only by pursuing a "Southern strategy"—attempting to put together a coalition of southern and western states—could the Republicans topple the New Deal coalition. Goldwater's defeat in 1964 had indicated the problems with this approach, but it remained to be demonstrated that in the wake of Johnson's landslide the Republicans could carry the large cities of the Northeast. Prominent moderate Republicans saw a Lindsay candidacy for mayor of New York as a means of demonstrating that a "Northern strategy" was still feasible, thereby providing a major boost to their efforts to regain control of the GOP. In their effort to persuade Lindsay to run, Governor Rockefeller and Walter Thayer, publisher of the moderate-Republican *New York Herald Tribune*, each pledged to raise a half-million dollars among their associates for his campaign, and Senator Jacob Javits pledged to raise a quarter-million dollars from his political contacts. A month before the election, three leading moderate Republican businessmen from outside New York— Leonard K. Firestone of Los Angeles, H. J. Heinz of Philadelphia, and Charles P. Taft of Cincinnatti—sent a letter to four thousand out-of-state moderate Republicans urging them to contribute to Lindsay's campaign.[57]

The chairman of the Republican national committee and wealthy Republican businessmen could not of course alone grant Lindsay the party's mayoral nomination. The authority to do that lay in the hands of New York City's GOP county leaders and county committeemen. However, the pledges of Republican fat cats were crucial, because Lindsay had made the raising of a large campaign fund a precondition of his agreeing to run for mayor. Once he decided to make the race, GOP party leaders in the city fell over themselves in their haste to pledge their support. Even apart from the question of whether they would have been in any position to resist pressure from Governor Rockefeller on behalf of Lindsay, they were jubilant about the prospect of his running because an attractive candidate at the top of their ticket could help GOP candidates for lesser offices—especially the state senate and assembly— regain positions the party had lost in the Johnson landslide. The expectation of receiving some City Hall patronage also could not have been entirely absent from their calculations, because many were chagrined when Lindsay announced—well after receiving the GOP nomination— that he would appoint no district leaders to positions in his administration.[58]

Evidently these considerations were sufficiently compelling to outweigh whatever hesitance GOP party leaders might have had about nominating a candidate whose record in Congress placed him to the left of the GOP's hard-core supporters in the outer boroughs, and about renewing an alliance with the Liberal party that had lain dormant for sixteen years.

The Organization of Reform

In sum, many of the conditions that historically led to the emergence of fusion movements were present in New York during the early and mid-1960s, and many of the political forces that historically joined fusion coalitions turned against the city's postwar regime. There were, however, two important and interrelated differences between the events of the 1960s and earlier fusion episodes with regard to what can be termed the "organization of reform." First, New York's postwar regime fragmented into an unusually large number of pieces, as groups that traditionally had acted in tandem went their separate ways, and then entered into and abandoned a kaleidoscopic series of new alliances. Second, important changes occurred in the balance of power among the political forces that rallied under the banner of reform and in the character of the organizations through which these political forces attacked the city's regime.

One of the most notable differences between the 1960s and earlier reform episodes was an increase in the number of political forces that played an independent and important role. The young men who launched reform crusades between 1894 and 1933 were a fairly homogeneous group. Generally, they shared a similar set of concerns, came from wealthy families, and operated through organizations—the City Club and the Citizens Union—that were financed by the WASP upper class. By contrast, the reform crusades of the 1960s were launched by three separate groups of young men and women—Democratic activists, journalists, and "advocacy professionals"—who opposed different aspects of New York's postwar regime and were not as closely tied to the city's upper classes as previous reform vanguards had been.

Small property owners were another group that acted with greater independence in the 1960s than their counterparts had in previous decades. In 1961, Comptroller Lawrence Gerosa ran as an independent candidate for mayor on a low tax platform and received 13 percent of the total vote, chiefly from this tax-conscious segment of the city's electorate. In 1965, the recently organized Conservative party, which appealed to this same segment of the electorate, refused to endorse fusion candidate John Lindsay and ran a slate of candidates of its own, headed by William F. Buckley. Buckley also won 13 percent of the total mayoral vote. In previous reform episodes this segment of the city's electorate had not acted so independently, and a greater proportion of it had joined with large property owners in supporting fusion slates.

Public employees also acted with greater independence in the 1960s than they had in earlier decades. Prior to the creation of municipal employee unions, which possessed most of the prerogatives of their counterparts in the private sector, city employee organizations were constrained from acting too independently of the machine politicians upon whom they depended for favors. In 1961, however, the city employee unions backed Robert Wagner's reform candidacy. And in the 1965 general election, when their nemesis John Lindsay seized the banner of reform, the majority of New York's public employee organizations jumped back into bed with the Democratic county organizations and supported the mayoral candidacy of Abe Beame.

Organized labor, too, acted with greater independence in the 1960s than it had in earlier decades. From the turn-of-the-century through the postwar period, New York's craft unions—especially those in the construction trades—had close ties to the city's Democratic machine politicians. But in 1961, the city's Central Trades and Labor Council organized the Brotherhood Party as its political vehicle and threw its weight behind Mayor Wagner's campaign against "bossism." Unions in the garment trades had no such ties with the machine, but prior to the mid-1930s they involved themselves only sporadically in New York City politics. This changed in 1937 when the American Labor party (ALP), which had been organized the year before, supported Fiorello LaGuardia's candidacy for a second term. The ALP's successor, the Liberal party, went on to play a crucial role in the reform movements of the 1960s, supporting Robert Wagner's bid for a third term in 1961 and then switching to John Lindsay in 1965, providing the slim margin of votes that elected him mayor.

Important differences also existed between the 1960s and most previous reform episodes regarding the character of the organizations through which reform coalitions attacked the city's regime. From 1871 through Fiorello LaGuardia's first election in 1933, the chief vehicles for fusion campaigns were "citizens committees" led by prominent members of New York's civic and economic elite. No such committee was organized in the 1960s. Rather, it was the support of organizations identified with New Deal liberalism—the Committee for Democratic Voters and/or the Liberal party—that enabled Robert Wagner in 1961 and John Lindsay in 1965 to call themselves the "reform" candidates for mayor. Moreover, it was these mayoral candidates, rather than the leaders of the organizations that draped the mantle of reform upon them, who played the major role in selecting the other candidates on the reform slate, bringing other political forces into the reform coalition, and constructing a campaign organization to turn out the vote on election day.

These changes in the structure of New York politics signified and contributed to an erosion in the power of the city's upper classes relative to other participants in reform coalitions and to the professional politicians who ran for office on the fusion slate. As other groups acquired the capacity for independent political action, their leaders were able to insist that anyone seeking their support pay heed to their distinctive concerns. Moreover, the fragmentation of New York's postwar regime contributed to the disorganization of the upper class by reducing the major incentive its members formerly had had to unite. It was the very unity of the machine that had led the majority of upper-class New Yorkers to conclude during earlier reform episodes that the problems they and the city faced stemmed from a common source, and that it therefore was in their common interest to join forces in a campaign to defeat the machine.

In addition, changes in the ideological climate of New York, which had roots in the 1930s, made it inconceivable that a committee of the city's wealthiest residents could present themselves as spokesmen for the citizens of New York. It had been possible for such committees to do so when a political machine that served the interests of its constituents largely by performing favors for them as individuals was successful in presenting itself as "the true home of the working classes"—Tammany's favorite self-description in the mid-nineteenth century. In a city that had elected to its highest office a co-sponsor of the Norris-LaGuardia Act, outlawing the use of injuctions in labor disputes, and the namesake of the Wagner Act's sponsor, this was no longer conceivable.

Finally, the willingness of New York's Republican leaders and of many leaders of the downtown business community to make the concessions entailed by this shift of the city's political spectrum to the left—that is, to support a mayoral candidate who was the nominee of the Liberal party—led many marginal homeowners who could not afford to make such concessions to reject the fusion slate and vote for independent candidates running on low-tax platforms that resembled those of nineteenth-century reformers.

These differences between the character of reform politics in New York in the 1960s and earlier decades had major implications for the fiscal policies pursued by Mayor Lindsay after he entered City Hall. This is epitomized nicely by a question that the leaders of the Liberal party posed to candidates seeking their party's nomination in 1965. Recognizing that a major complaint of many of Mayor Wagner's critics was his fiscal irresponsibility, and that many of these critics above all wanted a fusion administration to balance the city's budget, the Liberal leaders asked prospective candidates whether they placed a higher priority upon balancing the city's budget or "meeting human needs." Candidate John Lindsay gave the required answer: he pledged not to give priority to the former goal. As we shall see, he kept his pledge.[59]

4

Reform and Accommodation

AFTER entering City Hall, Mayor John Lindsay undertook to pursue policies that would deal with the problems that, in his view, New York's postwar regime had failed to alleviate, and sponsored a set of administrative reforms that would extend his administration's control over the agencies of municipal government. Lindsay's efforts were furiously resisted both by political forces that opposed the mayor's policies and by those whose influence would be reduced by his administrative reforms. This led to bitter conflicts that threatened civil order and Lindsay's future in New York City politics. To restore order and secure reelection in 1969, Lindsay came to terms with a number of his former opponents—the city's public employee unions and many Democratic machine politicians—greatly reducing the reformist thrust of his administration. In a number of ways, the last four-and-a-half years of Lindsay's mayoralty resembled earlier postreform regimes more than previous fusion administrations. This was ratified by the 1973 election of Abe Beame, who had the open support of New York's Democratic county machines. In contrast to earlier post-reform administrations, however, the regime over which Mayors Lindsay and Beame presided from 1969 to 1974 was not fiscally viable, and this laid the groundwork for fiscal crisis.

Reforming Municipal Policy

Like almost everything else having to do with New York City, the Lindsay administration has been subject to analysis from a variety of perspectives. One view, expounded by political scientist Stephen David, explains the administration's behavior in terms of the mayor's efforts to construct an electoral majority. Others explain the administration's behavior by reference to the mayor's political values or his governing style. For example, Charles Morris, who served in Lindsay's Budget Bureau, attributes many of the administration's policies to the mayor's "good intentions," while political scientist Douglas Yates attributes them to the mayor's penchant for acting as a "crusader" on behalf of the causes to which he was committed.[1]

Although there are elements of truth in these analyses, none can satisfactorily account for the behavior of the Lindsay administration during its first three years. Interpretations of the policies or administrative reforms proposed by Mayor Lindsay as efforts to build an electoral majority ignore striking characteristics of his administration's behavior during this period. One is that Lindsay and his associates often sought to alter established policies and to redistribute governmental benefits by creating, or relying upon, institutions that were *not* responsible to elected city officials. Another is that the mayor was often prepared to pursue policies opposed by a majority of the city's electorate, if they were supported by outside political forces that controlled resources crucial for either governing New York or realizing Lindsay's ambition for higher office.

As for the goals, commitments, and governing style of John Lindsay, there is no reason to doubt the sincerity of his commitment to the causes he crusaded for (in particular, racial justice). The policies he pursued during his early years in office did embody a vision of how the good of the city as a whole could be advanced. However, the goals and values of the Lindsay administration should not be treated as givens. First, these changed over time as political conflicts in the city strengthened the mayor's commitment to some goals and led him to abandon others. Second, many of the administrative reforms advocated by Mayor Lindsay and his allies differed greatly from those advocated by previous fusion mayors—John Mitchel in the 1910s and Fiorello LaGuardia in the 1930s—and these differences require explanation. Third, the conception Mayor Lindsay and those who shared his views had of the character of

83

the city had such blind spots that one must ask how anyone could have found it plausible.

The vision Mayor Lindsay and his allies had of the city, and the policies he pursued during his early years in office, embodied an *ideology*, a view of the common good grounded in the interests of those who profess it. This does not mean that the policies and reforms Lindsay advocated simply reflected the views that his supporters brought into the political arena. The Lindsay administration played an independent role in persuading the groups whose support it courted that they had interests in common, and a creative role by formulating policies that served those common interests. The differences between the policies and administrative reforms advocated by Lindsay and previous fusion mayors were a function of the distinctive composition and resources of the alliance of political forces, both inside and outside of New York, that Lindsay was seeking to forge. The reforms he proposed also reflected differences between the pluralist regime that he sought to drive from power and the machine-dominated administrations attacked by previous fusion movements.

Nothing better epitomizes the Lindsay administration's ideology—and its blind spots—during its early years in office than the title, composition, and slogan of an organization the mayor himself played an important role in founding: the Urban Coalition. As its name indicates, the Urban Coalition purported to speak for the city, and yet its membership was quite unrepresentative of the population of New York. Most of its members were executives of national corporations, non-profit organizations, or civil rights groups; there were few representatives of working- and middle-class whites, who comprised the majority of New York's population. The organization's claim to have its views heeded despite its unrepresentative character was based upon its members' self-proclaimed concern for the plight of the city's least fortunate residents—black and Puerto Rican slum dwellers. This ·vas expressed in the Urban Coalition's motto, "Give a Damn."[2]

The segments of the city's population represented by the Urban Coalition were central to the Lindsay administration's view of New York's character, prospects, and problems. The administration's policy initiatives were predicated on the view that the strongest sector of New York's economy was composed of the national corporations and business service firms in the downtown and midtown office districts and that the city's major social problem was the existence of a large nonwhite population locked in a cycle of poverty. The Lindsay administration sought to foster prosperity by making New York an attractive place for national corporations and the firms that served them to locate and for their employees to live. At the same time, it sought to promote justice and social harmony by enacting policies that would help the city's racial minorities escape from poverty.[3]

It would take us too far afield to describe here all the programs the Lindsay administration advocated and enacted in pursuing these goals. Suffice it to say that many involved controversial departures from the policies of previous administrations. For example, the Lindsay administration moved to reduce street congestion, air pollution, and noise in the downtown and midtown office districts by encouraging commuters to enter Manhattan by subway rather than by automobile. Toward this end, the mayor sought to use the surplus revenues of the Triborough Bridge and Tunnel Authority to finance the operation and extension of the subway system rather than the construction of additional highways, bridges, or tunnels. Not surprisingly, Robert Moses opposed this idea. And to make Manhattan a more attractive place for the cosmopolitan middle and upper classes to live and work, Lindsay's City Planning Commission granted variances to developers to erect office buildings with 40 to 50 percent more floor space than permitted by the zoning code of 1961. In return, the developers agreed to construct such "urban" amenities as open plazas, pedestrian arcades, and theaters, or to alter the building's design to make it (in the Commission's judgment) more aesthetically pleasing. Again with upper-middle- and upper-class residents in mind, the Lindsay administration abandoned a policy adopted by the Wagner administration in 1962 that excluded luxury housing from development projects.[4]

The Lindsay administration also proceeded in a number of controversial directions in coping with the problems of poverty and alienation among the city's racial minorities. In contrast to the procedures the Wagner administration had followed for selecting the members of neighborhood community action agencies—procedures that favored representatives of established local institutions, such as settlement houses, YMCAs, and churches—those formulated by the Lindsay administration gave greater representation to the "unaffiliated poor." Over the course of Lindsay's first term, the focus of the poverty program shifted away from the provision of social services to the poor, toward a strategy of community organization and protest. Lindsay also attempted to increase the proportion of black and Puerto Ricans holding jobs on the city's payroll by altering procedures for the recruitment of public employees and increasing the size of the municipal workforce. At the end of the mayor's first term, the administration adopted a policy of "open enrollment" at the City University, and enrollments of blacks and Puerto Ricans were greatly increased.

The city's welfare rolls also shot up during the first three years of the Lindsay administration. As welfare grant levels were increased, the number of people eligible for public assistance increased. Changes in procedures for getting onto the welfare rolls that the Lindsay administration adopted on its own initiative, or in response to court orders, made it far easier to obtain public assistance. Finally, welfare rights organizers on the staffs of community action agencies informed thousands of New Yorkers of their entitlements and encouraged them to demand all the benefits for which they qualified.[5]

In his 1965 campaign Lindsay had criticized the Wagner administration's fiscal irresponsibility—in particular, its use of borrowed funds to finance operating expenditures. During his early years in office, Mayor Lindsay increased the funds available for his programs and policies in a number of ways. He pressed the state and federal governments to grant additional aid to New York City. Intergovernmental aid to New York City increased dramatically during Lindsay's first three years in office (between the 1966 and 1969 fiscal years state and federal aid to New York City more than doubled, going from $1.3 billion to $2.9 billion, and as a proportion of the city's operating revenues it rose from 35.6 percent to 47 percent). Largely this occurred because there was a substantial overlap between the programs and political commitments of the Lindsay administration in New York City and the Rockefeller and Johnson administrations in Albany and Washington. Mayor Lindsay also obtained new taxes—most important, personal and corporate income taxes—the proceeds of which increased as the city's economy flourished.

Finally, Mayor Lindsay attempted to reduce expenditures that benefited or reflected the influence of the political forces he opposed. In particular, Lindsay, as well as business groups such as the Citizens Budget Commission, were convinced that the political alliance between Mayor Wagner and municipal employee unions had resulted in excessive wage settlements and a failure to implement managerial reforms and changes in work rules that would increase productivity. Lindsay attempted to alter this pattern of labor relations by demonstrating to city employee union leaders that he was a hard bargainer who was prepared to take strikes rather than bow to demands he regarded as outrageous. This resulted in a series of lengthy and bitter walkouts by municipal employees.

86

The mayor attempted to rally public opinion against the striking workers (during a strike by sanitation workers in 1968 he also asked the governor to call in the National Guard), but this tactic repeatedly failed.[6]

Reforming Municipal Administration

The Lindsay administration expended at least as much political capital, and provoked at least as much controversy, in trying to alter the administrative structure of the municipal government as in attempting to implement new public policies. These two efforts toward reform were not unrelated. Through various reorganization plans the mayor sought to (1) reduce the influence of political forces opposing his policies; (2) extend his own and his allies' control over the agencies of municipal government; (3) reallocate the benefits of municipal government to the advantage of his allies; and (4) endow the municipal government with the organizational capacity to implement his administration's policies.[7]

Dethroning the Opposition

Traditionally, the most important political forces that reformers weakened when they gained control of City Hall were the county Democratic machines. To accomplish this they deprived these machines of the patronage that was vital to their life and health. But the pluralist regime Lindsay attacked rested upon a more varied political base, and accordingly the new mayor's efforts to dethrone the "power brokers" of the Wagner regime led him to fight on a broader front.

As late as 1961, patronage controlled by the county machines continued to be a central target for reformers. A new city charter enacted that year deprived the borough presidents of their richest source of patronage—control over the construction of streets and sewers—centralizing this function in a new, citywide Department of Highways. Mayor Lindsay also wanted to limit the prerogatives of the borough presidents, but this was a minor theme in his administration. Moreover, racial considerations, rather than patronage, were most often the motivation in this attack. For example, the Lindsay administration altered the procedures for selecting sites for low-income housing projects in an effort to deprive borough presidents of the veto they effectively exercised over such decisions. That veto had enabled middle-class whites to block construction of public housing for low-income blacks in their neighborhoods.[8]

87

More significant was the attack Lindsay launched against other individuals and organizations that wielded power during the Wagner administration. One of the power brokers the mayor was out to dethrone was Robert Moses. Lindsay attempted to do this by asking the state legislature for authority to absorb the independent Triborough Bridge and Tunnel Authority (TBTA), controlled by Moses, into a new Transportation Administration that was to be headed by an official responsible to the mayor. This would enable City Hall to use the TBTA's revenues to construct the transportation facilities the mayor favored. Lindsay's proposals got nowhere, however, when Moses's constituency of contractors, construction unions, bankers, Democratic party politicians, and public officials rallied to defend the TBTA's autonomy.[9]

Mayor Lindsay also proposed a set of administrative reforms to reduce the influence of municipal employee unions. As Lindsay was convinced that political ties between these unions and Mayor Wagner had placed excessive burdens on the city's budget, he sought to "depoliticize" municipal labor relations through the creation of an "impartial" Office of Collective Bargaining (OCB). The OCB's procedures, however, turned out to be more beneficial to the unions than the informal practices they replaced. Because the members and staff of the OCB were committed to collective bargaining to resolve labor disputes, many issues Mayor Wagner had refused to negotiate—such as class sizes in the city's schools or manning levels of fire companies—were declared by the OCB to be subject to negotiation.[10]

Gaining Control of the Municipal Government

Mayor Lindsay pursued three different strategies to extend his administration's control over governmental activities in the city: centralization, circumvention, and community participation. The first strategy involved regrouping the city's myriad departments, commissions, and boards into ten "superagencies." The rationale was to coordinate the programs of the departments within the superagencies' jurisdiction. What this meant in practice was that the cadre of administrators, deputy administrators, assistant administrators, and staff at headquarters would monitor and seek to reorient the activities of the departments under their supervision. In addition, the city's Bureau of the Budget implemented various program-budgeting techniques designed to shake the bureaucracy out of its familiar routines and ensure that municipal agencies acted in accord with the mayor's objectives.[11]

The second strategy Mayor Lindsay and his associates used to accomplish their goals was circumventing the existing agencies of municipal government and relying upon—or creating—other organizations and institutions to perform public functions. For example, between 1965 and 1969 the city's expenditures on contracts with outside consulting firms increased from $8 million to $70 million. The use of consultants provided a means of hiring people whose social and educational backgrounds and points of view generally were closer to those of the mayor's chief associates than were the backgrounds and views of the city's regular civil servants. Consultants also had no stake in the established routines of the municipal bureaucracy and generally could be counted on to offer the administration solutions to problems that reflected its own predilections.[12]

Another example of the strategy of circumvention was the Model Cities program, which established institutions in nonwhite neighborhoods that paralleled many of the regular agencies of the municipal government. Their purpose was to influence how city departments provided services in these neighborhoods and to provide some of the services themselves. For instance, when efforts to get the Department of Sanitation to hire more nonwhites failed, the Model Cities boards hired "sanitation aides" to sweep the streets of Harlem, Bedford-Stuyvesant, and the South Bronx.

Community participation was the final strategy of reorganization pursued by the Lindsay administration and its allies. One mechanism for this was a proposal to decentralize the city's school system by creating thirty community school boards that would exercise substantial control over the elementary and junior high schools in their neighborhood and whose members would be selected by neighborhood residents.[13]

Participatory community institutions served a number of functions for the mayor and his allies. They lent legitimacy to the administration's efforts to extend its influence and added pressure from below—which shaded into violence in the Ocean Hill-Brownsville school decentralization controversy—to the attack upon the educational and other bureaucracies. Most important, community participation provided a conduit for blacks and Puerto Ricans in the Lindsay coalition to influence the allocation of public benefits and the behavior of municipal agencies. This helps explain an apparent contradiction in Lindsay's proposals for administrative reform—his advocacy of measures both to centralize and decentralize the municipal government. It is only a slight simplification to say that centralization was a technique with which the administration sought to enhance the influence of its upper- and upper-middle-class allies and decentralization was a technique for enhancing the influence of its nonwhite allies. The Lindsay administration, however, was unable to control the political forces that its decentralization proposals unleashed.

Reallocating Public Benefits

The changes in administrative practices and procedures sponsored by Mayor Lindsay to gain control of the municipal government were also designed to reallocate benefits to the advantage of his political constituency. In contrast to earlier fusion administrations, which brought ever larger numbers of city jobs into the classified civil service, the Lindsay administration increased the number of positions in the so-called "exempt" class. During his first two-and-a-half years in office this number grew eightfold, from 1,500 to 12,800. Many of these positions were in the city's antipoverty programs, and had been placed in the exempt class because their very purpose would have been defeated if they had been classified as ordinary civil service positions. Had these jobs been awarded to candidates who scored highest on competitive written examinations, there would have been no guarantee of distribution to the intended clientele of the antipoverty programs—namely, blacks and Puerto Ricans.

There were also differences between the career aspirations of the middle-class cadres who supported the Lindsay administration and their counterparts in the fusion administrations of Fiorello LaGuardia and John Purroy Mitchel. The employees of consulting firms that the Lindsay administration contracted with for services and the professional personnel who worked in social service programs financed by federal grants almost certainly did not aspire to lifetime careers working for New York City. Indeed, the very purpose of these arrangements was to draw on the talents of people who would not otherwise work for the city. Consequently, there was no political constituency within the Lindsay coalition advocating the expansion of the classified civil service. And because patronage had not played as central a role in the Wagner administration as it had in previous machine-backed administrations, Lindsay and his associates did not acquire the same commitment as did previous fusion mayors to what reformers had once called the "merit system."[14]

Increasing Governmental Capacity

The administrative reforms sponsored by Mayor Lindsay were also designed to increase what can be termed the "technical" and "social" capacity of the municipal government to accomplish the goals of the mayor and members of his support coalition. Through linear programming, queuing theory, and other abstruse analytical procedures, the systems analysts working for Lindsay's Budget Bureau and for the consulting firms under contract with the city sought to increase the technical efficiency of municipal operations. In addition, the mayor and his allies argued that municipal agencies were not adequately performing their functions in black and Puerto Rican neighborhoods because most of their employees were outsiders to the communities in which they worked, and were more dedicated to the perquisites of their jobs and established bureaucratic routines than to serving their clients. Besides this, existing civil service rules and administrative arrangements made it almost impossible to hold municipal employees accountable for their failure to perform satisfactorily on the job.

The Lindsay administration tried to bridge the chasm between "the bureaucracy" and "the community" by increasing the number of non-whites employed by the city and by establishing neighborhood boards to oversee the operations of some municipal programs. The most important example of this involved the mayor's proposal to decentralize the school system. The proponents of decentralization argued that it would improve the quality of education in ghetto schools by making teachers and administrators responsible to the people with the greatest stake in the education of black and Puerto Rican children—their parents.[15] Members of the Lindsay coalition doubtlessly found the case for decentralization persuasive—despite clear lacunae in the arguments made on its behalf and glaring weaknesses in the evidence cited to support these arguments—because it would transfer control of the schools into their own hands.[16]

But these proposals were more than a naked power grab. They involved a genuine effort to increase the bureaucracy's capacity to perform functions it manifestly was failing to serve. It is scarcely surprising that the most ardent proponents of school decentralization—the black activists who expected to control the school boards in ghetto neighborhoods; the blacks who sought to obtain jobs as paraprofessionals, teachers, and administrators in these neighborhoods; and the staff of institutions such as the Ford Foundation and local universities who expected to supplant the personnel at the Board of Education as the architects of educational programs in these neighborhoods—all believed that they would do a better job educating ghetto children than would the teachers, supervisors, and administrators who currently ran the city schools.

The Reaction to Reform

Mayor Lindsay's efforts to restructure municipal agencies and redistribute the benefits of city government were fiercely resisted by the interests adversely affected by them—particularly, municipal employee unions and working-class and lower-middle-class whites. Because Lindsay and his allies had not mobilized a mass constituency that could reelect him, this opposition was especially threatening. As a consequence, to secure election to a second term in 1969 Lindsay had to come to terms with some of his opponents. His part of the bargain was to abandon many of his more far-reaching plans to alter the policies and structure of the municipal government. Even with this, Lindsay managed to win reelection in 1969 only because Mario Procaccino, the Democratic mayoral nominee that year, was unusually weak. In 1973, when his probable Democratic opponent, Abe Beame, was a candidate who had close ties to the groups Lindsay had come to terms with four years earlier, Lindsay's political prospects were so bleak that he did not run for reelection.

Municipal employees were most immediately affected by Mayor Lindsay's first-term efforts to redistribute the benefits of municipal government, and when push came to shove they defended themselves by staging strikes. These were threatening to Lindsay for a number of reasons. Strikes contributed to the atmosphere of turmoil surrounding his administration, voters generally blamed the mayor more than the striking workers for the inconveniences caused by the interruption of municipal services, and labor confrontations tended to alienate voters belonging to the ethnic groups from which the unions involved drew their members.

All of these negative elements were present in the most politically significant confrontation between Mayor Lindsay and a civil service union—the series of strikes staged by the United Federation of Teachers (UFT) in the fall of 1968. These were initiated after a community school board in the Ocean Hill-Brownsville neighborhood in Brooklyn removed a number of teachers—an action that violated, the UFT claimed, the union's contract. The fundamental issue in the Ocean Hill-Brownsville controversy was the extent to which the union or the community school board would control the hiring and firing of teachers. The strikes closed down the city's schools for more than two months, and because the membership of the UFT was predominantly Jewish and the Ocean Hill governing board and student body were predominantly black, the controversy inflamed relations between blacks and Jews in the city. (Indeed, the Ocean Hill controversy was probably the most ethnically divisive episode in New York's history since the Orange Riot, pitting Irish Catholics against Protestants, in 1871.) Inasmuch as Mayor Lindsay was a proponent of school decentralization, and his appointees to the citywide Board of Education generally sided with the Ocean Hill governing board, the controversy cost Lindsay substantial support among the city's Jewish voters, and many other white voters as well.[17]

Lindsay's policies also generated substantial opposition among working-class and lower-middle-class Catholics. These voters quite accurately regarded Lindsay's actions as efforts to reallocate the benefits of city politics to blacks and upper-middle-class whites, at their expense. The Democratic mayoral nominee in the 1969 election, Mario Procaccino, referred to this as the "Manhattan arrangement," and criticized Lindsay for ignoring the "outer boroughs." Opposition from these quarters was especially dangerous to Lindsay because the majority of the city's registered Republicans were lower-middle-class Catholics who lived in the outer boroughs, and alienating them could cost him the GOP nomination. And that is precisely what happened in the 1969 Republican primary—Lindsay won a majority of the vote only in Manhattan, while his opponent in the primary, John Marchi, carried Brooklyn, Queens, the Bronx, and Staten Island, and with them, the Republican mayoral nomination.[18]

Lindsay also faced grave difficulties when he ran for reelection in 1969 because he and his allies failed to mobilize sufficient electoral support among the black and Puerto Rican beneficiaries of his administration's policies to counterbalance these defections among whites. Lindsay did win an overwhelming 80 to 85 percent of the vote among those blacks who went to the polls in 1969, a dramatic increase from the 40 percent of the black vote he had won during his first mayoral campaign four years earlier, and his share of the Puerto Rican vote increased from 33 percent to 63 percent. But turnout rates among nonwhites remained the lowest in the city. Although blacks and Puerto Ricans composed 30 percent of the city's population in 1969, only 21 percent of the voters in that year's mayoral election were nonwhite.[19]

Why did Mayor Lindsay behave in ways that so threatened his prospects for reelection? And why did he and his allies fail to mobilize more extensive support among blacks and Puerto Ricans? For answers one must look at the structure of incentives confronting both the mayor and the black activists he allied with. Central to this was the new

93

relationship between national and local political institutions that emerged in the 1960s.

In the late 1960s, the mayors of large cities had strong incentives to appeal to what political scientist James Q. Wilson termed the mayor's "audience"—composed of executive officials in Washington, national opinion leaders, the national news media, and voters living outside their cities—even when this appeal involved pursuing policies that alienated many voters within their own city. The mayor's audience controlled two resources that mayors found vital for governing their cities, establishing a record for themselves, and, perhaps, moving on to higher office. One was money. By pursuing policies designed to lift blacks from poverty and regarded as "innovative" by the officials of federal agencies that administered the numerous grant-in-aid programs of President Johnson's Great Society, mayors could obtain substantial sums of federal money for their cities. With considerable success, Mayor Lindsay assiduously sought such financial aid, bringing people into his administration who were skilled in the art of federal "grantsmanship."[20]

The second benefit this audience could confer upon a mayor was a national reputation and the concomitant opportunity to become a serious contender for national office. Lindsay pursued these goals as avidly as he sought federal grants for New York City—it was an open secret that he aspired to the presidency—and during his first years in office he appeared to be making steady progress toward realizing his ambitions. The actions he took as mayor may have infuriated many voters in Brooklyn and Queens, but they won Lindsay recognition as a leading spokesman for the nation's cities. Appointed by President Johnson to serve on the National Commission on Civil Disorders, Lindsay was often mentioned as a candidate for the United States Senate and as one of the leading presidential prospects of the Republican party's liberal wing.[21]

The support of a national audience not only provided Lindsay with an incentive to initiate programs that might be opposed by important groups within the city, it also made it possible for the mayor to implement such programs. Insofar as the mayor was able to use federal grants to finance programs that provided benefits to blacks and Puerto Ricans, he did not have to induce members of the Board of Estimate and the City Council— who were more reluctant to invite the displeasure of voters in the outer boroughs—to appropriate local revenues for this purpose. The availability of this external support explains how Lindsay could believe it was possible to reorder municipal priorities without mobilizing the beneficiaries of these new priorities into the electorate.

The black and Puerto Rican leaders Mayor Lindsay allied with also

94

had no compelling incentive to mobilize more nonwhites into the electorate. In contrast to the Irish politicians with whom Tammany's leaders allied in the mid-nineteenth century, or the Jewish trade unionists in the American Labor party with whom Mayor LaGuardia allied in the mid-1930s, the major benefit Lindsay received by working with black and Puerto Rican community activists was legitimation, not votes. In the view of Lindsay's chief supporters in New York City and, he hoped, in the view of an attentive national audience, the policies and administrative reforms he sponsored were justified as a means of improving the conditions under which blacks lived—an act of racial justice that, Lindsay claimed, was good in itself and a prerequisite for preserving civil order.

Because the legitimacy that black and Puerto Rican activists conferred upon the Lindsay administration was not dependent upon their organizing a broad following within the city's ghettos and barrios, the administration was prepared to grant them control over neighborhood community action agencies or kindred programs, as well as influence over municipal projects and policies, even if they could demonstrate that they enjoyed the support of only a miniscule proportion of their putative constituency. To complete the circle, because black and Puerto Rican leaders were not rewarded in proportion to the number of followers they mobilized, they had no overriding incentive to mobilize large numbers of followers. Political scientists Norman and Susan Fainstein have estimated that only fifty people on average regularly participated in the various institutions the Lindsay administration and its allies in federal grant-giving agencies created to obtain "input" from "the community."[22] Also, it was rare for the turnout in the elections conducted by community action agencies to exceed 2 or 3 percent of those eligible to vote. Because their leadership did not rest on a broad base, black and Puerto Rican leaders who allied with Lindsay were not in a position to offer much in the way of useful support to the mayor when he desperately needed it in 1969.

Post-reform Accommodations, 1969–74

Alliance Patterns

Municipal employee unions were the first and most important of John Lindsay's opponents with whom the mayor came to terms in his quest for reelection. To ensure that public employee strikes would not mar his

95

campaign for reelection, in 1969 the mayor negotiated generous contracts with the civil service unions. That year, the city and the Transport Workers Union (TWU) agreed on the most expensive contract in the union's history without the TWU even threatening a strike. The city granted District Council 37 of the American Federation of State, County, and Municipal Employees (AFSCME) its long-sought goal of a minimum salary of $6,000 per year for clerks and hospital workers; sanitation workers were granted a 10 percent salary increase plus a commitment that they would receive enough overtime pay to increase their income close to parity with those in the police and fire departments; police officers and fire fighters were granted longevity increments, increased overtime benefits, night shift differentials, and increased city contributions to pension and welfare funds; and, for the first time in its history, the United Federation of Teachers concluded its contract negotiations before the school year began. The city also signed an agreement with the Patrolmen's Benevolent Association (PBA) concerning the ratio of sergeants' to patrolmen's salaries that for technical reasons (too complex to describe here) ultimately cost the city between $150 million and $215 million in additional payments to police, fire, and sanitation personnel.[23]

The dollar-cost to the city of the 1969 labor agreements was extremely high, but the political benefits to Mayor Lindsay were great. Lindsay's bid for reelection was endorsed by the Uniformed Sanitationmen's Association, the Transport Workers' Union, Local 237 of the Teamsters, and District Council 37 of AFSCME. The UFT, whose opposition to the mayor's reelection seemed a foregone conclusion during the Ocean Hill strike, decided less than a year later to remain neutral, and though the unions for police and fire personnel remained officially neutral, both contributed money to Lindsay's campaign.

Mayor Lindsay also made a number of overtures to white, middle-class voters—especially Jewish voters, whose support he needed to win the 1969 general election. In the course of his campaign, Lindsay spoke to hundreds of such audiences, and, as the *New York Times* said in a post-election analysis, in "an almost ostentatious display of humility" Lindsay conceded that he had made serious mistakes during his first term. In particular, he acknowledged that crime was a genuine problem, rather than a phony issue raised by racists to defame blacks, and, at great expense, his administration paid overtime rates to 3,000 policemen assigned to a new tour of duty during high-crime hours. The mayor announced that his top priority in 1969 would be improving the delivery of services to the city's "neighborhoods"—a code word for white residential areas in the outer boroughs. Toward this end, the Sanitation

Department's budget was increased and a campaign to clean litter from the streets was launched with much fanfare. The city also broke ground on scores of visible and popular construction projects—schools, libraries, and playgrounds—throughout the city.[24]

Perhaps the most remarkable alliance the mayor formed to win reelection was with Democratic machine politicians in Brooklyn, Queens, and Manhattan. (The Democratic organization in the Bronx had close ties with Mario Procaccino, the Democratic mayoral candidate; it supported him strongly, as did the Staten Island party organization.) Despite Lindsay's denunciations of the machine Democrats four years earlier, they had reasons to come to terms with one another in 1969. The mayor's motives were simple: the less vigorously the Democratic county organizations campaigned for Procaccino, the fewer votes Lindsay would need to defeat him. Democratic machine politicians, for their part, recognized that Procaccino was a weak candidate, and as the campaign progressed and a Lindsay victory seemed increasingly likely, they had every incentive to come to terms with the probable winner. One sign that a deal was in the offing was that on October 30, with less than a week to go before election day, precinct captains in Brooklyn and Queens had yet to receive their traditional $25 "walking around money" to cover their expenses on election day. Lindsay's part in this deal involved distributing patronage to Democratic machine politicians during his second term.[25]

Lindsay was only in a position to ally with his former opponents because Mario Procaccino did not preempt him in this endeavor. Most important, the Democratic mayoral nominee was unable to capitalize on the widespread dissatisfaction with Lindsay among the city's Jewish voters, stemming from the role he had played in the Ocean Hill controversy. Ethnic and class antipathies help explain Procaccino's inability to exploit this—his institutional affiliations, personal associates, and demeanor enabled him to be dismissed as someone who was not of "mayoral stature."[26]

Procaccino had been able to win the Democratic mayoral nomination because of divisions among, and a general weakening of, the city's Democratic county organizations. This encouraged a large number of candidates to enter the Democratic primary—five candidates competed for the Democratic mayoral nomination in 1969, compared to three in 1965 and two in 1961. The wide field of candidates split the liberal and moderate vote, enabling Procaccino to come in first even though he won only 32.9 percent of the total vote (the election law then required only a plurality to win the primary).

Lindsay recognized that he owed his reelection in 1969 to his opponent's inability to forge a coalition among the major groups the mayor had alienated during his early years in office. He knew he could not count on being so fortunate again—especially because the election law was changed after 1969 to provide for a run-off if no candidate won an absolute majority in the first round of the primary—and therefore Lindsay did not stand for reelection in 1973. That year's mayoral election was won by Abe Beame, a candidate with close ties to many of the groups—civil service unions, the Democratic county organizations, and Jewish voters—that had only reluctantly supported Lindsay in 1969.

Beame's candidacy in 1973 won the backing of another set of politicians who almost unanimously had supported Mayor Lindsay's bid for a second term in 1969—black elected officials. In return, Beame promised to appoint large numbers of blacks to important positions in his administration and intimated that he would clear these appointments with the city's black elected officials, thereby buttressing their leadership of the black community in New York City. There was also a tacit understanding that in return for their support, Beame would back New York's leading black politician, Manhattan Borough President Percy Sutton, for mayor in 1977.[27]

A final similarity between the elections of 1969 and 1973 and previous post-reform accommodations is that important Democratic and Republican politicians colluded with one another. In the early 1970s, relations between Mayor Lindsay and Governor Rockefeller had grown increasingly strained because Lindsay had waged a public campaign to get Albany to increase state aid to New York's six largest cities. He did this at the very time that Rockefeller was trying to shed his reputation as a big spender in order to keep his presidential prospects alive, despite the growing conservatism of the national GOP. To ensure that Lindsay would not be in a position to embarrass him when he next made a bid for the presidency, Rockefeller pressured a majority of New York City's Republican district leaders to endorse a prominent Democrat—former mayor Robert Wagner—as the GOP's mayoral nominee in 1973. In the end Wagner declined the proffered nomination, and Rockefeller tacitly backed the Democratic mayoral nominee, Abe Beame.[28]

Essentially, there was a two-stage process of accommodation between established political interests in New York and the new political forces of the 1960s. In 1969 a reform mayor (John Lindsay) came to terms with some of the interests he had fought during his early years in office, and in 1973 a candidate with close ties to the city's Democratic county machines (Abe Beame) reached an accommodation with a number of the political forces that had supported his fusion predecessor. Nonetheless, there were significant differences between the regime that governed New York from 1969 to 1974 and previous post-reform administrations. These differences had important implications for the fiscal policies the city pursued during the early 1970s.[29]

Patronage and Party Organization

The patronage practices of Mayors Lindsay and Beame in the period from 1969 through 1974 reflected the political accommodations that had secured their respective elections.

During his second term, Mayor Lindsay did not completely abandon his efforts to increase the flow of municipal benefits to blacks or to enhance the influence of his upper-middle-class allies over the agencies of municipal government. But, with only a few exceptions, he no longer sought the drastic changes in the conduct or structure of city government that had embroiled him in conflicts with the groups adversely affected by these changes.[30] In addition, to maintain a base of political support in his second term, Lindsay made extensive use of patronage and tolerated its use by his political allies. The number of municipal employees holding provisional appointments tripled during Lindsay's mayoralty until it reached 27,813 in 1973, and in many cases these appointees were shifted from agency to agency in order to avoid the requirement of taking a civil service examination. This patronage was channeled through the John V. Lindsay Associations that had been established in 1969 to conduct the mayor's reelection campaign, and these groups, in turn, heeded the recommendations of Democratic machine politicians in distributing jobs. For this reason, many of Mayor Lindsay's patronage appointees were kept on after Abe Beame entered City Hall.[31]

A related phenomenon became increasingly evident during Mayor Lindsay's second term—the conversion of the resources of neighborhood antipoverty organizations into patronage. The mayor was loathe to intervene if the leader of a faction won control of an organization and then distributed jobs to his followers, compelling these subsequently beholden antipoverty workers to canvass for him if he ran for public or party office. The politicians who were most successful exploiting the patronage of antipoverty agencies in this manner were Ramon Velez, head of the Hunts Point Multiservice Center and a Democratic district leader in the Bronx, and Samuel Wright, who gained control of the Ocean Hill-Brownsville community school board in 1970 and was a state assemblyman and a Democratic district leader. Nothing so strikingly illustrates the difference between the first and second Lindsay administrations than the contrast between the radical advocates of community control who ran the Ocean Hill school district in 1968 and 1969 and the machine politicians who subsequently took it over.[32]

Mayor Beame exploited the patronage resources of the municipal government with an alacrity even greater than his predecessor's. Under Beame, municipal agencies were compelled to clear with City Hall every single appointment that was not filled by examination. In contrast to Lindsay, however, the new mayor distributed the bulk of his patronage directly through the Democratic county organizations in an effort to strengthen them. As Thomas Roche, Beame's chief patronage aide explained, "The mayor wants to strengthen and revitalize the Democratic party, and patronage is the way to do it. There has to be some inducement for people to go out and ring doorbells."[33]

An especially significant facet of Beame's campaign to strengthen the city's old-line party organizations was his effort to buttress their positions within New York's black and Puerto Rican communities. There were important differences between the structure of politics in these two racial communities, however, and the Beame administration's behavior toward them varied accordingly.

A central feature of black politics in New York City in the 1970s (which still exists today) was its intense factionalism. Black elected officials were independent political entrepreneurs who were elected by their own efforts and who recognized no common leader. What black politicians most wanted from their white counterparts was that they acknowledge the leadership of incumbent black officials and that they do nothing to undermine the position of black elected officials in their home constituencies.[34]

The regular Democratic county organizations and the Beame administration were prepared to do this. They recognized and came to terms with almost any black who won a public or party office in an overwhelmingly black constituency. And, for their part, most of the city's black officials were prepared to accommodate the regular party organization and the Beame administration. Democratic organizations would not sponsor challenges to black officials who had initially been elected as insurgents as long as they did not join forces with white reformers seeking to depose the incumbent party leadership. Mayor Beame also consulted with the city's black political establishment in selecting blacks for high positions in his administration. Notable in this regard was Beame's selection of James Dumpson as Human Resources Administrator. Dumpson's opposition to sectarian control of adoptions led Catholic and Jewish charitable organizations to fight his appointment. Sectarian forces had been dominant during previous machine-backed administrations, but Beame evidently concluded that it was worth his while politically to stick with Dumpson. Beame's decision reflected the hegemony of a new constellation of political forces in the field of welfare policy.[35]

The implicit quid pro quo for this consideration was that black politicians defer to the regular Democratic leadership in their borough in areas of its greatest concerns. This meant that black delegates voted for the regulars at judicial nominating conventions and supported the reelection of the regular county leaders in the face of challenges by reformers. An indication of the extent to which black politicians worked out a mutually agreeable arrangement with the county Democratic machines in the early 1970s was the frequency with which a number of them were denounced as sell-outs in the pages of New York's reformist newspaper, the *Village Voice*.[36]

The differences between the structure of politics within New York's black ghettos and Puerto Rican barrios led the Beame administration to deal somewhat differently with the Hispanic community. Among New York's Puerto Ricans Herman Badillo occupied a position of preeminence that had no parallel among New York's blacks in the 1970s. Badillo's position was most similar to that occupied by Adam Clayton Powell in New York's black community in the 1930s and 1940s, or the role Fiorello LaGuardia played among the city's Italian-Americans in the 1920s and 1930s.

Like Powell and LaGuardia, Badillo was a congressman who was regarded as a spokesman for members of his ethnic group regardless of whether or not they lived in his congressional district. Also, Badillo rose to prominence outside the regular Democratic party organization. He harshly criticized the machine for failing to provide Hispanics with their fair share of benefits from the municipal government, and he cultivated alliances with the machine's opponents.

The very political weakness of New York's Puerto Rican community (as late as 1973 there were no Puerto Rican city councilmen and only four Hispanic state legislators) was a source of Badillo's strength in that it gave him great recognition among his countrymen. Badillo was able to rely on this reputation to win elections; accordingly, he did not need to construct a political organization. Rather than commanding an organization, Badillo led a following—other Puerto Ricans with political aspirations found his support useful in securing election or appointment to public office.[37]

In the 1960s, two channels had opened up through which Puerto Ricans could get ahead in New York politics independently of Badillo. One was the city's antipoverty apparatus—Ramon Velez in the South

101

Bronx and the Del Toro brothers in East Harlem, to cite the most important examples, used the resources of community corporations, neighborhood school boards, and kindred groups to build political bases for themselves. A few other Puerto Rican politicians relied on the sponsorship of regular Democratic clubs to get ahead.[38]

After entering City Hall, Mayor Beame began a systematic campaign to undermine Badillo's position within the city's Puerto Rican community as well as to strengthen the regular Democratic organization in Hispanic neighborhoods. The Beame administration provided Velez, who had formed an alliance with the Bronx machine, with a steady flow of resources for his antipoverty empire. Beame also appointed a special mayoral assistant to serve as chief patronage dispenser to the city's Hispanic community. Beame's project was less than completely successful. Ramon Velez challenged Badillo in the 1974 Democratic congressional primary but was unable to defeat him, and the 1975 fiscal crisis restricted the quantity of patronage available for strengthening the machine in Hispanic neighborhoods.[39]

Although Mayor Lindsay formed an alliance with the regular Democratic county organizations at the end of his first term, and Mayor Beame strengthened them after he entered City Hall, the county organizations did not play as large a role as they had after previous reform episodes. True, in the early 1970s the majority of officials in New York City who represented district constituencies—city councilmen, state assemblymen, state senators, and civil court judges—were party regulars. Outside of Manhattan, the regular organizations also dominated offices elected at the borough or county level. The three most important of these offices were borough president, district attorney, and judge in the surrogate court. Following the 1973 election, eleven of the twelve occupants of these positions in the outer boroughs were party regulars. New York's Democratic machine and its affiliated clubs no longer had control over more than a half-million votes, as they had in the mid-1940s, but in elections for offices that had little public visibility they generally could place more campaign workers in the field than could most insurgents, raise more money, and draw on the talents of lawyers who knew how to use the incredibly (and deliberately) complex election law to get political novices thrown off the ballot.

Although the Democratic county organizations maintained their control over the majority of borough and district elective offices outside Manhattan in the early 1970s, their grip was not as tight as it had been twenty-five years earlier. Candidates who were in a position to spend a great deal

102

of money, devote a great deal of time, or campaign on issues that were of vital importance in their districts were able to seriously threaten party regulars even in some of the machine's strongholds. For example, in 1970 the deans of the U.S. House of Representatives (Emmanuel Celler) and the New York state assembly (Max Turshen)—both Brooklyn regulars who had served for forty-eight and thirty-six years respectively—were defeated by young insurgents who waged lengthy and, in the latter case, costly campaigns against them. Two years later, Congressman James Scheuer, a reformer who had been redistricted out of his seat in the Bronx, waged an expensive and successful campaign as an insurgent in a district in Brooklyn and Queens that included the home club of Brooklyn Democratic leader Meade Esposito. The Conservative Party also won an increasing number of votes in districts with large numbers of Irish and Italian homeowners during the early 1970s.

Democratic machine politicians attempted to ward off threats from these quarters as much by colluding with the Republicans and striking deals with insurgents as by trying to overwhelm them at the polls. The most extreme example of bipartisan collusion occurred in 1971 in Queens. In return for the Democrats' endorsement of Republican candidates for three vacant seats on the state Supreme Court in the judicial district encompassing Queens, the Republicans agreed to endorse the Democratic candidates for the three other Supreme Court seats, as well as the three top offices in the borough—borough president, surrogate judge, and district attorney. The way this deal was carried out is as significant as its scope. The incumbent borough president and surrogate judge, whose terms still had two years to run, resigned from their seats *after* the deadline had passed for candidates to enter that year's primary elections. In this circumstance the law provided that the Democratic and Republican candidates in the general election were to be designated by the executive committees of the two parties. The Democratic and Republican county leaders had now ensured that their jointly endorsed candidates could not be challenged in either party's primary. Evidently, they were suffi- ciently uncertain of their ability to defeat potential insurgents in a primary election that they were prepared to go to these lengths to guarantee that voters would play no meaningful role in the selection of the highest offices in their borough.[40]

When insurgent candidates did defeat party regulars, the leaders of New York's Democratic county organizations were likely to strike a deal with the insurgent. This was especially true of Brooklyn's Meade Esposito, who was as willing to negotiate mutual noninterference treaties with victorious white insurgents (such as James Scheuer) as with blacks. He

103

agreed not to sponsor challenges to these officials in subsequent primary elections if they agreed not to join with other insurgents to challenge his position as county leader or the machine's control over other elective offices.[41]

The city's regular party organizations also did not play as large a role in the *governance* of New York as they had after previous reform episodes. Party leaders in the state legislature and city council found it difficult in the early 1970s to get legislators and councilmen to vote for tax increases, and this contributed to the city's reliance upon borrowed funds to finance its budget. In addition, the mayor's power relative to the leaders of the county party organizations was greater during these years than had been the case in the years following LaGuardia's departure from City Hall. It was John Lindsay and Abe Beame—not party leaders—who brokered the deals that kept the city's governing coalition together. They decided, for example, how the claims of machine politicians for patronage would be balanced against the demand of civil service unions that all discretion be removed from the process of appointing and promoting municipal employees. One indication of Mayor Beame's power in making top appointments is the number of such appointees in his administration whose chief claim for preference was that they were personal associates of Beame's from his days as Budget Director or Comptroller, or even merely relatives of Beame's old associates. Another indication is that Beame was able to depose a county Democratic leader who crossed him. The victim of Beame's purge was Matthew Troy, who was both leader of the Queens Democratic organization and chairman of the city council's Finance Committee. In the latter capacity, Troy refused to rubber stamp Beame's budget in 1974. Infuriated, the mayor informed Democratic district leaders in Queens that he would not distribute any patronage to them unless they replaced Troy, which they dutifully did. Beame's ability to depose Troy had some important implications for New York City's fiscal politics.[42]

5

Sources of
the Fiscal Crisis

ALTHOUGH the regime Mayors Lindsay and Beame presided over from 1969 through 1975 was politically viable, it was not fiscally viable. Holding together their political coalitions required that their administrations spend more than the city collected in taxes and state and federal aid. The city could do this only as long as it could borrow money to cover the difference. When the market for New York City securities collapsed in 1975, the ensuing fiscal crisis was far more severe than the one that had contributed to John Lindsay's election as a fusion mayor in 1965.

Three factors distinguished the political system headed by Mayors Lindsay and Beame from earlier post-reform administrations and generated the 1975 fiscal crisis. The first involved changes in New York's position in the national and international economy; the second, changes in the relationship between national and local politics; and the third, changes in the composition of political coalitions in the city and in the structure of local political organizations and institutions. This combination of changes made it difficult for New York City's mayors to heed the political imperatives they faced without violating the economic and fiscal imperatives confronting local officials.

An Overview of Fiscal Politics in New York City, 1965–75

When he first ran for mayor in 1965, John Lindsay repeatedly denounced the Wagner administration for failing to balance the budget and for relying upon borrowed funds to close the gap between the city's operating expenditures and revenues. During his first three years in office, Mayor Lindsay pretty much kept his promise to put the city's finances back in order. The municipal government's operating expenditures increased by more than 50 percent during this period (rising from $3.9 billion in fiscal 1966 to $6.1 billion in fiscal 1969), but the enactment of new taxes, increases in the revenue generated by existing taxes, and increases in state and federal aid enabled the mayor to balance his budget without relying heavily upon borrowed funds.[1]

Between 1969 and 1973, however, in every year but one the city ran a large budget deficit which it papered over with various accounting gimmicks. It financed these deficits by selling short-term notes and long-term bonds, and when its notes fell due they were redeemed by selling additional notes.

Abe Beame's accession to the mayoralty in 1974 did not alter this pattern. While serving as city comptroller during Lindsay's second term, Beame had advocated an even greater reliance upon fiscal gimmicks— and therefore on borrowed funds—than Lindsay proposed in his budgets. The first budget that Beame prepared as mayor concealed another enormous deficit.

By 1975, New York City had amassed a cumulative operating deficit of more than $3 billion. Carrying this in addition to its other financing needs required that the municipal government sell an average of $750 million in short-term notes *each month.* The resulting flood of New York paper made it clear to participants in the municipal credit markets that the city was engaged in deficit financing and that a significant proportion of its outstanding notes were not, as they were purported to be, backed by tax revenues and intergovernmental aid that the municipal government would collect within a year's time.[2]

Investors came to fear that short of firing large numbers of its employees, the municipal government would be unable to redeem its notes even if a court ordered it to. And if push came to shove, they could not be certain that a judge would decree that the claims of New York's creditors had to be met, even at the expense of the safety and welfare of the city's residents. As the city's banks became increasingly skittish in late 1974 and early 1975, they reduced the holdings of New York City securities in their own accounts, further depressing the market for the city's notes and bonds. Mayor Beame's announcement that the gap between projected expenditures and revenues in the city's 1975–76 expense budget was $1.7 billion compounded the problem. The *coup de grace* was delivered in April 1975 when the attorneys for the banks indicated that if New York was unable to meet its debt service obligations, the institutions that underwrote the city's notes might be held liable for the losses suffered by the investors who purchased these securities. The refusal of the banks to serve as underwriters for the city made it impossible for the municipal government to borrow the funds needed to meet its payroll and redeem outstanding notes as they fell due, precipitating the fiscal crisis.[3]

New York in the National and International Economy

The most commonly offered explanation for New York City's fiscal problems in the 1970s focuses on the demographic and economic changes that increased burdens on the city's budget and reduced revenues. During the 1950s and 1960s, roughly one million poor blacks and Puerto Ricans moved to the city, and an equal number of middle-class whites left for the suburbs. Moreover, after experiencing a period of modest growth in the early and mid-1960s, the city's economy turned sharply downward in 1969. The sector whose economic growth had accounted for much of the city's prosperity in the 1960s—national and multinational corporations and the banks, law firms, advertising agencies, and real estate firms that served them—stopped growing. And the economic decline accelerated in the sector that had been weakest in the 1950s and 1960s—light manufacturing, primarily the garment industry. Traditionally, this latter sector had employed persons at the bottom of the city's social scale, and as light manufacturers moved from the city or went out of business, unskilled blacks and Puerto Ricans found it increasingly difficult to secure jobs. This rise in unemployment exerted upward pressure on the municipal government's social welfare expenditures at the same time that the growth of tax revenues was slowing.[4]

There is a substantial element of truth in this analysis of the sources

107

of New York City's fiscal problems. In the aftermath of the two fusion administrations that had preceded Mayor Lindsay's (1918–29 and 1946–60) New York's economy had been healthy enough to enable the post-reform regimes to finance the extensive social coalitions they were built on without drastically increasing tax rates, which would have provoked opposition from businessmen and homeowners, and without resorting to deficit financing, which would have precipitated a fiscal crisis. But sharp recessions in 1969–70 and 1973–75 reduced the market for goods manufactured in New York; the emergence of centers of light manufacturing in low-wage areas domestically and abroad (Taiwan, Hong Kong, and South Korea) increased the competition the city's firms faced in the remaining markets; and changes in transportation and communications technologies reduced some of the unique advantages New York had enjoyed as headquarters for giant corporations.

The cycle of prosperity and recession New York City experienced in the 1960s and early 1970s had other implications for municipal finances. The decline of the city's economy after 1969 made it more difficult for elected officials to finance expenditure increases by raising tax rates or enacting new taxes. In 1972, Mayor Lindsay was able to get Governor Rockefeller and the state legislature to grant additional aid and new taxing authority to the city only after a bitter, protracted fight, and then found it impossible to get the Board of Estimate and City Council to pass the full range of new taxes the state legislature had authorized. To paper over that year's budget gap, Lindsay accepted Comptroller Beame's unduly optimistic estimate of the tax revenues and federal aid the city could expect to collect and then borrowed heavily when these estimates did not pan out. Rather than face similar bruising battles in 1973 and 1974, when it was evident that prospects for victory were slim, Mayor Lindsay and then Mayor Beame did not even request new taxing authority from the state, but simply sold enormous sums of short-term notes and long-term bonds to finance operating expenditures.[5]

Why were New York's major commercial banks prepared to underwrite the sale of these securities in the early 1970s and then unwilling to do so in 1975, thereby precipitating the city's fiscal crisis? The most immediate explanation for their initial behavior is that the healthy fees and commissions they earned for their services made them loathe to ask municipal officials too many embarrassing questions about the city's financial practices. Beyond this, the cyclical pattern of New York's economy in the 1960s and 1970s explains why it was feasible for the banks to act on the basis of such short-run considerations, and why they ultimately concluded that the risks of such behavior outweighed the rewards.

108

The prosperity in the 1960s of the corporations with which the large commercial banks did business convinced members of the financial community that the city's economy was basically healthy, that New York had a future it could borrow against. In 1970, the major bond-rating agencies, Moody's and Standard & Poor's, expressed concern about the municipal government's financial practices by lowering New York's credit rating. But that same year, the First National City Bank published a rosy survey of New York's economy, and in 1972–73 the bond-rating agencies raised the city's rating back to "A," with Moody's citing the "amazing resiliency" of New York's economy.[6]

The recession of 1973–75—the deepest the United States had experienced since the 1930s—shattered this complacency. The nation's banks were caught in an exposed position with loans to financially shaky corporations and real estate investment trusts, and the billions of dollars of debt they carried from Third World countries that, in the wake of the 1973 oil shock, were in precarious financial positions. The banks had more reason now to be uneasy about New York's financial practices and to reconsider the advisability of continually rolling over New York's short-term debt.[7]

Although the importance of these economic conditions in explaining New York's fiscal problems cannot be denied, it is not the whole story. Policies pursued by the federal and municipal governments also contributed to New York City's economic problems. And the effect of economic changes upon the city's budget was mediated by politics. After all, unemployed men, single mothers, and abandoned children do not have the authority to appropriate funds from the city treasury or to float municipal bonds. To account for the rapid growth of New York City's budget and debt, one must explain why public officials responded as they did to changes in the city's demographic and economic base.

National–Local Political Linkages

Changes in national political alignments, in the institutions linking Washington to local governments, and in the policies pursued by the federal government also played a part in making the regime that governed New York from 1969 through 1974 less viable fiscally than previous post-reform administrations had been. Traditionally, political parties had served as the institutions linking national and local politics, and the distribution of patronage was the central focus of that relationship. As long as this was operative, federal-local relations did not have a major impact upon the fiscal health of the municipal government.[8] The situation was fundamentally altered, however, by the New Deal realignment in the 1930s, Washington's turn to internationalism in the 1940s and 1950s, the concessions that liberal Democrats made to other political forces during those decades, and the programs the Republican party sponsored to overcome the Democratic majority.

Federal policies grounded in the political alignments of the New Deal and postwar period were instrumental in the exodus of many white, middle-class taxpayers to the suburbs and the migration of poor Southern blacks into New York and other Northern cities, as well as in the decline of the manufacturing sector of the city's economy. Especially influential were policies that (1) financed the construction of highways linking central cities with suburban areas; (2) channeled private savings and investment capital into the financing of single-family homes in these areas; (3) fostered the mechanization of agriculture in the South (while abandoning efforts to reform the Southern land-tenure system); (4) delegated authority to the states to determine welfare grant levels and to outlaw union shops; and (5) created an international regime of free trade encompassing low-wage regions abroad and that also extended America's defense perimeter to these regions.[9]

Besides having adverse consequences for the revenue side of New York City's budget, federal policies rooted in New Deal and postwar alignments placed burdens on the expenditure side of the budget. The federal program that imposed the greatest burden was Aid to Families with Dependent Children (AFDC). Washington covered half of the cost of AFDC, but required that states—which then could pass on part of the cost to local governments—cover the other half. Albany required New York City to finance half of the nonfederal share, so that every four dollars spent on AFDC in New York City cost the municipal treasury one dollar. However, for reasons to be explained later, prior to the mid-1960s this burden was not onerous. In 1964, the total cost of AFDC to the municipal treasury was only $151 million, which amounted to less than 7 percent of the city's total tax levy budget.[10]

Changes in national politics that occurred during the 1960s led New York City's expenditures to grow rapidly in 1965–75. Most directly, the landslide victory of the Democrats in the 1964 presidential and congressional elections overwhelmed the conservative coalition of Republicans and Southern Democrats in Congress, which for a quarter century had

110

blocked new federal social programs. Following the 1964 election Congress enacted a number of new grant-in-aid programs that, by virtue of matching requirements, placed additional burdens on New York City's budget.

The Democratic ascendancy of the 1960s altered not only the balance of power in national politics between conservative Republicans and Southern Democrats and the more liberal Nothern Democrats, it also sparked a struggle for influence within the latter faction of the majority party. This struggle was directly related to political conflicts occurring then in the nation's major cities and led to significant changes in the institutions linking Washington to urban governments. These changes, in turn, contributed to sharp increases in municipal expenditures in New York and other large cities.[11]

In the early and mid-1960s, the Democratic party drew the bulk of its support outside the South from blue-collar workers, city dwellers, Catholics, blacks, and Jews; and its cadres were an amalgam of machine politicians, public officials, union leaders, and middle-class liberals. The influence of this last group was greater at the peak of the political system than at its base. Middle-class professionals played a major role in staffing and in drafting the legislative programs of the Kennedy and Johnson administrations, but in most large Northern cities Democratic machine politicians, businessmen, union officials, civil servants, and tax-conscious homeowners exercised considerably more control over municipal governments and bureaucracies.[12]

Middle-class liberals used the influence they enjoyed in the Kennedy and Johnson administrations to influence the policies, practices, and fiscal priorities of city governments. The presidential task forces that drafted New Frontier and Great Society legislation—composed of academics, foundation officials, representatives of professional associations, and so forth—argued that municipal governments did not command the resources, the talent, or the intiative necessary to solve the "urban crisis." They proposed that the federal government extend grants-in-aid to local governments on the condition that they adopt "innovative" programs to deal with the problems of the poor. To obtain these grants, cities had to hire administrators whose educational backgrounds and institutional affiliations were similar to the officials in Washington who dispensed federal funds, and who would propose to spend these monies for purposes their Washington counterparts favored. Essentially, the grant-in-aid programs of the Kennedy and Johnson administrations were the means by which middle-class liberals and their political allies used their

111

access to the executive branch of the federal government to influence the programs, hiring practices, and expenditure patterns of city governments.

Blacks played a crucial role in this process. Racial minorities received less than their share of municipal jobs and services in most Northern cities, and the effort of middle-class liberals to alter the behavior of city governments was animated in part by a desire to remedy this. Equally important, that effort was legitimated by the liberals' claim that municipal bureaucracies were "insensitive" and "unresponsive" to the needs of the black community. Blacks joined in this attack because the mechanisms of community participation attached to almost all Great Society programs provided them with channels to obtain access to federally funded resources and with a means to influence the behavior of the regular agencies of municipal government.

Federal urban programs had a major impact upon municipal expenditures in New York and other large cities, enabling the political forces that wanted urban governments to alter their fiscal priorities to exert pressure upon cities from both Washington and from the cities' streets. One of the clearest examples—but by no means the only example—of this involved the AFDC program. Prior to the mid-1960s, New York City's welfare department did little to encourage those eligible for benefits to apply for them. In addition, the department rejected the applications of a substantial proportion of those who did seek AFDC assistance and made systematic efforts to purge its rolls of persons who might no longer be eligible—going so far as to stage midnight raids on AFDC recipients to see if there were a man in the house who could be held financially responsible for supporting the family.

Activists affiliated with federally financed antipoverty agencies played a major role in overturning or swamping AFDC procedures. Antipoverty lawyers successfully challenged in the courts the rules and practices welfare bureaucracies used to limit the growth of the AFDC rolls in New York and other cities. Antipoverty workers informed poor people of their entitlements and encouraged them to apply for public assistance. The subsequent torrent of applicants in welfare offices made it impossible for social workers to follow the lengthy procedures they had formerly used to determine client eligibility. Finally, welfare rights organizers—the majority affiliated with federally financed community action agencies—organized demonstrations at welfare offices by AFDC recipients demanding the full range of benefits to which they were entitled. In the volatile late 1960s, welfare officials commonly acceded to demands to avoid incidents that could escalate into full-scale ghetto riots.

Even after the threat of riots passed and the welfare rights movement collapsed, expenditures on public assistance remained at a high level. The expansion of the welfare rolls brought about by the events of the 1960s reduced the stigma attached to being on welfare that had formerly kept many poor people from applying for public assistance. Also, the judicial decisions striking down the procedures welfare departments had employed to reject applicants and throw people off the rolls remained the law of the land.[13]

The interaction between the national and local political actors who played leading roles in these events, it should be noted, occurred through judicial and administrative, rather than party, channels. Moreover, the quest for votes was not a central concern of these antipoverty lawyers, federal judges, community organizers, and officials in the federal Office of Economic Opportunity. This carried an important implication: because these actors had few ties to the elected officials responsible for city finances, they did not have to concern themselves with the question of how the city was to pay for the changes in social welfare policies and procedures that they helped to bring about.[14]

Local Political Coalitions and Institutions

The fiscal policies of New York in the early 1970s were also heavily influenced by changes that occurred in the composition of the city's dominant political coalition and in the organizations and institutions linking important political forces to the municipal government. Three features of New York politics were especially important in leading the city's operating expenditures to increase at a faster rate than its annually recurring revenues: the increasing power of nonwhites and their political allies, reflected in the rapid growth of expenditures on programs serving black and Puerto Rican clienteles; the inability of mayors, for political and institutional reasons, to finance these increases by holding the line on expenditures flowing to other segments of the city's population, especially white working- and middle-class voters and municipal employees; and changes in the structure of New York politics that reduced the influence of taxpayer interests relative to those demanding expenditures.

113

Racial Minorities and their Allies

A major source of budgetary inflation in New York in the 1960s and early 1970s was the growing power of the city's racial minorities and their political allies. Table 5.1 shows that total expenditures on the four basic functions (police, fire, sanitation, elementary and secondary education) serving most residents grew far less rapidly between fiscal 1961 and 1976 than did expenditures on redistributive functions (social services, hospitals) serving a predominantly nonwhite clientele. New York City's expenditures on higher education also rose greatly after open admissions increased the number of black and Puerto Rican students at the City University. As for tax-levy expenditures, social services and higher education again rank on top, but the growth rate of these expenditures in the municipal hospital system declined after the enactment of Medicaid in 1965, which enabled the city to use federal dollars to cover costs it had formerly financed with local revenues.

These expenditure increases resulted in part from changes in the relationship between the local and national political systems. By no means, however, were these expenditures forced upon a reluctant City Hall. Mayors Lindsay and Beame advocated increasing welfare grants, despite the additional burdens this would place on the municipal treasury. And the open enrollment admissions policy in higher education was adopted without prodding by federal officials. Therefore one must look

TABLE 5.1
Increase in New York City Expenditures
for Seven Major Functions, 1961–76

	Total Expenditures (%)	Tax-Levy Expenditures (%)
Basic Functions		
Police	277.6%	278.4%
Fire	216.9	224.7
Sanitation	178.0	148.5
Education	304.8	189.4
TOTAL	274.5	212.1
Redistributive Functions		
Welfare	940.2	749.1
Hospitals	569.7	150.8
Higher Education	1,224.3	614.0
TOTAL	829.7	399.6

SOURCE: City of New York, Temporary Commission on City Finances, *Eighth Interim Report to the Mayor*, 1977, p. 19.

114

at political changes within the city to account fully for these budget increases.

Politicians that they were, Mayors Wagner, Lindsay, and Beame doubtlessly gave consideration to whether increased social service spending would be politically beneficial, neutral, or suicidal. But it is unlikely that they adopted these priorities to win the votes of welfare recipients, whose electoral turnout rates were so low that to risk alienating taxpayers for this purpose would have been political madness. The mayors were more concerned with the reactions of opinion leaders who believed the city should not be mean-spirited in its treatment of the poor and who could influence the votes of liberal whites and middle-class blacks.

New York's mayors also increased public benefits to blacks to preserve civil order during the late 1960s and early 1970s. In particular, the city adopted its policy of open admissions at the City University in response to a student sit-in that threatened to ignite a riot in the surrounding black neighborhood. This fear of civil disorder was not unfounded. In 1971, a demonstration in Brooklyn's Brownsville against possible cuts in municipal programs serving blacks began a riot that lasted three days.[15]

Middle-Class Whites and Municipal Employees

Another reason why New York City's budget grew so rapidly in the 1960s and early 1970s is that increases in expenditures on programs serving nonwhite clienteles were not financed by reducing or, at least, restricting the growth rate of expenditures serving other clienteles in the city. The data in table 5.1 indicate that expenditures on the basic municipal services most salient to working- and middle-class whites did not grow as rapidly as expenditures serving the city's nonwhite communities, but they were not stagnant: between fiscal 1961 and 1976 basic municipal service expenditures increased by 274.5 percent.

Actions taken by city officials in the interests of the residents of publicly subsidized middle-income (Mitchell-Lama) housing projects also contributed to the explosive growth of New York's short-term debt. As interest rates climbed during the early 1970s, city officials were reluctant to finance the construction of the cooperative Mitchell-Lama projects with long-term bonds, as this would require residents to bear relatively high monthly mortgage payments. Anticipating that interests rates would decline, Comptroller Abe Beame used short-term bond anticipation notes (BANs) to finance Mitchell-Lama, with the intention of converting these into long-term bonds when rates came down. When interest rates continued to climb, however, BANs that matured were redeemed with the proceeds of new, and larger, note sales.[16]

115

Mayor Lindsay went along with such measures because he did not command a political organization strong enough to elect himself and a majority on the Board of Estimate and city council without the support of the voters who benefited from these measures. Consequently, Lindsay could not finance expenditures benefiting the core groups in his own constituency by reducing the flow of expenditures to, or increasing the taxes of, these other voters, another reason why New York City's expenditures grew more rapidly than its revenues.

In addition, the unionization of municipal employees in the 1960s greatly increased the city's labor costs. The data in table 5.2 assess the extent to which increased labor costs contributed to the rise of municipal expenditures in New York between 1961 and 1975. This table reports the city's "expenditures by object," that is, the size of the city's payments to the ultimate recipients of municipal expenditures—city employees, welfare clients, the holders of New York City bonds, and business firms and nonprofit organizations from which the city purchased goods and services.[17]

Between 1961 and 1975 New York City's labor costs quadrupled. This was less than the rate of increase in the city's social welfare expenditures, but because the salaries of municipal employees are higher than the benefits received by welfare recipients, rising labor costs accounted for 45.1 percent of the total increase in the city's budget between 1961 and 1975, whereas social welfare expenditures accounted for a smaller rise— 27.1 percent—in the total increase in municipal expenditures during this

TABLE 5.2

New York City Operating Expenditures by Object: Percentage Increase and Proportion of Total Increase, 1961–75

| | Expenditures in Millions | | Percentage Increase | Proportion of Total Increase |
	1961	1975	1961–75	1961–75
Wages, Pensions, and Fringe Benefits	$1,334.7	$5,520.6	313.6%	45.1%
Social Welfare	303.9	2,822.0	828.6	27.1
Hospitals	159.4	631.5	296.1	5.1
Debt Service	386.7	1,383.5	257.7	10.7
Contracts, Supplies, Equipment, Other	180.2	1,296.7	619.6	12.0
TOTAL	$2,364.9	$11,654.3	392.7	100.0

SOURCES: City of New York, *Annual Report of the Comptroller*, 1960–61 and 1974–75; Temporary Commission on City Finances, *The City in Transition*, Appendix III, table 4.

period. If one adds to these figures the payments to the municipal hospital system (whose patients were largely poor and nonwhite), it becomes evident that more than 75 percent of the increase in the city's budget between 1961 and 1975 was due to increases in benefits to municipal employees and programs that served the poor.

The most proximate explanation for the rapid rise of municipal labor costs is that the size of the city's workforce grew by almost 50 percent between 1961 and 1975—from 200,706 to 294,522—and the average cost to the city for each employee (salary, pension, and fringe benefits) almost tripled during these years, rising from $8,234 in 1961 to $22,283 in 1975. Growth of the city's workforce was partly a consequence of the process that led expenditures on programs serving largely nonwhite clienteles to increase rapidly during this period. Employment in the city's welfare agencies increased by more than 200 percent between 1961 and 1975, and employment in the City University system increased by more than 300 percent. Employment in the third municipal agency that came to serve a predominantly nonwhite clientele—the city hospital system—grew more slowly (by 21 percent), but taken together the city's welfare, higher education, and health agencies accounted for 45 percent of the increases in municipal employment between 1961 and 1975.

Unionization of city workers is another reason why municipal employment grew rapidly in the 1960s. As the Ocean Hill-Brownsville dispute demonstrated, civil service unions ensured that the interests of their current members would not be impaired by efforts to increase the number of nonwhites on the municipal payroll. Consequently, the city could only hire additional blacks and Puerto Ricans if it increased the size of its workforce. And the unionization of the municipal labor force was the major reason why the wages, pensions, and fringe benefits of New York's employees rose in the 1960s and early 1970s—at a more rapid rate than inflation.[18]

In addition, unionization enabled civil servants to act as an independent force in the electoral arena, most notably in state legislative races. In return for campaign assistance, members of the city's delegation to the state legislature supported bills benefiting civil servants—in particular, increasing pension benefits—that were extremely costly to the municipal treasury. In mayoral elections, the unionization of municipal employees was significant not so much in the provision of campaign assistance, but because strikes could disrupt the administration of the incumbent mayor. It was to avoid municipal employee strikes—and the tumultuous atmosphere these had imparted to his first three years in office—that Mayor Lindsay granted expensive concessions to the city's unions during the

117

1969 round of contract negotiations. For similar reasons, Mayor Beame refused to implement major cutbacks during his first year in office, even though the skein of municipal finances was beginning to unravel.[19]

Finally, the very municipal labor relations apparatus that Mayor Wagner had established during his last years in office, and which Mayor Lindsay extended to avoid strikes and institutionalize the relations between his administration and civil service unions, greatly increased labor costs. It took little time for the unions to learn that the "impasse panels" that were convened to break deadlocks in collective bargaining generally split the difference between the city's last offer and the union's last demand. By simply inflating their initial demands the unions were able to get the benefit increases they wanted. Also, the work rules established through collective bargaining limited the ability of managers to deploy personnel in a manner designed to increase output per employee. The only way a mayor could maintain a constant level of services under these conditions was to increase the size of the municipal workforce—at great expense to the public treasury.[20]

The forces driving up public expenditures in the 1960s and early 1970s were by no means unique to New York City. The unionization of civil servants, the growing assertiveness of blacks, and the alliances formed between blacks and Washington were nationwide phenomena and, consequently, expenditures increased elsewhere. Table 5.3 shows that in 1975 New York's per employee labor costs (salaries plus pensions) were well above average, but not out of line with those borne by some of the nation's largest cities: Detroit's labor costs per employee were higher and Los Angeles's only 5 percent lower. Indeed, looking only at the salaries of municipal employees performing comparable functions, Chicago, Washington, and Los Angeles, as well as Detroit, rank higher than New York.[21] However, New York's civil service unions were able to win unusually generous pension benefits, pushing labor costs per employee up to the second highest position among the twelve most populous cities in the United States.[22]

As the data in the second column of table 5.3 indicate, New York's work force per capita was larger than those in all but two of the twelve major cities. The number of municipal employees per thousand population in New York was significantly lower than Washington's and essentially the same as Baltimore's, but was from two to five times greater than those of the other major cities. (Washington's work force is larger than any other city's because it performs functions that are performed elsewhere by state governments.)[23]

The figures in the third and fourth columns reflect the combined effect

118

TABLE 5.3

Municipal Labor Costs in Twelve Largest U.S. Cities in 1975

	Labor Costs Per Employee	Employees Per 1,000 Population	Labor Costs Per Capita	Labor Costs As Percentage of Personal Income
New York	$19,543	45.5	889	19.9%
Chicago	15,102	15.4	232	5.5
Los Angeles	18,638	17.1	318	6.8
Philadelphia	14,013	20.4	286	7.4
Detroit	23,424	14.8	346	8.4
Houston	10,387	10.8	112	2.9
Baltimore	11,278	46.2	521	14.1
Dallas	11,411	16.3	186	4.0
Washington, D.C.	16,724	62.4	1044	20.7
San Diego	15,326	9.1	140	3.6
San Antonio	8,709	14.6	127	4.7
Indianapolis	8,244	15.8	130	3.1

SOURCES: Labor costs from U.S., Bureau of the Census, *City Government Finances 1974–75*, table 5; full-time equivalent employees from U.S., Bureau of the Census, *City Employment in 1975*, table 4; personal income from U.S., Bureau of Economic Analysis, *Local Area Personal Income*, 1977.

of New York's moderately high labor costs per employee and unusually large work force. New York's per capita labor costs in 1974–75 were $889. This sum was about 15 percent lower than Washington's, but was from 1.7 to 7.9 times greater than in the other largest cities. The fourth column shows that New York's municipal wage bill amounted to 19.9 percent of the total personal income of the city's residents. Again with the exception of Washington, municipal labor costs relative to the local economy loomed from 1.4 to 6.9 times greater in New York than in any of the nation's other major cities.[24]

Service-Demanders versus Money-Providers

Changes also occurred in New York during the 1960s and early 1970s in the relative power of service-demanding and taxpayer interests and in the organizations linking these political forces to the municipal government. These further weakened constraints upon municipal budgetary inflation.

In 1975, New York's total expenditures—the costs of all the functions it performed—were much higher per capita than those of any other large city (with the exception of Washington). However, as the figures in the first column of table 5.4 indicate, New York's per capita expenditures in 1975 on what the U.S. Census defines as *common* municipal functions—

119

TABLE 5.4
Per Capita Operating Expenditures
in Twelve Largest U.S. Cities, 1974–75

	Common Functions	All Functions
New York	215	1,330
Chicago	163	266
Los Angeles	183	247
Philadelphia	227	423
Detroit	215	370
Houston	113	155
Baltimore	269	823
Dallas	144	196
San Diego	143	186
San Antonio	96	131
Washington, D.C.	392	1,710
Indianapolis	122	264

SOURCE: U.S., Bureau of the Census, *City Government Finances in 1974–75*, tables 5 and 6.

police, fire, sanitation, and other basic services—were not so different from those of other large cities. The reason why New York's expenditures on all functions were so much greater than those of other cities, even though its expenditures on common functions were less out of line, is that far larger sums were spent on *noncommon* functions—functions that most city governments do not perform. These include elementary and secondary education, higher education, welfare, health care and hospitals, and subsidized housing programs. To a considerable degree, the New York City programs and agencies whose clienteles became increasingly black and Puerto Rican in the 1960s and early 1970s, and whose budgets grew the most rapidly, involved these noncommon functions. If these are performed at all in other cities, they generally are conducted and financed by state governments, county governments, or special districts (for example, school districts) with their own revenue-raising and spending authority.[25]

The explanation for this difference in expenditure patterns between New York and other major cities is partly historical and juridical. New York entered the 1960s performing a broader range of functions than other cities, especially within the realm of social welfare policy. Hence, demands for increased expenditures for programs serving blacks that elsewhere were focused on county or state governments were focused on the municipal government in New York City.

There was, however, a political foundation underlying these expenditure differences between New York and other cities. Elected officials in New York found it politically useful prior to the 1960s to enact social welfare programs, and in ensuing years they increased expenditures on a number of these more rapidly than did officials having jurisdiction over such programs in other cities. This does not mean, though, as political scientist Paul Peterson has argued, that New York City's financial problems resulted from a long-standing propensity of its officials to enact programs that redistribute income to the poor. The source of this propensity, Peterson argues, is the unusually important role special interest groups have long played in the city's political process—a characteristic of New York politics that was a central theme of Wallace Sayre's and Herbert Kaufman's 1960 classic, *Governing New York City*.[26]

It is true that interest groups played a central role in New York City politics prior to the 1960s, but Sayre and Kaufman observed that these groups divided into two camps, the "service-demanders" and the "money-providers." The most important members of the latter camp were homeowners and small businessmen in the outer boroughs, whose political vehicles were the Democratic county party organizations; and real-estate, banking, and business interests in downtown and midtown Manhattan, whose leading spokesman on issues of municipal finance was the Citizens Budget Commission (CBC). Prior to the 1960s, these groups enjoyed privileged access to the bloc that dominated the Board of Estimate.

Figure 5.1 suggests that an equilibrium existed between service-demanding and money-providing interests in the 1950s. The figures on the vertical axis are the municipal government's locally financed operating expenditures as a percentage of the total personal income of New York City's residents.[27] These data indicate that, relative to the city's economy, locally financed municipal expenditures grew slowly between 1952–53 and 1961–62; it took seven years to increase from 6.8 to 8 percent. This equilibrium was shattered during Mayor Wagner's third term. Between 1961–62 and 1965–66 municipal expenditures relative to the total income of the city's residents rose from 8 to 9.5 percent, a larger increase than during the previous period, in less than half the number of years. Locally financed operating expenditures relative to the private sector remained on this new and higher plateau during Mayor Lindsay's first three years in office, but between 1968–69 and 1974–75 they shot up from 9.9 to 15.4 percent—more than three times faster than in Wagner's last term and Lindsay's early years in office.

Changes in the size of the municipal budget relative to the local economy were a consequence not only of the growing assertiveness and

121

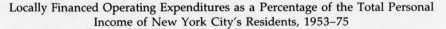

FIGURE 5.1

Locally Financed Operating Expenditures as a Percentage of the Total Personal Income of New York City's Residents, 1953–75

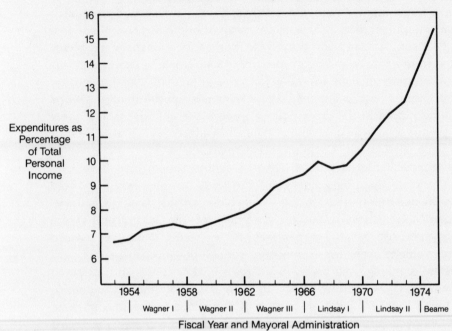

Fiscal Year and Mayoral Administration

SOURCES: Locally financed operating expenditures from City of New York, Citizens Budget Commission, master sheets for *Pocket Summary of New York City Finances, Fiscal Year 1977-78*, table 4; income data from New York State, Department of Commerce, *Personal Income in Counties in New York State, 1953–1975*.

power of expenditure-demanding groups, but also of the declining cohesiveness and power of the coalition of forces that had slowed the pace of budgetary growth in the 1950s. Cleavages over municipal financial policy developed within the downtown business community during the 1960s. The CBC continued to adhere to the old-time religion of fiscal restraint, but other groups that counted prominent businessmen among their members—most notably, the Urban Coalition—preached another gospel: that New Yorkers must atone for the historical injustices inflicted upon the city's racial minorities, even if this meant increasing municipal expenditures and taxes.[28]

In addition, however united or divided leaders of the business community might be, New York's business elite was a less influential force in the 1960s than it had been during previous reform periods. In contrast to those earlier periods, when citizens' committees formed by the most prominent members of New York's upper class had bestowed the imprimatur of reform on anti-machine candidates, it was the support of

122

the Liberal party in 1961 that helped Mayor Wagner present himself as a reformer, despite his long association with Carmine DeSapio and other machine politicians. More important, it was John Lindsay's nomination by the Liberal party in 1965 that enabled the Republican congressman to campaign as a fusion candidate, rather than as simply the GOP nominee. The Liberals granted their nomination to these candidates because they were identified with liberal programs and policies, not because they had strong commitments to fiscal restraint. In 1969, Lindsay found himself even more dependent on the support of expenditure-demanding groups to win reelection and govern the city. In the 1960s, then, the only terms upon which it was possible for a reform mayor to put together a winning coalition involved a commitment to higher, rather than lower, levels of municipal expenditure.

The influence that homeowners and small businessmen from the outer boroughs exerted over municipal fiscal policy also changed in important ways in the 1960s, and the declining strength of New York's regular Democratic party organizations played a major role in this. During the 1950s, leaders of the Democratic county machines had put together slates of candidates that provided representation to tax-conscious home-owners. Robert Wagner's election to a third term in 1961, in opposition to a slate backed by the regular Democratic party organization, and Lindsay's election under similar circumstances in 1965, severed—or, at least, loosened—this tie between tax-conscious voters and the mayor. The tacit alliance that many Democratic machine politicians entered into with Mayor Lindsay during and after his campaign for reelection in 1969, and the election in 1973 of Mayor Beame, whose administration also rested upon a grand coalition of expenditure-demanding groups, signaled the machine's recognition that the only terms upon which a governing coalition could be held together at the citywide level entailed increases in municipal expenditures.

Tax-conscious homeowners were acutely aware that their chief concerns were not foremost in the minds of Democrats and Republicans alike in City Hall during the 1960s and early 1970s, and this contributed to a rise in the Conservative party vote in councilmanic and state legislative districts in Brooklyn, Queens, the Bronx, and Staten Island. This, in turn, created a disjunction between the imperatives that confronted politicians representing citywide constituencies and those confronting politicians representing many neighborhood constituencies. The former found it politically useful to increase municipal expenditures, whereas the latter found it increasingly difficult to vote for revenue measures sufficient to finance these expenditures.

Although representatives of the city's small homeowners were unable

123

to limit the growth of municipal spending during the 1960s and 1970s, they could and did fight the mayor's efforts to raise the taxes their constituents had to bear, requiring the mayor to expend a lot of political capital to secure tax increases. After 1969, when the city's economy entered a deep recession, the resistance Mayor Lindsay had to overcome to raise city taxes increased. Consequently, he relied more heavily upon the sale of short-term notes and long-term bonds to close the city's annual budget gaps. The pace of borrowing became even greater during Mayor Beame's first year in office—setting the stage for New York City's 1975 fiscal crisis.[29]

PART III

THE POLITICAL CONSEQUENCES OF NEW YORK CITY'S FISCAL CRISIS

6

The Fiscal Crisis and
Its Budgetary
Consequences

THE SUMS New York City borrowed to cover its budget deficits grew to be so great by the mid-1970s that major participants in the public credit market came to doubt the municipal government's ability to redeem its securities. In March 1975 the market closed to the city. Because the prospect of New York going bankrupt was so threatening to the most powerful political forces in the city, they were compelled to accept a bail-out plan that required major changes in both the city's fiscal policies and the institutions controlling the city's finances. Once these new financing arrangements were established and the threat of imminent bankruptcy passed, however, the city's fiscal politics and policies settled into a pattern that is not as unique as many observers of New York City politics have alleged. This pattern of politics and policy resembles in many ways the pattern characterizing previous post-reform regimes.

1975: A Year of Crisis

"Crisis" is a much overused term, but even under the most restrictive definition, New York was in a state of crisis in 1975. When the financial markets closed to the city it became impossible for the municipal government to function as it had previously, gravely endangering the groups and individuals whose interests were deeply affected by what the city government did or failed to do. New York City needed to borrow money to conduct its day-to-day operations. If the city's notes could not be sold—or some alternative source of financing found—the municipal government would not be able to pay its employees, purchase supplies, issue public assistance checks, or redeem its maturing securities.[1]

The most immediate consequence of the city's inability to meet its obligations would have been that the value of New York securities held by the city's banks would have plummeted, municipal employees would have faced payless paydays, and, if the employees refused to work without being paid, the public would have been deprived of municipal services. If vital services such as policing, firefighting, and garbage collection were interrupted, social chaos might have erupted. And if New York City had defaulted on its $11 billion in outstanding debts, serious damage might have been done to the national and international banking systems. State and federal officials could scarcely be indifferent to these possibilities.

To avoid these catastrophes, influential figures on the city, state, and national levels proposed a variety of drastic actions: declaring a moratorium on some or all of the city's debt service payments; firing tens of thousands of municipal employees and reducing the wages of those remaining; eliminating a number of municipal services and cutting back on others; and increasing local taxes and subway fares. Public officials were compelled to implement some of these proposals and to consider the others— thereby threatening the interests of almost every important political force in the city.[2]

When groups and individuals find it impossible to defend their vital interests through existing institutions and practices, they characteristically act outside those institutions and violate those practices in an effort to protect themselves. As political scientist Samuel P. Huntington notes, in Third World countries whose political institutions are incapable of channeling the demands voiced by major social forces, "the wealthy bribe; students riot; workers strike; mobs demonstrate; and the military

128

coup."[3] So far as one can judge, the level of bribery did not increase in New York in 1975, nor did the police department attempt to take control of City Hall. Nonetheless, a number of groups and individuals took some extraordinary steps to protect their interests that year. The city's major commercial banks, for instance, engaged in something close to financial blackmail. Rather than underwriting or purchasing New York's securities in exchange for a fee (in the form of commissions and interest payments), they refused to do so unless the municipal government adopted the financial policies and practices that they—as interpreters of what "the market" demanded—wanted it to pursue.[4]

The behavior of the banks, however, was only a particular instance of a more general phenomenon. Others used whatever leverage they could command in an effort to avoid bearing the costs of the city's financial problems. Convinced that New York's largest bank, First National City, was leading the drive to fire city workers, several municipal employee unions withdrew $15 million from the bank in June 1975, and staged a demonstration at the bank's headquarters that was attended by 10,000 city employees. In October 1975 a number of municipal union leaders threatened to stage a general strike if the mayor went ahead with a plan to lay off thousands of employees and impose a three-year freeze on the wages of those remaining on the city payroll. The police and fire unions attempted to pressure the municipal government into rehiring members who had been discharged, by threatening the city's tourist trade—distributing leaflets at bus, train, and airline terminals describing New York as "fear city," and warning out-of-towners that it was no longer a safe place to visit. Municipal employees also staged wildcat strikes and disruptive demonstrations. For example, several hundred discharged policemen disrupted rush hour traffic on the Brooklyn Bridge, and employees of the Highway Department blocked traffic on the Henry Hudson Parkway.[5]

Partisan acrimony also escalated during the early months of the crisis, and public officials went beyond the usual boundaries of political give-and-take to put pressure on one another. To get the Republican-controlled state senate to pass a bill granting the city additional taxing authority, for example, Mayor Beame threatened to cut public services in the neighborhoods represented by the city's seven Republican state senators. The senators agreed to support the legislation only if the mayor pledged to limit layoffs in the police and fire departments—agencies that employed and served the largely lower-middle-class Catholic homeowners the senators represented.[6]

The 1975 fiscal crisis, then, led to a suspension of politics-as-usual in

129

New York. Established institutions were unable to channel (and thereby contain) the efforts of key political forces to influence the municipal government, and public officials ignored the norms of comity they heeded in more normal times. This posed additional threats to groups whose interests were most affected by the city's financial policies. Bankers and union leaders each feared that their opponents would succeed in convincing the public that they were responsible for the city's financial problems, enabling public officials to implement drastic measures at their expense. Public officials feared that once conflicts spilled outside institutional channels, a chain reaction might be set off—union leaders could lose control of their members, demonstrations by public employees trying to protect their jobs could spark demonstrations by minority groups seeking to protect the benefits they received from the municipal government, and so on. Further, this potential threat to public order would be compounded if it convinced investors that it would be madness to purchase New York City securities. Finally, the power play of the Republican state senators could lead representatives of other groups to insist that their constituents be spared the full costs of retrenchment; in fact, the black caucus in the state legislature did attempt to extract such concessions as a condition for its support of one bail-out plan, and a group of liberal politicians formed a caucus called Elected Officials for Social Justice in an effort to do the same. Fragmentation like this could make it impossible to implement any bail-out plan.[7]

Despite these potential dangers, public officials and other influential figures in New York politics regarded as untenable the most obvious solutions to the city's financial problems—default or bankruptcy. (Default would have involved the city's failing to make scheduled interest or principal payments on its securities, and bankruptcy would have involved asking a federal court to assume control of the city's finances and to release the municipal government from some of its financial obligations.) Both default and bankruptcy would have compounded the problem of obtaining the additional loans the municipal government needed to continue functioning. Moreover, the procedures called for in the federal bankruptcy statute operative in 1975 would probably have been impossible to follow in the New York case. Public officials also could not expect city employees, welfare recipients, and the consumers of municipal services to sit quietly and patiently for the months or years it would take for a federal judge to determine which of the benefits they had received would now have to go.[8]

Commercial banks also regarded default and bankruptcy as unacceptable

130

options. They could not assume that if push came to shove a judge would give priority to the city's note holders if it meant firing half the city's workforce and cutting vital municipal services. And if the municipal notes the banks had underwritten were not redeemed at full value when they fell due, the banks might be held liable for any losses sustained by investors. The banks also might be charged with failing to meet fiduciary obligations to trust department clients for whom they had purchased New York City securities.[9]

The leaders of New York's municipal employee unions also dreaded bankruptcy. If the city went bankrupt, a federal judge would have the power to abrogate municipal labor contracts—cutting the wages and fringe benefits of municipal employees, altering work rules, and perhaps reducing pension benefits. This would mean the end of collective bargaining in New York—and, for all intents and purposes, the destruction of public employee unionism in the city.[10]

Because default or bankruptcy were considered unacceptable alternatives, it was possible for the architects of the plan that ultimately bailed out the municipal government to compel city officials, bankers, and municipal union leaders to acquiesce to arrangements that imposed substantial burdens on them. In contrast to previous fiscal crises, New York's bankers did not take the lead in designing the 1975 bail-out plan, because they no longer commanded resources sufficient to the task. The municipal government had grown so much since the fiscal crisis of 1932–33 and had engaged in such extensive fiscal gimmickry during the early 1970s, that in 1975 it required $12.96 billion in cash and credit to deal with its cash-flow problem, finance its current deficit, refund outstanding short-term notes used to finance previous operating deficits, and meet its minimal capital construction needs. This sum exceeded the combined gross capital of the eleven major commercial banks belonging to the New York Clearing House Association.[11]

Mayor Beame was also unable to take charge of events in 1975. Early in the year he announced a series of budget cuts and employee lay-offs which he hoped would restore investor confidence in New York securities. These efforts failed because in the eyes of the "market"—meaning the banking and business leaders who reputedly knew what investors were thinking—Beame was too closely identified with the coalition of political forces and the fiscal practices that had led the city to near-bankruptcy. Moreover, the behavior of the Beame administration as the crisis unfolded did nothing to alter this identification. When city agencies were ordered to lay off several thousand civil servants, they filled their quotas by

131

counting employees who had voluntarily retired months before. Beame used these inflated figures in his press releases. Such ploys were a standard procedure for administrative agencies in New York politics, but the mayor and his associates failed to recognize that the fiscal preconditions for politics-as-usual no longer existed in 1975. This only reinforced the financial community's judgment that the Beame administration was unwilling and unable to change its ways.[12]

Under these circumstances it was Governor Hugh Carey who took the initiative in rescuing New York City from bankruptcy, because the state government's credit would have been seriously impaired if the city had defaulted on its financial obligations. Also, the state ultimately would have been called upon to pick up the pieces—by calling out the National Guard—if New York City's government ceased functioning. Carey was successful because he was prepared to make a sharp break with the past and to heed the counsel of a small group of advisors—the most important of whom was Felix Rohatyn—who had extensive experience as brokers within or between the worlds of business and government. In varying combinations, this group operated through an advisory committee that Carey appointed in May 1975, and then through the Municipal Assistance Corporation and the Emergency Financial Control Board, agencies established in June and September of 1975 to monitor New York City's finances. The group consulted frequently with New York's leading bankers, to whom they turned for loans to tide the city over and to check out ideas concerning the changes in municipal financial practices and policies that might reopen the credit market to New York securities. Carey's financial advisors were not, however, mere frontmen for the banks. Because the banks could not supply the city with all the credit it needed, Rohatyn and his associates could only rescue New York from bankruptcy by working out deals acceptable to the municipal employee unions and state and national officials, as well as the banks.[13]

Governor Carey and his advisors confronted two tasks: obtaining the cash the city needed to avoid defaulting on its obligations in the remaining months of 1975, and helping the city find a long-term source of financing. The former was achieved with loans from public and private institutions that had a major stake in the city's solvency—the state and federal governments, the city's commercial banks, and municipal employee pension funds. This required that concessions be made to these institutions. The second task was to be achieved—or so Governor Carey and his advisors initially believed—by the city's reentry into the regular credit markets. This required that the municipal government reform its financial practices so investors would be assured that New York City bonds were, in fact, redeemable. The differences between these two imperatives had important consequences because, contrary to expectations, New York City did not regain access to the credit market in 1975. Nonetheless, the concessions the city was compelled to make for the loans it desperately needed in 1975 led to some dramatic changes in the institutions and the personnel controlling the city's finances, as well as in the financial policies and practices the city pursued.

The most visible and enduring change in 1975 was the creation of a new set of institutions to supervise New York City's finances: the Municipal Assistance Corporation (MAC) and the Emergency Financial Control Board (EFCB), already mentioned, the Office of the Special Deputy Comptroller for New York City (OSDC), and the Office of New York City Finance in the U.S. Treasury Department. The first to be created was MAC. It still exists today, and is an independent public corporation authorized to sell bonds to meet the city's borrowing needs. To provide investors with an ironclad assurance that MAC would be able to meet the debt service payments on these bonds, the state legislature converted the city's sales and stock transfer taxes into state taxes. The proceeds from these taxes flowed directly into a special account, inaccessible to city officials, from which MAC could withdraw funds to make interest and principal payments on its bonds. A majority of MAC's directors were selected by the governor, and MAC was authorized to revamp the municipal government's accounting practices and oversee the city's finances for a period of ten years. MAC's structure was intended to assure investors that New York City was progressively reducing its use of borrowed money to finance its operating expenditures, thus enabling the city to reenter the market on its own by September 1975.[14]

Despite MAC's legal and fiscal independence from the municipal government, investors shunned its bonds, which led Governor Carey's financial advisors (now speaking through MAC) and his aides to propose even more stringent restrictions on the city. The restrictions were administered by a new agency of the state government, the EFCB. The EFCB, which was composed of the governor and state comptroller, the mayor and the city comptroller, and three additional members appointed by the governor, was granted plenary authority over the finances of New York City. The state law creating the EFCB required the city to balance its budget within three years using accounting principles specified by the state, and to submit a three-year financial plan indicating how it would do so. The EFCB was given the power to review—and reject—the city's financial plan, its expense and capital budget, the contracts negotiated with municipal employee unions, and all municipal borrowing. If the EFCB believed that city officials were not complying with the financial plan, it had the authority to take control of the city's bank accounts and give direct orders to city officials. The EFCB could even remove from office and press criminal charges against city officials who violated its edicts.[15]

Even these drastic measures failed to reopen the market to MAC securities (let alone to New York City's own notes and bonds). Therefore, Governor Carey asked the federal government to intervene as a lender of last resort. For a while, the Ford administration rejected this request, but in November 1975 it relented. With the condition that the city's employees and creditors as well as the state's taxpayers make additional sacrifices, the White House supported legislation extending up to $2.3 billion in short-term loans to the city per year during the 1976 through 1978 fiscal years. The legislation authorizing these loans required the Secretary of the Treasury to certify on a regular basis that the municipal government was making reasonable progress toward a balanced budget. To ascertain whether this condition was being met, yet another monitor was created—the Office of New York City Finance in the U.S. Department of the Treasury.

In 1975, two other potentially significant institutions were created. The first was the Mayor's Management Advisory Board, staffed largely by businessmen, whose mission was to advise city officials how to increase the efficiency of municipal agencies. The second was the Temporary Commission on City Finances, which, between 1975 and 1977, conducted and published sixteen studies and a three-hundred-page final report analyzing, criticizing, and recommending changes in the city's long-range taxation and expenditure policies.

Together these new institutions had the potential for sharply limiting the control that local officials exercised over the municipal government. The extent to which this potential has been realized in the years since 1975 will be analyzed later. It is worth noting here, however, that in 1975 an additional limitation was placed on Mayor Beame's ability to control his own administration: Governor Carey's financial advisors insisted on the resignation of several top officials in the Beame administration, and that the mayor appoint persons in whom they had greater confidence as First Deputy Mayor, Deputy Mayor for Finance, and Budget Director.[16]

Municipal officials were not alone in making sacrifices to rescue New

York from bankruptcy. The consumers of municipal services also had to bear major burdens. To convince investors that the municipal government was mending its ways, the architects of the city's bail-out plan called for the slaughter of three sacred cows of New York politics—cheap subway fares, free tuition at the City University, and low-rent housing for apartment dwellers. For three-quarters of a century no politician could expect to win elective office in New York without expressing a firm resolve to maintain a low subway fare; consequently, from the subway's opening in 1904 to 1975, the fare had been increased only five times. By contrast, following the fiscal crisis of 1975 the fare was raised three times in six years. The tradition of free tuition at the City University was a century old in 1975, but within a year of the fiscal crisis tuition was imposed. As for the third of the sacred cows—low rent for apartment dwellers—while the rent-control program was not abolished, as the city's banks and the private members of the EFCB had wanted, Mayor Beame did proclaim a five-year moratorium on municipal construction of subsidized middle-income housing.[17]

Major burdens were also placed on municipal employees in 1975. First, 25,000 city workers were fired. In addition, a 6 percent wage increase that city employees were scheduled to receive in 1975 under existing labor contracts was partially deferred for low-wage employees and fully deferred for high-wage employees, and take-home pay was reduced by requiring workers to pay a greater proportion of the contributions to their pension funds. Finally, under pressure the municipal employee unions agreed to accept the risks and costs of investing up to 40 percent of their pension fund assets in New York City and MAC bonds.[18]

Cuts in municipal services and personnel had especially adverse consequences for the city's poor and racial minorities. In some instances explicit decisions were made to cut programs that exclusively or disproportionately benefited the poor—such as nutrition programs for welfare clients or the open admissions policy at CUNY. In other instances adverse consequences were implicit in decisions made for other reasons. Cuts in the city's payroll had a far more deleterious impact upon nonwhite city workers than their white counterparts, because blacks and Puerto Ricans on average had less seniority and were more likely to be let go under the "last hired, first fired" rule. Between mid-1974 and the end of 1975, the number of Hispanic workers on the payroll of mayoral agencies was halved and the number of blacks fell 35 percent, while the number of white municipal employees fell by only 22 percent.[19]

Major burdens were also placed on New York's banks in 1975. The various financing packages arranged to get the municipal government through its monthly cash crises required that the city's major commerical banks purchase additional New York City or MAC securities, and/or lengthen the maturities and accept lower interest rates on the securities in their portfolios. Even more distasteful to the financial community was one of the conditions the Ford administration set for extending seasonal loans to the city—that the holders of New York's outstanding short-term notes be compelled to either exchange them for ten-year MAC bonds or face a three-year moratorium on the repayment of principal on these notes. This moratorium amounted to the city's defaulting in all but name on its obligation to redeem its notes on time.[20]

A final condition set by the White House for extending loans to the city was distasteful to business interests. Although MAC had extracted a pledge from a very reluctant Mayor Beame that a three-year cap be placed on municipal expenditures and taxes—so that the city's budget would be balanced by cutting expenditures rather than by raising taxes— the Ford administration insisted that the city and state levy an additional $200 million in taxes to demonstrate that they were doing as much as they possibly could on their own to solve New York City's problems.

It is important to note that New York City did *not* regain full access to the credit markets in 1975. For the loans needed to avoid full-scale default, the three-year financing package put together in November had relied primarily upon the institutions with a substantial stake in the municipal government's solvency—public employee unions and banks, and the state and federal governments. Only after these institutions committed themselves to providing this credit was it possible for MAC to enter the market and sell enough of its bonds to meet the balance of the city's financing needs.

By committing the unions and banks to provide the municipal government with credit, this mode of financing further increased the stake of these institutions in the city's solvency. In return, however, the institutions were able to insist on limits to the sacrifices they would have to make. The unions won assurances that the city would, whenever possible, rely upon attrition rather than further layoffs to reduce the size of its payroll, and that collective bargaining and union grievance procedures would not be scrapped. And in the process of spelling out the size, rate of interest, and maturity of the loans the banks would extend to the city, the November 1975 bail-out plan delimited their obligations. The banks were assured that they would not be called upon repeatedly to invest more and more of their funds in New York City and MAC bonds in order to protect their existing investment in these securities. These considerations gave the unions and the banks a strong incentive to avoid doing anything that might upset the delicately balanced structure that was keeping the city from bankruptcy.

Once it appeared possible to negotiate a social contract that would prevent a full-scale default, New York politicians stopped seeking to protect their constituents from bearing the burdens of retrenchment. They closed ranks behind the bail-out plans drafted by Governor Carey's financial advisors, joined across party lines to press for further assistance from the Republican administration in Washington, and accepted the harsh conditions the White House attached to the aid it ultimately granted the city. The burdens this imposed on their constituents and the limitations placed on their own authority were evidently preferable in their eyes to contending with a Hobbesian war of all against all that a full-scale default could precipitate. The closing of ranks by municipal union leaders, bankers, and public officials helps explain how order was restored in a situation that showed signs of degenerating into widespread chaos.

New York's brush with bankruptcy in 1975 brought about some enduring changes in the institutions controlling the city's finances, in patterns of political activity in the city, and in the city's fiscal practices and policies. It makes sense to examine who has benefited and lost as a consequence of the city's new financial policies before analyzing how and why these changes were produced by the political processes that have prevailed in New York since 1975.

The Budgetary Consequences of the Fiscal Crisis: 1975–84

New York's budgetary policies changed dramatically after 1975 as the city's use of borrowed funds to finance operating expenditures was gradually reduced. In 1981 its expense budget was balanced according to generally accepted accounting principles, and it remained balanced in each subsequent fiscal year.

One reason the municipal government has been able to balance its budget is that between 1975 and 1984 state and federal aid to New York City increased from $4.9 billion to $6.3 billion—a rise of 28 percent. The state also assumed the full costs of financing the City University's senior colleges and the Supplemental Security Income program, along with some of the costs of the city's court system. The state also tightened controls over Medicaid reimbursements to health care providers, thereby

FIGURE 6.1

New York City Operating Expenditures in Inflation-Adjusted Dollars and as a
Percentage of Total Personal Income, 1975–84

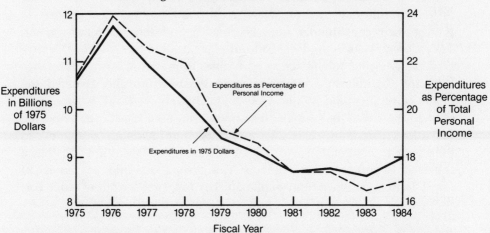

SOURCES: Charles Brecher and Raymond Horton, "Expenditures," in *Setting Municipal Priorities, 1984,* ed. Brecher and Horton (New York: New York University Press, 1983), table 3.1; City of New York, Office of the Comptroller, *Annual Report, Fiscal Year 1984,* pp. iv, 245; Citizens Budget Commission, *Five-Year Pocket Summary of New York City Finances, Fiscal Year 1984–85* (New York: Citizens Budget Commission, 1984), table B-3; U.S., Department of Commerce, Bureau of Economic Analysis, *Survey of Current Business,* November 1984, table 7.1.

reducing the costs of the Medicaid program to the city, and committed itself to gradually assuming the full costs of this program.[21]

Partly because the state relieved the city of costs and partly because local officials controlled expenditures for which the municipal government retained responsibility, the city's operating expenditures in inflation-adjusted dollars declined every year between 1976 and 1981, as indicated by the solid line in figure 6.1.[22] Operating expenditures rose only modestly over the next three years, so that, controlling for inflation, these expenditures were 15.9 percent lower in 1984 than they had been in 1975. Municipal operating expenditures as a proportion of the total income of the city's residents (that is, the size of the local public sector relative to the private sector) also declined every year between 1976 and 1981, and remained essentially unchanged between 1981 and 1984—a dramatic reversal of the pre-1975 pattern (compare figures 5.1 and 6.1).

The changes that occurred in New York City's capital budget in the years following 1975 were even greater than the changes in the expense budget. Between 1975 and 1978 capital expenditures, measured in inflation-adjusted 1975 dollars, fell from $1.7 billion to $422 million, a decline of 75 percent. From that nadir in 1978, they rose to $751 million in 1984—56 percent lower than they had been in 1975.

These changes in New York's fiscal practices and policies did not go unnoticed by participants in the credit markets. The city, however, failed to meet the goal set by the state and federal government of regaining access to the market by 1978; consequently, New York sought further federal assistance. A condition the federal government attached to its assistance was an extension of the Emergency Financial Control Board (with "emergency" dropped from its title) into the twenty-first century. In 1979, the city was first able to sell short-term notes in the open market, and in 1981 it sold a small issue of long-term bonds. Following its initial entry into the market, the city increased the size of its bond issues gradually each year, but it was not until 1985—ten years after the fiscal crisis erupted—that New York no longer had to rely upon bond sales by MAC to help meet its financing needs.

A retrenchment program as profound as the one New York City implemented in the years following 1975 cannot but have differential effects upon the interests of those individuals and institutions with a substantial stake in the city's fiscal policies. The following analyzes retrenchment in greater detail, assessing who has benefited from it, and who has borne the greatest burdens.

The Banks

The city's avoidance of bankruptcy has reduced the primary danger the banks confronted—the liability that might have been imposed by the courts for losses sustained by investors whose New York City securities had been underwritten by the banks. It is true that additional burdens were placed on New York's major commercial banks after 1975. In 1977 they were pressured into lengthening the maturities of the MAC bonds in their portfolios, and Congress insisted, as a condition of authorizing federal participation in the New York City financing package of 1978, that the banks purchase additional MAC securities. However, the steady progress toward balancing the city budget after 1975 sufficiently enlarged the market for MAC securities to make them a liquid investment that the banks could sell or retain as their business interests dictated.[23]

Municipal Employees

New York's municipal employee unions have not fared as well as the banks, but the burdens they have had to bear in recent years are fewer than those confronting them in 1975. The unions have achieved what had been their primary goals since the onset of the fiscal crisis— preserving the institution of collective bargaining and defending the principle that past contractual gains are inviolable, enabling unions,

139

rather than the city, to set the agenda of collective bargaining.

In 1975, these labor practices and principles were seriously compromised. The unions were compelled to negotiate a deferral of some or all of a wage increase provided by existing labor contracts. The state legislature also authorized the EFCB to extend this wage freeze for two additional years. The unions accepted these burdens and did not stage a general strike, as a number of labor leaders had threatened to do when these measures were initially proposed, for fear that the municipal government would go bankrupt.

New York City's avoidance of bankruptcy has enabled collective bargaining—and hence the unions—to survive. Since 1975, municipal unions have in fact made further organizational gains. In 1977 the city granted them the right to collect dues from nonmembers as well as members, and in 1982 the city council passed a law requiring the municipal government to deduct political contributions (for use in federal elections alone) directly from the paychecks of city employees who wished to contribute to their union's campaign fund.

The steady progress made toward balancing the city budget between 1975 and 1982 removed constraints on the benefits civil service unions were able to negotiate for their members. In the 1976 round of labor negotiations the EFCB established guidelines prohibiting general or automatic wage increases for city employees, and the U.S. Department of the Treasury insisted that the unions consent to the elimination of $48 million in fringe benefits for their members. However, the EFCB did permit city workers to receive cost-of-living adjustments as long as these were funded by increases in labor productivity, and hence imposed no additional costs on the city. The unions were not at all happy with these guidelines because they required municipal employees to give up monetary gains or work-rule changes won in earlier labor negotiations, but having no alternative, they complied.

In the labor negotiations of 1978, 1980, and 1982, municipal employees fared better than they had in 1976. In 1978 the unions won automatic wage increases (4 percent in each of two years) and cash bonuses ($750 a year) that were not tied to increases in labor productivity. Moreover, the fringe benefits given up two years earlier were restored and workers were granted the unpaid portion of the cost-of-living adjustments they had been granted conditionally in 1976. The contracts negotiated in 1980 provided the same bonuses, with larger wage increases than in the 1978 contracts (8 percent in each of two years for nonuniformed, 9 percent the first year and 8 the second for uniformed personnel). The 1982 contracts provided wage increases of 8 percent the first and 7 percent

140

the second year for nonuniformed, and 8 percent in each year for uniformed employees. They also provided for payment of the wages that had been deferred in 1975, restoring the last of the major concessions that had been imposed upon city workers in 1975.

In a detailed study, policy analyst Mary McCormick estimated that between 1975 and 1982 municipal pay raises, cost-of-living adjustments, and bonuses, plus the automatic longevity increments built into the municipal wage structure, yielded increases in earnings ranging from 38 to 64 percent for municipal employees in a representative range of job titles.[24] (Earnings increases varied because the lump sum payments to city workers between 1976 and 1982 constituted a proportionately greater share of the income of workers near the bottom of the city's occupational hierarchy than of those near the top and because the longevity increments paid to municipal employees vary among job titles.) During this period, the cost of living increased by 67 percent; therefore, in inflation-adjusted dollars the earnings of these employees fell by amounts ranging from 1.8 percent (in the case of clerks) to as much as 17.2 percent (in the case of police officers). The decline for workers in median categories, such as custodial assistants, computer operators, and administrative assistants, ranged from 8.5 to 8.9 percent. The labor contracts negotiated in 1982, however, provided city workers with pay increases that turned out to be well above the rise in the cost of living during the life of these contracts. Consequently, between 1975 and 1984 the change in the real wages of city workers occupying the job titles referred to earlier ranged from a decline of 6.7 percent (for police officers) to a gain of 12.9 percent (for clerks), with employees in the median categories gaining from 3.4 to 4.3 percent. In other words, all New York City employees suffered a decline in real wages in the early years of the fiscal crisis, but its magnitude varied among employees and has diminished over time. By 1984 the real earnings of many (but not all) city workers were roughly at the level that they had been when the crisis first erupted.[25]

In assessing both how city employees have fared and changes that have occurred in the municipal government's labor costs since 1975, pensions and fringe benefits should also be factored in, as they are major components of the standard of living of municipal employees and of the city's expenditures for personal services. (A 1981 study conducted by the Urban Institute calculated that fringe and retirement benefits as a percentage of the salaries of New York City employees ranged from 29.3 percent in the case of typists and stenographers to 70.1 percent in the case of firefighters.) Between 1975 and 1984 New York City's total labor costs per employee—the average cost to the municipal government of the wages, fringe benefits, and retirement benefits of each city worker—rose from $24,447 to $42,692.[26]

One way that New York City financed these increased labor costs was by reducing the size of its workforce, which was cut by 44,000 positions—from 273,474 to 229,192—between 1975 and 1981.[27] After 1975, the chief technique the city relied upon to accomplish this reduction was attrition—that is, not replacing all of the municipal employees who died, retired, or resigned—which meant that remaining employees had to shoulder a heavier workload. This option, however, was less onerous than the alternatives city workers were given—outright pay cuts, layoffs of employees performing nonessential functions, and increases in the managerial prerogatives of supervisors.[28]

Because such alternatives have not been implemented, and efforts to increase employee productivity have had limited success, the city's practice of financing pay hikes by failing to replace employees who left its workforce has led to a deterioration in several basic municipal services. This, in turn, has had important implications for how other segments of the city's population have fared since the onset of the fiscal crisis.[29]

Downtown Business Community

If the final report of the Temporary Commission on City Finances (TCCF) is representative of opinions in the downtown business community, its record since the fiscal crisis has been mixed. Patterns of public expenditure and public policy in New York have been more favorable to business since 1975 than they had been prior to the fiscal crisis, yet business has not fared as well as many had expected when the crisis first erupted.[30]

From the perspective of the downtown business community, a number of developments in New York since 1975 have been encouraging. The local public sector has shrunk in size relative to the local economy. The city's real estate tax rate has remained fairly stable, and a number of local business taxes have been reduced or repealed. The municipal government has provided generous tax abatements to encourage the construction or renovation of both commercial and residential buildings. And the city has sponsored—or joined with the state in sponsoring—a number of projects designed to invigorate the local economy, most notably a new convention center, the Westway highway project, and the Times Square development project.

Conversely, the opportunity the fiscal crisis presented for reordering municipal priorities was, from the business vantage point, at least partly squandered. In the face of complaints by business groups and the city's

142

fiscal monitors, the municipal government failed to eliminate nonessential services and failed, during the eight years following the fiscal crisis, to bring its recurring expenditures into line with recurring revenues. Rather, the city used unanticipated or potentially nonrecurring revenues—and, in 1982, tax increases—to cover increases in its labor costs. With the notable exception of the Department of Sanitation, the municipal government failed to implement most of the managerial reforms and changes in municipal labor relations recommended by the TCCF and the Mayor's Management Advisory Board. Indeed, it even failed to implement the changes in the city's managerial structure and personnel practices mandated by the 1975 amendments to the city charter.[31]

The fiscal policies and managerial practices the municipal government pursued after 1975 led to a reduction in some of the public services that make New York City an attractive place for business. (Since 1981, however, there have been improvements in a number of municipal services.) The attractiveness of New York has also been impaired by the deterioration of the city's physical infrastructure, as the municipal government used a significant portion of its capital funds for current expenditures—a practice not fully phased out until 1981. The city's failure to maintain its capital facilities has directly created problems for business firms in the city—by slowing the movement of people and goods to and from work sites, for example. It also contributed to the deterioration of city services, because municipal agencies did not provide their employees with the up-to-date facilities and equipment that would enable them to work more productively as their numbers declined.[32]

Service Consumers

New York City's retrenchment policies also have worked to the disadvantage of the city's residents as consumers of municipal services. The size of the municipal workforce and the city's expenditures in inflation-adjusted dollars hit their post-fiscal crisis lows in 1980 and 1981—at lowest ebb they were 15 to 20 percent lower than they had been in 1975—and between 1981 and 1984 they increased only moderately. Although studies have found improvements in the quantity and quality of some municipal services since 1981, many remain below pre-fiscal crisis levels because many city agencies have not made changes in the way they produce and deliver services radical enough to compensate for the budgetary and personnel cuts they have experienced.[33]

Four considerations have influenced how expenditure and payroll cuts have been distributed among municipal agencies providing services to the public. First, a number of municipal agencies are protected by federal and state laws, guidelines, or judicial decrees limiting the ability of local officials to cut their budgets. To cite an extreme example, in the face of a general decline in the payrolls of municipal agencies the payroll of the Department of Corrections actually increased by 74 percent between 1978 and 1984 because the department is subject to a judicial decree specifying in great detail the services that must be provided to prisoners in the city's jails.

A second consideration influencing the locus of retrenchment is the varying distribution of financial responsibility for different municipal programs among the federal, state, and municipal governments. Other things being equal, the city has a greater incentive to reduce expenditures on programs it bears full financial responsibility for than on those financed in whole or in part by the state or federal government, because every dollar it cuts from the budget of city-funded agencies saves the municipal treasury a full dollar (whereas the same reduction in a program that is, say, 75 percent financed by the state and federal governments saves the city only 25 cents).

A third factor in retrenchment is the commitment that city officials and New York's fiscal monitors made in November 1975 to rely upon attrition to reduce the size of the municipal workforce. To a considerable degree attrition removes control over the composition of the city's workforce from public officials. (When fiscal conditions permit officials to replace employees leaving the municipal payroll, however, they are able to determine which vacancies will and will not be filled.) The limitation the policy of attrition imposes on city officials is reinforced by those provisions of collective bargaining agreements and state civil service laws that forbid transferring municipal employees among different job titles and that establish manning levels for various municipal programs that city officials cannot alter unilaterally.[34]

The final consideration influencing the distribution of cuts is that, within the boundaries established by these other constraints, elected officials can allocate the burdens of retrenchment according to their judgment concerning which municipal services are most or least dispensable and their assessment of the relative political costs of reducing the flow of the city's resources to various municipal agencies.

What has this welter of conflicting considerations, incentives, and constraints added up to? A useful standard for assessing patterns of retrenchment is the alternatives outlined by the Temporary Commission on City Finances in its 1977 final report—not because the commission's recommendations are beyond questioning, but because these alternatives were based upon an intellectually coherent analysis of the city's finances

144

TABLE 6.1

Changes in the Work Force of Municipal Agencies, 1974–84

		Greater than Average Reduction (%)		Less than Average Reduction (%)
Basic Services	Sanitation	−20.6%	Fire	−3.8%
	Police	−16.1	Education	−9.8
Other Services	Social Services	−16.8	Hospitals	−6.5
	Other	−13.6		

SOURCES: Mary McCormick, "Labor Relations," in *Setting Municipal Priorities, 1982,* ed. C. Brecher and R. Horton (New York: Russell Sage Foundation, 1981), table 7.5; City of New York, Office of the Comptroller, *Annual Report, Fiscal Year 1984,* pp. 241–44, 248.

and endorsed by reputedly powerful political forces. The commission recommended that the city should reduce its operating expenditures, but that such cuts should be less severe in agencies performing basic services—services it deemed vital for the health of the local economy—than in agencies performing less essential functions. The TCCF placed the fire, police, and sanitation departments and the Board of Education in the former category. The latter category includes services that either serve as a drag on the local economy or are economically neutral. The largest agencies in this category are hospitals, social services, and a residual group.[35]

In table 6.1, municipal agencies are located at the right or left according to the depth of the workforce reductions they experienced between December 31, 1974, and June 30, 1984. Had New York followed the retrenchment strategy recommended by the TCCF, most agencies would be clustered in the upper-right and lower-left quadrants. But in fact they are scattered among the four quadrants. The reason for this is that most of the considerations that have influenced the incidence of retrenchment in New York since 1975 bear little relation to the concerns of the TCCF.[36]

Intergovernmental mandates primarily protect programs in the fields of health, education, and welfare. This helps explain why the Health and Hospitals Corporation and the Board of Education have been subject to relatively small payroll cuts, and why the Police and Sanitation Departments experienced heavier than average personnel cuts. (The Department of Social Services and the Fire Department stand as exceptions to this rule.)

The second influence on retrenchment—the allocation of financial responsibility for services among different levels of government—reinforces the effects of intergovernmental mandates. Federal and state aid

145

provide much of the financing for the city's hospitals, schools, and social service programs, whereas the city must rely almost entirely on its own resources to cover the expenses of the Police, Fire, and Sanitation departments. Moreover, because uniformed personnel are among the most highly paid city workers, the city reduced the number of uniformed employees in the Police and Sanitation Departments even more sharply than indicated by the data in table 6.1. Between 1974 and 1984 the number of uniformed police officers declined by 23 percent and the number of uniformed sanitation workers by 48 percent. (Personnel cuts in the Fire Department, however, did not conform to this pattern.)

The third consideration shaping the incidence of payroll cuts—the city's reliance upon attrition to pare its payroll—also does not protect basic services at the expense of others. This provides a partial explanation for why, while the city was reducing the number of police officers and sanitation workers, employees who ran municipal radio and television stations and who calculated a cost-of-living index that duplicated one published by the U.S. Department of Labor, were kept on its payroll.

The final influence on retrenchment, judgments public officials have made concerning the substantive merits and political value of different municipal programs, is the only one favoring basic services. As the analysis in the next chapter will indicate, the 1975 fiscal crisis significantly altered the balance of power in New York politics and the ideological climate in the city—one reason why the city has allocated the bulk of its discretionary expenditures, which are not subject to federal or state mandates, to basic services. This has not been sufficient, however, to counterbalance other considerations influencing the pattern of payroll cuts in New York between 1974 and 1984, as the scattering of agencies among the four quadrants of Table 6.1 shows.[37]

The figures in table 6.2 suggest a similar conclusion, indicating how the city's total workforce was distributed among the largest municipal agencies in 1974 and 1984. Among the agencies suffering declines in their share of the city's work force were the Police and Sanitation Departments. The agency experiencing the largest increase was the Health and Hospitals Corporation.

The Dependent Poor

The impact of retrenchment upon the consumers of municipal services has to this point been analyzed by examining the distribution of cuts in the *workforce* of various municipal agencies. In the case of one municipal program, public assistance to the poor, however, service consumers are affected much more by *expenditure* levels than by the number of civil

146

TABLE 6.2
*Distribution of City Employees
Among Major Municipal
Agencies, 1974 and 1984*

	Distribution (%)	
	1974	1984
Police	12.9%	12.3%
Fire	5.1	5.6
Sanitation	5.2	4.7
Education	30.0	30.7
Hospitals	17.1	18.1
Social Services	9.8	9.2
Other	19.8	19.4

SOURCES: Mary McCormick, "Labor Relations," in *Setting Municipal Priorities, 1982,* ed. C. Brecher and R. Horton (New York: Russell Sage Foundation, 1981), table 7.5; City of New York, Office of the Comptroller, *Annual Report, Fiscal Year 1984,* pp. 241–44, 248.

servants who administer the program. And as a result of reductions in real expenditures for public assistance, New York's retrenchment program imposed a greater burden on the dependent poor than on any other segment of the city's population.

From 1974 through 1981, New York's basic welfare grant was frozen, as the cost of living rose by 68 percent. The increase in the basic welfare grant for a family of four enacted in 1981 amounted to 15 percent, an allotment that remained unchanged between 1981 and 1984, despite continued increases in the cost of living. By 1984, the purchasing power of the allotment was almost 40 percent lower than it had been in 1974. Also, the housing allowance for welfare recipients remained frozen from 1974 through 1984, despite steady increases in rents and even larger increases in the costs of providing adequate housing to poor New Yorkers. By 1984 60 percent of the city's welfare recipients found it necessary to use a portion of their basic grant to pay rent, which further lowered their standard of living. In addition, because tenants on welfare were unable to pay rents sufficient for maintaining the buildings they occupied, the city's housing stock deteriorated, and the supply of decent housing for New York's poor declined.

Since the onset of the fiscal crisis, New York City has also tightened the procedures for obtaining and retaining public assistance, contributing to a decline in the number receiving public assistance—from 991,000 in

1975 to 928,000 in 1984. Thus New York's retrenchment program imposed costs not only upon welfare recipients who remained on the rolls, but also upon poor people who would have received welfare had the old procedures for certifying eligibility for public assistance remained in force.

Of all the interests affected by New York's retrenchment program, the city's commercial banks have probably fared the best. Municipal employees have not done as badly as they had reason to fear, and the city's downtown business community has not fared as well as it had reason to hope when the fiscal crisis erupted. The heaviest burdens of retrenchment have been imposed upon the consumers of municipal services, and among these, the poor have fared the worst. The sources of these retrenchment patterns can be found by analyzing the changes that have occurred since 1975 in the composition of prevailing political coalitions in New York, and in the structure of the city's major political organizations and governing institutions.

7

The Fiscal Crisis and the Reorganization of New York City Politics

SINCE the onset of the 1975 fiscal crisis, many changes have occurred in the structure of New York City's governing institutions, and new alliance patterns have formed within and across important sectors of the city's public life. Together these changes have contributed to the emergence of three major centers of power, involving (1) the municipal government's private creditors—commercial banks and civil service unions; (2) the city's public creditors and its official and unofficial fiscal monitors; and (3) Mayor Ed Koch and his political following. These changes have created a regime capable of meeting the fiscal as well as the political imperatives confronting city officials.

New Institutions

The most obvious change in the governance of New York is that the agencies established in 1975 to monitor municipal finances have since

149

become permanent features of the governmental landscape.[1] Moreover, under the supervision of its fiscal monitors, New York has revamped its financial and budgetary procedures. The city now conducts its financial affairs and keeps its books according to generally accepted accounting principles, abandoning the budgetary gimmicks that enabled it to amass operating deficits and the accounting practices that concealed the true size of these deficits. The city now relies on sophisticated econometric models to estimate revenues and expenditures for the coming fiscal year, rather than relying on figures pulled out of the air by the mayor or comptroller. As municipal policy analysts Charles Brecher and Raymond Horton note,

The City has improved its information systems and integrated them into a financial planning process with a long-term perspective. The City that literally did not know how many people it employed in 1975 now projects staffing levels, borrowing and cash flow for four-year periods, and has a ten-year plan for capital investments. The system ... is probably one of the best management information systems among large American cities and rivals the practices of well-managed private firms.[2]

New York's fiscal monitoring agencies have not, however, fully exploited their authority over the city's finances. Had the Financial Control Board (FCB) broadly interpreted powers granted by the Financial Emergency Act of 1975 (and had the courts upheld a broad construction of this statute), the Board could have dictated the content of the annual financial plan the city is required to submit by refusing to approve any plan that did not accord with its preferences, seized control of the city's bank accounts, and withheld all funds from the municipal government to compel local officials to comply with every jot and tittle in the plan. The Board also might have attempted to make use of the power of approving or rejecting municipal labor contracts to shape the terms of municipal labor settlements.

That the FCB chose to be less intrusive does not mean that it has been inconsequential. By insisting that the city make steady progress toward balancing its budget and keeping it balanced, the Board has enabled the mayor to say "no" to agency heads seeking larger appropriations and union leaders seeking larger pay increases. When the staff of the FCB has questioned revenue or expenditure projections in the city's financial plan or the city's ability to finance new labor contracts, the Board as a rule has not rejected the plan or contract in question. Instead it has asked that the mayor submit a document, known as a Program to Eliminate the Gap, indicating how the city would cut its expenditures (or increase

150

its revenues) if its financial projections proved incorrect. However, under some conditions the Board has fought openly with municipal officials and ordered them to take steps they would not otherwise have taken.

Officials in Washington also continued to supervise New York City's finances between 1975 and 1982, the period when the municipal government relied upon the U.S. Treasury to meet a portion of its financing needs. (And until the last of the city's federally guaranteed bonds are redeemed—that is, until 1987—the Treasury will retain an interest in the municipal government's financial affairs.) Statutes providing seasonal loans to the city and federal guarantees for New York City bonds required that, before releasing funds to the city, the Secretary of the Treasury certify that the municipal government was pursuing policies that in time would enable it to return to the capital market on its own. Leaders in New York City politics also were acutely aware that congressional committees with jurisdiction over these loan programs had to be satisfied that the city was setting its financial house in order to ensure further credits to the municipal government. These considerations had especially important implications for municipal labor relations. In effect, new labor contracts had to be approved by the Secretary of the Treasury and key members of Congress. This helps explain why municipal union leaders were unable to negotiate contracts in 1976 and 1978 that ensured that the wages and benefits of their members would keep pace with inflation.

New Sectoral Alliances

Since 1975, leaders (or would-be leaders) of groups in a number of sectors have formed new organizations or coalitions to advance or defend the interests of their members in the new fiscal order. The most important are alliances that seek to speak for municipal employees, for the city's banking and business communities, and for the social groups that traditionally have served as the vanguard of New York reform movements.

Municipal Employees

The most significant of the new organizations or coalitions is composed of unions representing the majority of New York City's employees. Union leaders jointly negotiated the 1975 wage deferral agreement (described in chapter 6) and went on to negotiate municipal labor

151

contracts in 1976, 1978, 1980, 1982, and 1984. In 1975 and 1978 they also negotiated the terms under which their pension funds would purchase New York City bonds.

Coalition bargaining is the way that union leaders coped with the tensions between two imperatives after 1975. On the one hand, they had an enormous stake in ensuring that New York remained solvent. This required that the unions make concessions on wages, fringe benefits, and pension fund investments which state or federal officials demanded as a condition for providing the municipal government with the loans it needed to avoid defaulting on its obligations. On the other hand, contracts had to be ratified by the rank-and-file, and if union leaders were to remain in office they had to retain the support of the members. By forming a coalition and bargaining as a unit, individual leaders found it possible to make the concessions demanded by state and federal officials without being left in an exposed position by the refusal of other union leaders to go along.[3]

Although the unions' stake in New York's financial viability led them to make some major concessions, they have not been without leverage in their negotiations with the city. City officials depend on municipal union leaders to secure rank-and-file approval of labor contracts that do not exceed the tolerance of New York's fiscal monitors. And New York's reliance on municipal employees' pension funds for financing between 1975 and 1982 meant that the municipal government needed the cooperation of civil service unions and their leaders for its very functioning.[4] In return for their cooperation, union leaders could plausibly argue that they would be able to convince their membership to ratify contracts only if the terms were not too harsh. Indeed, to keep the control of their unions away from hotheads who would pay no heed to the financial constraints confronting the city, union members had to be assured that moderation was a two-way street rather than meaning that the municipal government would ignore the problems inflation was creating for city workers.

The consequences of these shared interests for municipal labor relations were clearly illustrated by the 1978 contract negotiations. The federal seasonal loan program that had been enacted in 1975 expired in 1978, and because the market remained closed to New York, the city needed additional federal financing assistance to avoid bankruptcy. To ensure that New York's banks, employees, local officials, and state government would contribute all they could to rescue the city—and to provide assurance to members of Congress who were reluctant to extend additional assistance to the city—the Secretary of the Treasury declared that the

152

administration would not submit a bill to Congress providing New York with federal loan guarantees until a number of conditions were met. The municipal employee unions and the city's major banks had to commit themselves to lending additional funds to the city; the state had to extend the life of the EFCB; and, most relevant here, the unions and the city had to complete their negotiations for a new labor contract. This deadline constrained the unions because it prevented them from seeking substantial wage increases that hostile senators and representatives could point to as evidence of New York City's continued profligacy. However, the deadline also constrained Mayor Koch. He had regularly denounced the civil service unions in his election campaign the previous year and initially insisted that he would provide pay increases to the city's employees only if the unions would agree to work-rule changes that would increase productivity. Union leaders insisted just as adamantly that their members would never relinquish gains they had struggled long and hard to achieve. In this face-off it was the mayor who ultimately retreated. He recognized that there was no way the Treasury's deadline could be met—and the city saved from a repetition of the crisis conditions of 1975—if he persisted in demanding that the unions agree to work-rule changes.[5]

In other words, given the cards each side holds in the game of municipal labor relations, the most stable solution is one involving minimal moves from the positions the players had occupied just prior to the fiscal crisis. However, this presupposes that union leaders who heed the city's financial constraints are able to remain in office and induce their members to ratify appropriate contracts, and that they do not attempt to pass on the costs of retrenchment to other unions. It cannot be assumed that these conditions will prevail indefinitely. Indeed, in the 1980 and 1982 municipal labor negotiations, the police, fire, sanitation, and corrections unions formed a coalition that bargained independently with the city. This coalition demanded—and received—a slightly better settlement than the one granted their nonuniformed counterparts. The possible implications of this development, and of other changes in municipal labor relations in New York, will be discussed in chapter 8.

The Banking and Business Communities

From the earliest days of the fiscal crisis, whenever New York's major banks faced threats to their vital interests, their top executives have formed a working group that has been able to commit their institutions to a common strategy. This is precisely what occurred in 1975, when the city lurched from cash crisis to cash crisis; in 1977, when the state's highest court ruled that the 1975 moratorium on the repayment of city notes was unconstitutional and the municipal government had to come up with $983 million to redeem them; and in 1978, when the city's inability to return to the public credit markets after the 1975 federal loan program expired made it necessary to put together a new financing package.

The banks had a strong incentive to join forces because they had a common stake in the city's avoidance of bankruptcy, while at the same time they shared an interest in minimizing the risks and costs imposed upon them by any bail-out plan. These interests were served by pooling their resources and demanding assurances or concessions in exchange for extending loans to the city. New York's major banks have been able to work together effectively because they are few in number (the New York Clearing House Association is composed of only eleven banks), because they have a long history of creating syndicates to underwrite New York City securities, and because public officials have sought their advice or made demands on them as a group. However, since 1975, as the sources upon which the municipal government has depended for financing have changed, the nature of their influence has changed.

The influence of the banks was greatest during the rather brief period in mid-1975 when (1) it was widely recognized that the city could not sell its securities in the public credit market unless there were substantial changes in its fiscal institutions and policies, and (2) it was also believed that such changes would in fact reopen the market to the city. During this period Governor Carey's fiscal advisors consulted with the banks to ascertain the fiscal controls and budgetary changes that in their judgment would enable the city to regain access to the market, and they compelled the city to acquiesce to much of what the banks recommended—most important, the creation of a monitoring agency with substantial supervisory powers over municipal finances.

After it became clear that nothing the city did in the short run could gain its reentry to the market, however, and the architects of New York's bailout plans turned to the municipal employee unions and the federal government for credit, the influence of the banks declined considerably. In fact, the banks were compelled to purchase additional New York securities when the federal government made this a condition of extending credit to the city in November 1975 and again in 1978, thereby increasing the risk they would be exposed to if the city were to go bankrupt.[6]

The limited scope of the influence that the banks have been able to exercise over New York's finances after the city turned to the union pension funds and the U.S. Treasury for credit was revealed clearly in

154

1977 when the municipal government had to raise close to $1 billion following the nullification of the moratorium on repayment of its short-term notes. The banks agreed to extend additional credit to the city only if a monitoring agency, more powerful than the EFCB, was created to supervise New York's finances after 1978, when the Control Board was scheduled to go out of business. Mayor Beame reluctantly agreed to this condition, but the municipal employee unions adamantly refused to go along, thus killing the banks' proposal. In the end the city came up with a financing plan that did not require bank participation; hence there was no need to resolve the deadlock between the banks and the unions. The banks have learned to live with these limitations on their influence. Shortly after their 1977 battle, the leaders of the city's largest banks and civil service unions began meeting on a regular basis to avoid future blow-ups.[7]

Organizations speaking for New York's general business community have also undergone significant changes in the years since the fiscal crisis. In 1977, New York's two leading business associations—the Chamber of Commerce and the Commerce and Industry Association—merged. In 1979, the New York Partnership, which counts the city's most prominent corporate executives among its members, was founded. The Partnership's founder and chairman, David Rockefeller, also served as chairman of the merged Chamber of Commerce and Industry and as chairman of the Economic Development Council, another leading business organization. Finally, in 1980 the Citizens Budget Commission reorganized itself, beefed up its staff, and redefined its mission.[8]

Since 1977, the Chamber of Commerce and Industry has rallied support for projects designed to bolster the city's economy, such as a new convention center. The Chamber also has persuaded major corporations to deploy executives for periods of twelve to eighteen months in the city's new Office of Operations, where they can bring business methods to the management of public agencies. The revitalized CBC now uses its traditional techniques of research and publicity to press the city into improving the delivery of those municipal services that will make New York a more attractive place to live and work. The New York Partnership performs some services that the municipal government has cut because of its fiscal problems, such as building middle-income housing in the city. Finally, several corporations have financed the upkeep of parks that, due to cutbacks, the municipal government could no longer afford to maintain.[9]

These activities reflect efforts by New York's business community to institutionalize the influence in municipal affairs that business leaders

155

had gained in 1975. The executive loan program to the city's Office of Operations is an outstanding example of this. The 1975 Mayor's Management Advisory Board—composed of top executives from nine of New York's largest corporations and chaired by Richard Shinn, president of Metropolitan Life Insurance Company—reported that the municipal government had "no viable organization structure, limited management talent . . . outdated systems and procedures, and no real planning systems or capabilities—as business knows them." The Board recommended the establishment of the Office of Operations to overcome these problems. This agency provides a regular channel through which the advocates of managing municipal affairs according to business principles can implement the administrative reforms recommended by the Shinn Commission.[10]

The New York Partnership's notion that the private sector can assume some of the responsibilities the municipal government no longer performs also can serve useful functions for businessmen who advocate reducing the size of the public sector. It can help make retrenchment more acceptable to the consumers of municipal services and help defuse popular resentment toward the business community in whose name budget cuts are being made. Significantly, the first public event sponsored by the Partnership was an address by President Reagan lauding efforts by the private sector to take up the slack left by his administration's reductions in social programs, and the first major project of the Partnership—the middle-income housing program—was announced in conjunction with the president's address. In this respect the activities of the New York Partnership may contribute to the stability of a regime that regards as one of its primary missions restoring investor confidence in New York securities and improving the city's business climate.

Although noteworthy changes have occurred since 1975 in the character and behavior of business organizations, and although New York's current regime is friendlier to business than its predecessor had been, business's influence over municipal affairs since 1975 is less than is alleged by such political scientists as Stephen David and Paul Kantor and such journalists as Jack Newfield and Paul DuBrul. Individuals representing the business community have found much to criticize in New York's retrenchment policies. Both the CBC and the Economic Development Council (EDC), for example, criticized a plan designed by MAC chairman Felix Rohatyn in 1977 to lower the city's debt service costs in the short-run by exchanging MAC bonds with long maturities for bonds with shorter maturities. A CBC report pointed out that this would substantially increase the total interest costs the city would have to bear over the life of these bonds, and in an article in the Chamber of Commerce and

Industry's newsletter, a vice president of the EDC asserted that this refunding was "nothing more or less than a postponement of the repayment of a debt—a form of reborrowing."[11]

In the areas of municipal labor relations and municipal service performance business organizations have repeatedly criticized City Hall for granting municipal employees what they believe are unaffordable wage increases. At the depth of the 1982 recession the CBC went so far as to call upon City Hall to renegotiate existing labor contracts. Even more troublesome to business is the adverse impact on municipal services of reducing the workforce to finance wage increases without securing work-rule concessions that would increase productivity. In 1980 the CBC was so alarmed by this practice that it declared that the city's fiscal crisis had become a service crisis. It was then that the CBC reorganized and shifted the focus of its activities, explaining in its annual report that the fiscal monitoring agencies established in 1975 had assumed the CBC's role of serving as the city's fiscal watchdog. These agencies had made it impossible for the municipal government to continue the unsound financial practices the CBC had been devoted to uncovering and denouncing. But, as the report went on to say, those who were keeping the city on the road to solvency had been unable "to capitalize on the opportunity provided by the fiscal crisis to improve, even revolutionize, the service delivery process." The CBC wants to change this state of affairs.[12]

Editorials and news analyses in the *Wall Street Journal* have indicated that there is tension between some elements of the general business community and New York's commercial banks over the retrenchment policies the city has pursued and failed to pursue since 1975. The *Journal* has criticized the banks for selling out the interests of the business community in order to protect their own narrow interests. To avoid the legal problems they would face if the city went bankrupt, the banks have helped finance municipal budgets that—according to the *Journal*—continue to provide excessive wages and fringe benefits for city employees and contain appropriations for unnecessary agencies and programs. The health of New York's economy and the interests of its business community would have been better served, the *Journal* has argued, if the city had been forced into bankruptcy, for this would have made it legally and politically possible to slash (rather than simply freeze) the salaries and benefits of city workers and abolish nonessential municipal programs.[13]

In the years since 1975 New York City certainly has pursued policies (such as reducing business taxes) and embarked upon projects (such as the redevelopment of Times Square) of benefit to the business community and warmly supported by business leaders. Most often, however, these policies and projects have been initiated by public officials who have then led the fight to secure their implementation. They have done this to revitalize the city's economy and to signal to the capital markets and firms considering locating in New York that the city's business climate has changed. Public officials have not embarked upon this course in response to pressure from the Chamber of Commerce or other business organizations. In many instances when business groups join a campaign in support of these initiatives, it is more correct to say that public officials have assumed the task of organizing the city's business community, rather than vice versa.[14]

The Vanguards of Reform

Since 1975 some important changes have also occurred in the political behavior of New York's reform vanguards. The three forms of organization through which middle-class professionals influenced the conduct of politics and government in New York prior to the fiscal crisis—good government groups, Democratic reform clubs, and civic associations— have all declined in power. A new political force drawn from this constituency has emerged since 1975, however, which has had some success in shaping the issues of city politics.

If anything should have enabled New York's traditional good government groups to seize the political initiative, it was the events of 1975. An administration with close ties to the city's Democratic machine had literally almost been declared bankrupt, and plans to reorganize the municipal government were proposed and enacted. Yet, the story of New York's fiscal and political crisis of 1975 can be told without even mentioning good government groups such as the Citizens Union and the City Club. The institutions established in 1975 to supervise New York City's finances were created on the initiative of Governor Carey, the legislation establishing MAC and the EFCB was drafted by the governor's fiscal advisors, and Carey consulted with the city's bankers and union leaders—not good government groups—to ensure that this legislation would achieve its purposes and be passed by the state assembly and senate.[15]

New York's Democratic reform clubs also have not played a significant role since the onset of the fiscal crisis. In the 1977 Democratic mayoral primary, Bella Abzug, whose candidacy was backed by the New Democratic Coalition, won only 17 percent of the vote, coming in fourth in a field of seven. And in 1981 the reform Democrats, along with other

158

opponents of Mayor Koch, were unable to recruit a candidate of any stature to challenge the mayor's bid for a second term.

The influence of the civic associations through which members of New York's upper- and upper-middle-classes have shaped municipal health, education, and welfare policies has declined as well. Despite their persistent complaints that inflation was sharply reducing the real income of the city's dependent poor, and despite the formation of an umbrella group—the Task Force on the New York Fiscal Crisis—which prepared a "counterbudget" designed to show it was fiscally possible to increase benefits, the basic welfare grant remained frozen for seven years. Moreover, to impose retrenchment upon agencies with jurisdiction over social welfare policies, Mayor Koch has appointed commissioners selected for their managerial abilities and commitment to his fiscal priorities, rather than, as civic associations have long demanded, specialists dedicated first and foremost to the mission of the agency in question.

The decline of these organizations does not mean, however, that upper-middle-class professionals have been without influence since 1975. In recent years a loosely knit group of policy analysts, many connected with universities and charitable foundations in New York, have established new organizations (or reoriented existing ones) concerned with municipal affairs, have cultivated new alliances, and have come to play a significant role in the city's politics by evaluating the municipal government's retrenchment policies and considering alternatives to them. This is not to say that these policy analysts have cynically taken advantage of New York's fiscal problems to engage in a power grab. By their own lights, they seek to use their skills to help the municipal government function as effectively as possible within the limitations imposed upon it. Moreover, the involvement of universities and other nonprofit institutions in efforts to increase the efficiency and effectiveness of New York City's government is a longstanding one; it goes back to the Progressive Era, and was a hallmark of the Lindsay years.

In his efforts to save New York from bankruptcy in 1975–76, Governor Carey turned to some individuals who previously had been involved in efforts to reform New York City's financial or managerial practices. MAC's first executive director was Herbert Elish, who had applied the techniques of operations research to the New York sanitation department while serving as that department's commissioner in the Lindsay administration. One of Carey's appointees to the MAC Board of Directors was Dick Netzer, dean of New York University's Graduate School of Public Administration, who had directed a study of New York City's finances for a commission established by Mayor Wagner in 1965. Netzer was also one of the designers of the Emergency Financial Control Board, along with Peter Goldmark, Carey's budget director, who previously had served as assistant budget director for program planning and analysis in the Lindsay administration. In 1976 the governor appointed Stephen Berger as the EFCB's executive director. Berger is a man of fierce intelligence who, as staff director of the Scott Commission, established to investigate New York City's government in the early 1970s, had criticized the prodigality of the Lindsay administration, and laid the groundwork for a series of amendments to the city's charter enacted in 1975.

In the initial stages of the fiscal crisis, then, when preventing the city from going bankrupt was the central concern, public officials and the leaders of institutions that could provide the city with credit dominated events, while academics and efficiency experts played roles only if they were tapped by these dominant figures. Once the threat of bankruptcy receded, however, and participants in New York politics could turn their attention to restoring the municipal government's long-term financial viability, the city's universities and private foundations carved out a position for themselves in the new political order. In 1977, the Center for New York City Affairs at the New School for Social Research began publication of a newsletter, the *Fiscal Observer*, that analyzed on-going fiscal events—labor negotiations, financing arrangements, the preparation of financial plans, and so forth—and summarized the numerous reports issued by New York's financial monitoring agencies. At roughly the same time the Twentieth Century Fund began a program of research and assembled a task force to make recommendations concerning policies the city might pursue to ensure its long-term vitality. And in 1982 the Fund for the City of New York, which had been working to improve municipal management and productivity for close to a decade, began publishing a series of occasional papers to "report on this work in a form useful to others."[16]

The most impressive of these endeavors, however, is the Setting Municipal Priorities project (SMP), a joint venture of Columbia University and the New School for Social Research, later joined by New York University. The project's directors are Raymond Horton of the Columbia Business School, who served as staff director of the Temporary Commission on City Finances (TCCF), and Charles Brecher, who has held research or teaching positions at each of the sponsoring universities and had served on the staff of the TCCF. In the preface to the project's first publication, Horton and Brecher explain that while working together for the TCCF they conceived of the project, with the following purposes in mind:

First, we perceived the need for an annual volume that dealt with major aspects of New York City's economy, government, and finances from a longer-range perspective than most official analyses could provide. While the New York City fiscal crisis had increased the volume and upgraded the quality of research on City finances, no group was responsible for providing the growing audience interested in New York City's future with a comprehensive analytical review focusing on where New York City had been, where it was heading, and what options were available to improve its development. It was, and remains, our belief that providing information to a broad audience would better inform policy debates and help produce better policy. . . . Our second goal was to contribute to the research community in New York City by helping to train other people in policy-oriented research.[17]

The project's annual volume of essays analyzing the city's economy, finances, and public policies is released in conjunction with a conference held in the early stages of the municipal government's budgetary process, because, as the foreword to the first volume explains:

Even the best policy research will prove sterile unless it engages the attention of those in the public arena who shape discussions and outcomes—the press, politicians, administrators, civic groups, and other actors. The present volume will therefore serve as an agenda for a conference of interested and concerned parties drawn from among the city's private and public sector leadership.[18]

The policy analysts affiliated with these different institutions do not hew to a single ideological line. Nonetheless, it makes sense to speak of a policy-oriented research community in New York. The focal point of this community is the SMP project, which is sponsored by New York's three major private, secular universities—institutions that traditionally have kept their distance from one another—and financed by several of New York's charitable foundations. The annual volumes of the SMP project are written by, and conferences primarily attended by, persons employed by the city's universities, foundations, civic associations, fiscal monitors, and other public agencies. In addition to their participation in this collaborative project, there has been considerable interchange of personnel among the institutions composing this community.[19]

Although members of this research community do not hesitate to disagree, a number of themes recur in their writings. They have criticized the city's failure to alter managerial practices and the modes of delivering essential municipal services in ways that would increase their quantity

161

and quality. Another theme is how imperative it is for the city to renovate its capital plant and equipment so as to increase employee productivity and improve the city's business climate.

Although the policy analysts affiliated with the institutions participating in the SMP project have stressed improving the city's business climate, they are by no means mouthpieces for business interests. The essay on economic development policy in the 1984 SMP volume, for example, argued that there is little reason to believe that the tax abatements the municipal government grants to encourage investment in the central business district serve any useful purpose. And in introductory essays in SMP volumes, Brecher and Horton have called upon the city to increase real estate assessments for tax purposes and raise the city's basic welfare grants.[20]

It must be emphasized that this community of policy analysts has not been a major force in the governance of New York to date. Its members have not been able to compel the municipal government to alter its budgetary priorities, nor have they provided forums at which New York's most powerful public officials, bankers, businessmen, and labor leaders can reach accommodations with one another. The SMP conferences are attended chiefly by individuals of the second rank, rather than by the leaders of New York's major institutions—that is, by the executive directors and staffs of MAC and the FCB, not by members of their boards of directors; by professors, research fellows, and deans, not by university presidents; by vice presidents for public affairs of commercial banks and younger partners of investment banks, not by the chief executive officers or managing partners of these institutions; by newspaper columnists and reporters, not newspaper publishers, and so forth.

Yet, New York's community of policy analysts has not been politically insignificant. In a number of respects, the SMP project serves as a standing successor to the Temporary Commission on City Finances. It was founded by members of the TCCF staff and many of the themes recurring in its volumes were present in the TCCF's reports. Most important, it provides the findings of policy analysts with a quasi-official aura they would not possess if they were published in professional journals, just as the TCCF's findings had more of such an aura than if they had been issued as reports of the Chamber of Commerce. Consequently, SMP conferences and volumes have generally received substantial coverage in the press, enabling its policy analysts to influence political discourse in the city. For example, Mayor Koch felt it necessary to respond to the assertion in the 1981 SMP volume that the dependent poor had borne a disproportionate share of the burdens of retrenchment, and the *New York Times* referred frequently in its editorials and news analyses to its argument that municipal services could be improved without increasing municipal expenditures.[21] Another indication of SMP's significance is that the Citizens Budget Commission, as part of its effort to revitalize itself in 1980, appointed Horton, Brecher, and a third SMP member, James Hartman, as, respectively, executive vice president and director of research, co-editor of a new CBC quarterly, and executive director. The new mission the CBC adopted—focusing as much upon improving municipal services as upon restraining municipal expenditures—was concordant with a theme receiving increased emphasis in the SMP volumes.[22] Finally, under conditions discussed in chapter 8, this community of policy analysts could provide the intellectual leadership for a new political coalition in the city.

Three Centers of Power

Since 1975 three major power centers have emerged in New York. Their influence stems from the important role their members have played in providing the municipal government with credit or political support.

The Bank/Union Nexus

The coalition of banks and municipal employee unions that helped bail out the city after the fiscal crisis became institutionalized in 1977 as the Municipal Union-Financial Leaders group (MUFL). Composed of the chief executive officers of six of the city's largest commercial banks and six of its largest civil service unions, its other members are Jack Bigel, the most important advisor and strategist for the unions on questions of municipal finance, and Felix Rohatyn, the chairman of MAC. Other bankers, businessmen, and public officials attend its meetings from time to time.[23]

Although MUFL has issued a number of statements and position papers supporting various public policies and projects—such as lowering the state's personal and corporate income taxes and constructing a convention center and the Battery Park City development project—its chief significance is not that it enables its members to pool political resources to fight on behalf of such measures. While a number of policies and projects endorsed by MUFL have been realized, there is little reason to believe they would have failed without MUFL's endorsement. Rather,

163

the chief significance of MUFL lies in what it has *prevented* its members from doing—namely, advancing or defending their interests in ways that the city's other creditors would not tolerate. This, in turn, has contributed to the survival of the arrangements that saved the city from bankruptcy in 1975.

The episode that led to MUFL's formation demonstrates the importance of this function. When the state Court of Appeals invalidated the moratorium on the redemption of New York City's short-term notes, the Clearing House banks said that they would only participate in a new financing package if the EFCB were replaced with a Budget Review Board that would exercise even more stringent controls over the city's finances. This demand infuriated municipal employee union leaders, whose leverage in dealing with the mayor was greater than it would have been with any such board, and they stormed out of the Gracie Mansion meeting at which the bankers presented their proposal. Because the city was able to raise the money needed to comply with the Court of Appeals decision without turning to the banks, this episode, which occurred in February 1977, did not drive the city into bankruptcy. It was ominous, however, because it almost certainly would be necessary for both the banks and the unions to extend additional loans to the city— and to reach agreement on the fiscal controls that would be placed upon the municipal government—in one year's time when the 1975 financing package would expire. Recognizing that the conflicts that flared up in February 1977 would have to be overcome if the city were to avoid bankruptcy, which both the unions and banks dreaded, Jack Bigel proposed to Walter Wriston, the chairman of New York's largest bank, that a committee of municipal union leaders and bankers be formed to discuss their common concerns. Each convinced his associates that such a committee would serve a useful purpose, and thus MUFL was created.

In discussions at their monthly meetings the members of MUFL have come to a better understanding of the constraints under which their counterparts on the other side of the table operate. The bankers now recognize that union leaders could not possibly get rank-and-file city employees to ratify contracts that would fail to protect their real incomes from the effects of inflation, or accept changes in the work rules they fought long and hard to obtain, and that efforts to force municipal workers to make such concessions would probably precipitate strikes that would impair the city's access to the public credit markets. For their part, union leaders now appreciate that banks operate in a competitive environment and under legal obligations that prohibit investing shareholders' money in inadequately secured paper, and that maintaining the city's credit requires placing external controls on the municipal government's fiscal autonomy. Recognizing these constraints, the banks and unions were less inclined to use the substantial leverage gained from serving as the city's creditors in their efforts to extract concessions from the municipal government that would benefit themselves but would not be countenanced by the other members of MUFL.

Still, there have been conflicts between New York's unions and banks since the founding of MUFL. In 1981, the municipal employee unions supported a bill in the state legislature that was vigorously opposed by the banks—a bill that would raise revenues for mass transit by imposing a tax on financial corporations. In 1978, when the state legislature was considering legislation to extend the life of the EFCB, a disagreement emerged between the banks and the unions concerning the conditions under which the city's chief fiscal monitor—which now would be called the Financial Control Board (FCB)—would be transformed from an active to a more passive monitor of the city's finances. The bill supported by the unions provided that the FCB would enter its passive mode after the city had balanced its budget for three consecutive years and all federally guaranteed city bonds had been retired. But the banks feared that the unions and city officials might collude to exchange the federally guaranteed bonds in union pension funds for city bonds and hold down wage increases enough to balance the budget for three years running. Then, after being freed from close supervision by the FCB, the unions and the city would return to their profligate ways. After a tense MUFL meeting the unions acquiesced to the banks' insistence that the statute extending the life of the FCB be amended to require that a third condition be fulfilled before the Board enters its passive mode—that the city regain full access to, and thereby be subject to the discipline of, the public credit markets.[24]

Despite these conflicts, the negotiations to put together a bail-out package in 1978 demonstrate that MUFL has been an institution of significance in the governance of New York. It has helped preserve the coalition of forces responsible for providing the municipal government with the loans it needed to keep functioning in the wake of the fiscal crisis. It is remarkable that only a year after refusing to countenance a proposal to extend the life of the EFCB beyond 1978, the unions agreed to legislation that will keep its successor alive beyond the year 2000. It is equally remarkable that the banks participated in a bail-out plan that included a labor agreement returning all the fringe benefits city employees

165

conceded in their previous contract and that completely abandoned the principle that pay increases should be based on increases in worker productivity.[25]

The accommodation between the banks and unions encouraged the municipal government to devote a substantial proportion of its revenues to servicing its debt and financing increases in its per employee labor costs while many important public services and facilities deteriorated. Thus, the emergence and influence of the bank/union nexus helps account for some of the central budgetary policies New York City followed after the fiscal crisis erupted.

With the benefit of hindsight, it is not so surprising that New York's major private creditors and public officials would unite behind this set of accommodations. Theirs was a "minimax" solution: it minimized the chances that the outcome yielding the maximum loss for each of them— municipal bankruptcy—would occur. The inability of the banks and unions to reach agreement on a bail-out plan in 1977 demonstrates, however, that it cannot be assumed that the players in New York's complex game of municipal finance would automatically arrive at such a solution. For this reason, the chief significance of the bank/union nexus is that it contributed to the capacity of the post-fiscal crisis regime to both meet its immediate financing imperatives and avoid the strife that would have erupted if either the banks or the unions had attempted to exploit their leverage fully.

Public Creditors and Fiscal Monitors

The second node of power in recent New York politics centers around the city's public creditors and fiscal monitors—the U.S. Treasury, MAC, and the FCB—and the political forces that comprise the constituency of these agencies. Because it provided New York with much of the credit it needed to continue functioning after 1975, and because it possesses extraordinary legal authority over the city's finances, the power of this nexus is enormous. If in their judgment municipal officials were not managing the city's finances in a responsible way, the U.S. Treasury could have withheld guarantees from city bonds, MAC could refuse to float bonds on the city's behalf, and the FCB could reject the financial plans submitted by city officials, formulate a plan of its own, take control of the city's accounts, and order city officials to implement the FCB plan.[26]

At various times since 1975 New York's fiscal monitors have used financial and legal sources of influence to become involved in numerous aspects of the city's governance—altering the structure of the city's

166

political institutions, extracting additional loans from the city's private creditors, establishing the terms and conditions of employment for municipal workers, imposing economies on the city's quasi-independent agencies, insisting that the mayor cut the expenditures of agencies directly subject to his authority, and changing the city's managerial personnel and practices. However, the intrusiveness of the city's fiscal monitoring agencies, and the magnitude of the sacrifices imposed on the individuals and groups with the largest stake in the city's fiscal solvency, have diminished over time and become remarkably limited relative to the full powers possessed by these monitoring agencies and the expectations of observers during the early years of the crisis.[27]

The most extensive intrusions of New York City's public creditors into the affairs of the metropolis occurred in 1975 and 1978. In 1975, state and federal officials insisted that MAC and the EFCB be established, institutionalizing the supervision of higher levels of government over municipal finances. In 1978, Secretary of the Treasury Michael Blumenthal indicated that the Carter administration would only agree to grant additional federal assistance to New York City if a successor to the EFCB was created with powers at least as great. The new Financial Control Board established by the state legislature pretty much met the Secretary's specifications. The powers granted to the FCB were the same as the EFCB's, except that it was not given the authority to administer a wage freeze or to set ceilings on the growth rate of municipal expenditures. The FCB was given a life-span of up to 30 years, however, whereas its predecessor had been designed as a temporary agency that would go out of business three years after its creation.[28]

New York's fiscal monitors also intervened quite actively in municipal labor relations during the early years of the fiscal crisis. In the summer of 1975, MAC ruled that the wage increases city employees were scheduled to receive be deferred. The next year, at the outset of the 1976 labor negotiations, the EFCB and the Secretary of the Treasury dictated the outlines of the settlement, indicating that there should be no general wage increase and that $50 million in existing fringe benefits should be eliminated.[29] Thereafter, the constraints New York's fiscal monitors imposed on the collective bargaining process progressively diminished. Treasury Secretary Blumenthal's insistence in 1978 that the unions and the city agree on labor contracts before loan guarantee legislation would be submitted to Congress carried the implicit threat that if these contracts were too costly Congress would balk at approval. And in 1980 Senator Proxmire indicated that unless the labor contracts negotiated that year were reasonable he would block the release of additional loan guarantees

167

to the city. These threats were imprecise enough, however, to permit the unions to win increasingly generous wage increases.

In a similar fashion, the EFCB steadily relaxed the conditions for granting cost-of-living adjustments (COLAs) to municipal employees. In 1976 the Board had insisted that the full cost of COLAs must be financed by savings realized through increases in worker productivity or reductions in fringe benefits. One year later it ruled that only half the cost of COLAs must be financed in this way, and in 1978 it permitted city employees to receive COLAs regardless of whether their productivity had increased.[30]

The EFCB also sought to reduce the expenditures of New York City's quasi-independent agencies (the Board of Education, City University, and Health and Hospitals Corporation [HHC]), organs of government not fully subject to the mayor's control and that had been the most adamant in resisting budget cuts. Stephen Berger, executive director of the EFCB throughout most of 1976 and 1977, fought vigorously to impose economies on these agencies. He criticized the Board of Education for negotiating a teacher's contract that could only be financed by reducing the length of the school day, castigated the HHC for refusing to consider closing even one of its eighteen hospitals, and blasted the administration of CUNY for spending its 1976 appropriation at a rate that required it to shut down two weeks prior to the regularly scheduled end of the academic year. Berger's successors have not taken on these agencies as directly as he had; rather, the FCB has provided Mayor Koch with support for his own efforts to control the expenditures of these agencies.[31]

The EFCB sought to ensure that cuts were imposed as well on the municipal agencies subject to the direct control of the mayor—the police and fire departments, the departments of sanitation, parks, social services, and so forth. During the early years of the EFCB, these efforts led to serious conflicts with Mayor Beame. Over the initial objections of the mayor, the Board ruled that the city should initiate no new capital construction projects and that the $200 million in revenues generated by new taxes levied in 1975 should be used to reduce the city's operating deficit, rather than to eliminate the need for further budget cuts. Conflicts between Beame and the EFCB also erupted over whether the Board should accept the revenue and expenditure projections in the city's financial plan, or whether it would independently estimate the revenues the city could reasonably expect to receive from the state and federal governments and local taxes, and the probable future costs of federally mandated programs such as AFDC and Medicaid. In June of 1976, the

168

Board went so far as to order Mayor Beame to cut $50 million from his budget for the forthcoming fiscal year, and in the first year of the EFCB's life there also were disputes over how closely the state's Office of Special Deputy Comptroller would monitor the city's compliance with its financial plan.[32]

Once it was demonstrated that the EFCB was not a paper tiger, a *modus vivendi* was established between the Board and Mayors Beame and Koch. With few exceptions, when there have been disagreements between the mayor and the Board over revenue and expenditure projections in the city's financial plan, these have generally been resolved in private negotiations between the FCB's and the mayor's staff. In reviewing the city's financial plan, the FCB has confined its attention to budgetary totals and has scrupulously avoided dictating which priorities local officials should establish within these totals.[33]

A conflict that occurred between the FCB and the city in June 1982 illustrates this point. The Board refused to approve the financial plan submitted by Mayor Koch because the city had yet to conclude its labor negotiations; hence, the labor costs it would bear could not be determined. In addition, the mayor's plan counted on state aid that had yet to be appropriated by the legislature. The FCB instead authorized the city to extend the previous fiscal year's budget for an additional six months, enabling it to conclude its labor negotiations and prepare a new four-year plan. During this grace period the 1982 recession deepened, and the city negotiated labor contracts that provided for wage increases considerably higher than the estimated rate of inflation. The FCB rejected the city's revised financial plan, but approved a third plan submitted by the mayor that provided for layoffs of as many as 6,600 employees and for cutting the city's workforce by as many as an additional 11,000 employees through attrition. In approving this plan, the FCB refused to heed the call of Felix Rohatyn and the CBC that the city's labor contracts be renegotiated so as to avoid the necessity of such deep cuts in its workforce. In rejecting that course of action, the FCB's executive director, Comer Coppie, asserted that the Board's refusal to approve the city's labor contracts would violate the integrity of the collective bargaining process.[34]

Two conclusions can be drawn from this example of FCB-city conflict. One is that the FCB is prepared to insist that the city do whatever is necessary to balance its budget, even if it involves actions that would sharply reduce municipal services. The other is that the FCB is reluctant to become involved in setting municipal fiscal priorities as long as the

169

city stays within the boundaries of a balanced budget, even if the priorities of city officials run counter to those advocated by organizations such as the CBC.

The efforts of New York's fiscal monitors to strengthen the city's managerial personnel and practices have also declined. In 1975 and early 1976, the monitors compelled Mayor Beame to replace the top financial and managerial personnel in his administration and adopt a new computer-based Integrated Financial and Management System that would enable city officials to instantaneously obtain complete information about the municipal government's financial position, and therefore make managerial decisions more intelligently. After this the city's fiscal monitors largely withdrew from this area. As Stephen Berger, who believed that all bureaucracies in New York City were undersupervised, observed in an interview, the EFCB "took a very moderate view of its statutory powers. Only in the case of severe hemorrhaging, such as in the Health and Hospitals Corporation, did we go beyond budget analysis to ensure that the budget lines were within the financial plan—at least formally. Only with HHC did we delve into real questions of personnel, management, organization, and policy."[35]

Why has the Financial Control Board been so restrained in exercising its extraordinary powers over New York City's finances? Or, more generally, what forces have influenced the behavior of New York's fiscal monitors? One consideration shaping the conduct of New York's fiscal monitors stems from the central mission of these agencies—namely, to help the city meet immediate financing needs while pressing it to make changes in fiscal policies and practices that will enable it to regain full access to the private capital markets. This mission led the FCB to insist that the municipal government make steady progress toward balancing its budget and keeping it balanced. If the city failed to do so, MAC would have found it impossible to sell the bonds the city needed to stay afloat, and the prospects for the municipal government's regaining full access to the credit markets on its own would evaporate.

At the same time, however, the FCB's mission has constrained its freedom of action. If the Board pressed for budget cuts so deep that powerful local groups would be required to make greater sacrifices than their members were prepared to absorb, they might dig in their heels and resist. By seizing control of the city's accounts and ordering local officials to implement the changes in municipal financial policy it wanted, the FCB might prevail, but its victory would be Pyhrric. The spectacle of such a battle could impede the city's efforts to regain full access to the market, because nothing is more likely to convince outsiders that the city remains a poor credit risk than such resistance to budget cuts.

The FCB has occasionally been willing to press for expenditure reductions in the face of resistance by vocal groups in the city. In 1976, for example, it was prepared to face considerable turmoil to impose reductions in expenditures upon the City University system. The Board was willing to risk such confrontations in the year following the eruption of the crisis, because the prospect of the city's regaining entry to the credit market was remote and the spectacle of conflict could do little damage. But as the municipal government's prospects for reentering the market became brighter, the FCB had an increasing incentive to come to terms with the major political forces in the city and to join with them in presenting a united front to the outside world.

The incentive to present a united front also has created restraints on the FCB's ability to usurp the full powers of locally elected officials. For one, the statute creating the EFCB asserts in its preamble that to deal with New York City's financial emergency "the state must . . . exercise controls and supervision over the financial affairs of the City of New York, but in a manner intended to preserve the ability of city officials to determine program and expenditure priorities within available financial resources." The Financial Emergency Act authorizes the FCB to reject a financial plan submitted to it by the mayor, or, in an extreme case, to seize control of the municipal government's accounts, only if the city is not making "substantial" progress toward balancing its budget. If the FCB took either of these steps, the mayor could challenge its action in the courts, claiming that the city was making the required progress. Whatever the outcome of such a suit, the legal shadow that would be cast over the city's finances while the case was being adjudicated, and the possibility that another suit might be filed at any point in the future, would make investors extremely reluctant to purchase New York City securities. Even without taking the FCB to court, a mayor could publicly charge that the Board's efforts to usurp the powers of locally elected officials were a violation of democratic principles. If this charge struck a responsive chord among the city's residents, there might be an eruption of popular resistance or turmoil that could impair the city's access to the market.

New York's fiscal monitors have, however, been prepared at times to risk confrontations with the mayor. Their willingness to do so is a function of two conditions: the relative strength of the constituencies of the mayor and of the monitoring agencies, and the extent to which fiscal policies pursued by the mayor are compatible with those advocated by the monitors. As for the first, the constituency of the FCB is composed

171

most immediately of the constituents of its members, the most important of whom is the chairman, the governor. The governor must be concerned with maintaining the state's credit, which is tied to New York City's, and with winning the support of voters throughout the state. During the early years of the fiscal crisis Governor Carey served both these ends by actively setting New York City's finances in order, presenting himself to the market and the state's electorate as a firm proponent of fiscal responsibility. In 1975 he led the effort to save New York City from bankruptcy, and in 1976 he appointed Stephen Berger as executive director of the EFCB and provided him with the political backing he needed to impose economies on Mayor Beame and the city's quasi-independent agencies. In 1977 Carey intervened in the city's mayoral election in an effort to defeat Beame's bid for a second term.

This, however, proved to be the high point of Governor Carey's intervention into New York City's affairs. By helping replace Beame with Ed Koch, a mayor more firmly committed to retrenchment, the governor relieved himself of the necessity for active involvement in efforts to impose budget cuts on City Hall. After Berger's resignation from the EFCB and Beame's defeat, Carey appointed as the Board's executive director Donald Kummerfeld, an official who was far less aggressive than Berger. When asked why he had not pressed Koch harder, Kummerfeld explained that the new mayor had campaigned as a proponent of retrenchment, and the Board was more than happy to let him take the lead in balancing the city's budget.[36]

In campaigning for reelection in 1978, Governor Carey pointed to the role he played in saving New York City from bankruptcy as a major accomplishment of his first term. A public official who must appeal to a statewide electorate, however, cannot be too actively involved in the city's governance. At the same time, since one third of the state's voters live in New York City, a governor also cannot afford to be indifferent to their views. Because policies likely to be popular downstate are often unpopular upstate, and vice versa, the safest course of action for a governor is to avoid heavy involvement in New York City's affairs.

The second element of the FCB's constituency is the credit market the Board wishes to make receptive to New York City securities, and it is the three private-sector members of the FCB who, in effect, represent these investors and potential investors in the city's securities. The governor's first appointees to these seats were the chief executives of billion-dollar corporations headquartered in New York, appointed in the hope that if businessmen of this stature gave their approval to the city's budget, the market would be reassued that New York was putting its affairs in order. The role FCB private-sector members thus play gives them the leverage to insist that the city's financial plans and budgets be based on conservative revenue and expenditure estimates.

Although New York City did not gain reentry to the market as scheduled, the early success of the EFCB's private-sector members is indicated by the decline in the risk premium that MAC needed to pay to sell its bonds, and by the fact that in 1976 the initial occupants of these seats on the Board felt that their task had been accomplished and they could resign. The men the governor appointed to succeed them were less prominent than their predecessors—an indication that this role had become institutionalized. That role, as one participant described it, was to serve as "the conscience of the Board," ensuring that the FCB continue to serve its mission of pressing the city to do what was necessary to regain full access to the private capital markets.[37]

Although the businessmen who serve on the FCB in this sense represent potential investors in New York City securities, it is important to note that no cleavage has emerged on the Board between its private- and public-sector members. The Board has strived for a consensus—and has regularly achieved it—because if investors perceived that locally elected officials were only balancing New York City's budget at the insistence of the businessmen on the FCB, they might well fear that elected officials twenty years from now would not be likely to redeem the city's securities. This impressive record of unanimity indicates that the FCB's private-sector members have gotten the city to pay heed to the concerns of the market, but at the same time it also indicates that they have been prepared to come to terms with powerful local political forces, such as New York's banks and public employee unions.

The third component of the FCB's constituency is the Board's "attentive publics"—notably, the Citizens Budget Commission, the SMP project, the city newspapers, and professional staffs of the OSDC, MAC, and the FCB itself. These institutions have regularly supported the FCB's efforts to impose economies on the municipal government, and frequently urge that the city implement greater economies, or more extensive changes in managerial practices, than the Board finds it prudent to demand. In the early months of the EFCB's life, Mayor Beame argued strenuously that the OSDC should not be permitted to release its audits and analyses of municipal programs until its findings and recommendations were approved by the Board. But Governor Carey insisted that the OSDC be permitted to do so, and he prevailed. Since 1975 the staffs of the OSDC and FCB have often issued reports criticizing City Hall, and these criticisms have been reported in the press.[38] This barrage of criticism—along with similar reports issued by the SMP project and the CBC—has made it easier politically for the FCB to exert pressure on City Hall.

The inclination of the FCB to battle City Hall is also a function of the extent to which the mayor's policies are compatible with the Board's and the strength of the forces the mayor can mobilize in his own defense. The FCB had a greater incentive to fight the Beame administration than the Koch administration because Abe Beame had originated many of the gimmicks that enabled the city to engage in deficit spending; he had resisted cutting expenditures drastically after the crisis erupted; and he remained closely allied with expenditure-demanding groups—notably, municipal employee unions. Consequently, there was reason for the FCB to fear that if it failed to supervise his administration closely, Beame would revert to his old ways.

The situation with Mayor Koch has been quite different. Koch has repeatedly stated that setting the city's finances in order is the top priority of his administration, and he has demonstrated his commitment by being prepared to make political enemies for the sake of achieving this goal. As one FCB private-sector member said of Mayor Koch in 1979, "One of the reasons I have confidence in the [city's financial] plan is that I have confidence in the mayor. The plan is only going to work if the officials responsible are committed to achieving its goals. Mayor Koch is committed to carrying out the mandates."[39] Even more significant than the contrast between the policy orientations of the Beame and Koch administrations are the differences in their respective political bases. These differences have made the FCB far less willing to fight Koch than Beame.

The Mayoralty

The Beame administration was discredited by the 1975 fiscal crisis in the eyes of the city's financial community and, as the outcome of the 1977 mayoral election indicated, in the eyes of the city's electorate as well. This provided Governor Carey and his financial advisors with a strong incentive to involve themselves in the city's governance, and it reduced the mayor's ability to resist such intervention. In 1975, when the mayor had to fire top officials in City Hall and replace them with appointees acceptable to the city's fiscal monitors, he relinquished some control over his own administration. In addition, during the first two years of the crisis he had to fire many of his lower-level patronage appointees. Between December 31, 1974, and September 1, 1976, the number of municipal employees in the provisional and exempt classes of the civil service fell from 9,335 to 4,163, a reduction of more than 50 percent. Beame was compelled to do this to demonstrate to the city's monitors and to the market that he was seriously committed to reducing expenditures and increasing the efficiency of the municipal government. By laying off these appointees, however, he was further weakened politically. A number of machine politicians asserted at the time that as the prospects for getting a patronage appointment diminished, attendance at local Democratic clubs declined. This was a serious problem for Beame, because the regular Democratic county organizations were a major political pillar of his mayoralty.[40]

Mayor Koch's election greatly altered the structure of politics in New York City. Koch assembled a political coalition that differed in some important respects from Beame's, and he was far more popular with most segments of the electorate than his predecessor had been. This has had significant implications for the policies the municipal government has pursued and for the balance of power between City Hall and the FCB.

One component of Mayor Koch's political constituency is the business community. Koch's bid for the mayoralty in 1977 was backed by a few businessmen who were personal friends of Koch, such as Kenneth Lipper of the investment banking house Salomon Brothers, as well as by William Ellinghaus and David Margolis of the EFCB (Margolis was also a close friend of the mayor). But as Lipper said of Koch in 1982:

When he first came into the mayor's office in 1977 the business community in general was skeptical. He didn't have much identifiable executive experience, and his record in Washington didn't focus on the hard issues that New York City faced, such as fiscal and budget issues. But he has demonstrated an exceptional competence in learning to manage a complex enterprise, in achieving stability and creating an environment in the city that allowed private enterprise to flourish.[41]

In both word and deed, Mayor Koch has indicated that revitalizing New York's economy is a top priority of his administration. Shortly after entering City Hall, Koch asserted that: "the main job of municipal government is to create a climate in which private business can expand in the city to provide jobs and profit. It's not the function of government to create jobs on the public payroll."[42] These priorities have been reflected in the city's budget during the Koch administration. In their study of municipal expenditure patterns in fiscal 1975, 1978, and 1982, Charles Brecher and Raymond Horton report that expenditures by agencies performing "developmental" functions (promoting the growth of the city's economy) fell from $1.17 billion in 1975 to $734 million at the end of Mayor Beame's term, but then rose to $1.27 billion at the end of Mayor Koch's first term. This 72 percent increase in developmental spending was considerably larger than either the 21 percent rate of expenditure growth on the part of agencies performing "redistributive" functions (public assistance, social services, and health), or the 36 percent growth of expenditures on "allocative" functions (those performed by all other agencies). These expenditure priorities indicate that Mayor Koch has backed up his warm words about business with cold cash.[43]

Mayor Koch has also strived to increase the efficiency of municipal agencies. The city now allocates a significant proportion of its capital expenditures to purchasing equipment or constructing facilities that will lower its operating costs, such as large-capacity, side-loading sanitation trucks that can be conveniently operated by crews of two, rather than three, refuse collectors, and that can handle long collection routes without having to take time out to dump their loads. The Koch administration has attempted, with mixed results, to amend the civil service laws governing New York City to enhance its control over the municipal labor force and to alter the managerial practices of municipal agencies to improve their performance. Again the most notable examples involve the Sanitation Department, which has hired civilians to perform jobs formerly filled by more highly paid uniformed employees, lengthened collection routes, improved procedures for maintaining and repairing equipment, and, as mentioned, reduced the size of the crews manning many sanitation trucks.[44]

More striking than the support that Ed Koch the *liberal* has received from New York's downtown business community is the alliance that Ed Koch the *reformer* has cultivated with the city's Democratic county machines. Koch entered New York politics in the 1950s through the Democratic reform movement and gained citywide prominence by defeating Carmine DeSapio for the Democratic leadership of DeSapio's home district, thus ending the public career of "the last of the big time bosses." Reformism was not a central theme in Koch's 1977 mayoral campaign, though he did criticize Abe Beame's clubhouse connections.[45]

But after entering City Hall, Koch signaled his willingness to make peace with the city's Democratic machines. He appointed men with ties to these organizations to a number of positions in his administration; he backed a party regular for the Democratic leadership of the Bronx in 1978 over the candidate supported by that borough's reformers; and the following year he tacitly supported the regular, rather than the reform, candidate for Bronx borough president. Koch's relationship with party regulars in other boroughs became equally warm, to the point that his

176

renomination in 1981 was backed by four of the city's five Democratic county party organizations. (The Manhattan organization, in which the reform faction was strongest, remained neutral in the race.) This support was repeated when Koch ran for the Democratic gubernatorial nomination in 1982 and for a third term as mayor in 1985.[46]

There is one other way in which Koch, despite his roots in the Democratic reform movement, became a practitioner of the old politics, and that is in the character of the relationship he established with major real estate developers and owners in the city. A significant proportion of Koch's campaign contributions in 1981 and 1985 came from these sources, and although there is no direct evidence that those who make such contributions are rewarded by City Hall, there is some indirect evidence suggesting such a linkage. In 1982 the front-runner for the Republican gubernatorial nomination, state comptroller Edward Regan, withdrew from the race, explaining that businessmen dependent upon the good will of the city and state governments were unwilling to contribute to his campaign, because Koch was assured of being either mayor or governor after the election, and because they feared that a Koch administration in either New York City or Albany would retaliate against businessmen who had contributed to his political opponents. As Regan phrased it, "People who contribute money have developed a very practical sense about things in life."[47]

Why did Mayor Koch ally with machine politicians and adopt these traditional practices? The answer is not that he would have been otherwise unable to be reelected. On the contrary, it is Koch's electoral strength that explains why the city's regular Democratic party organizations were so anxious to come to terms with him. Despite the high probability that he would win any contest against a machine-backed candidate, the mayor had no reason to welcome such a race, and because the county party organizations still commanded an electoral apparatus useful for circulating nominating petitions and getting voters to the polls, having these organizations on his side decreased the effort necessary to put together his reelection campaigns. Moreover, the regular party organizations were still important forces in the state legislature, city council, and, to a lesser extent, the Board of Estimate, and establishing a working relationship with them eased the task of governing the city. And because Koch would almost certainly win any direct confrontation with the county party organizations, the price he had to pay for their support was not high. For example, Koch is the first mayor in New York City's recent history who refuses to use judicial appointments as a form of patronage, and county party leaders are simply in no position to insist that they be granted influence over these appointments.[48]

As startling as the deal Ed Koch the reformer struck with New York's machine politicians is the alliance Ed Koch the *Democrat* cultivated with the city's Republican party. In the 1980 state legislative elections the mayor endorsed the reelection of two incumbent Republican state senators, and by staging a well-publicized meeting with Ronald Reagan during the 1980 national campaign, he provided the Republican presidential candidate with a means of countering the charge that his election would be a disaster for the nation's older cities. All of this was a prelude to four of New York City's five Republican county organization's supporting—with President Reagan all but endorsing—Koch's nomination in the 1981 GOP mayoral primary, a nomination the mayor handily won. The Republican county leaders endorsed Koch because he was prepared to offer them municipal patronage and assistance in raising money for their organizations. Most important, Koch was very popular with the major groups in their constituencies and the odds were overwhelming that he would win reelection even if they nominated someone to run against him. Unable to beat him, they joined him.[49]

Koch's popularity among New York City voters is the final, and most important, source of his political strength. In the 1977 mayoral election voters divided along ethnic lines to a considerable degree, and a prime reason that Koch emerged on top was that he belonged to the city's largest voting bloc, the Jews. Yet, after entering City Hall Koch became increasingly popular among other segments of the city's population, with the exception of racial minorities. Koch's popularity was especially remarkable because a number of municipal services and public facilities continued to deteriorate during his first term. The mayor managed to absolve himself of responsibility by arguing that the city simply could not afford to spend more of its own resources to improve services and renovate its physical infrastructure, by harshly castigating the state and federal governments for failing to provide the city with additional financial aid, and by blaming the city's employees and even some of his own appointees for failing to produce more with the resources that were available to them. Indeed, Koch's frequent and harsh verbal attacks upon others—being "feisty," as the mayor himself has termed it—is probably the chief source of his popularity: Koch is a politician who travels on his tongue. The mayor's rhetoric during his first term was especially feisty on racial issues, contributing to his popularity among the city's white ethnic groups and causing strains in his relationship with New York's racial minorities.

Tensions between Ed Koch and New York's black and Puerto Rican

178

political leadership emerged during the 1977 Democratic mayoral primary. Two of the major themes in Koch's campaign were advocacy of the death penalty and denunciations of "poverty pimps"—officials in community action agencies who used antipoverty funds for personal or political gain—themes that were regarded as thinly veiled racial slurs by most minority group politicians. Nonetheless, after Koch promised to appoint more blacks and Puerto Ricans to important positions in his administration than had Mayors Wagner, Lindsay, and Beame combined, a substantial proportion of minority politicians endorsed Koch in the second round of the primary. In selecting his deputy mayors, Koch was true to his word: he appointed Herman Badillo (the city's leading Puerto Rican politician) Deputy Mayor for Policy, and Basil Paterson (former state senator from Harlem and vice-chairman of the Democratic National Committee) Deputy Mayor for Labor Relations.

But shortly thereafter Mayor Koch did several things that caused his relations with black political leaders to deteriorate. In contrast to his predecessors, Mayor Koch did not select his black appointees from among the city's black political establishment, nor did he clear his selections with that leadership group, and this they denounced as an "act of political contempt." Second, the mayor reorganized the city's poverty program, evoking even louder protests from black political leaders and activists. The mayor and a top official in his administration were shouted off the stage at a public meeting in Harlem which had been called to explain this reorganization; the chairman of the state legislature's black caucus denounced Koch's plan as "genocide" and initiated a campaign to recall him. Third, the mayor proposed closing some municipal hospitals in black neighborhoods, and for this he was charged with being willing to sacrifice black lives for the sake of balancing the city's budget. Every bit as important as these deeds were Koch's words—when he was denounced in hyperbolic language by black political leaders, the mayor replied in kind.[50]

Black politicians responded with such fury to the behavior of the Koch administration because these actions withdrew concessions that black politicians had extracted from previous administrations and threatened the position of the existing black leadership. In particular, Koch's appointment of blacks who were not approved by New York's black political leadership violated the principle, first established by Adam Clayton Powell, that blacks, rather than whites, should determine who will speak for black New Yorkers.[51]

Mayor Koch's reorganization of the city's poverty program also presented a serious threat to many black politicians. The autonomy that

179

previous administrations had conceded to community corporations in poor neighborhoods had enabled those who controlled these agencies to distribute jobs and other benefits to their personal and political supporters. Many black and Puerto Rican politicians relied upon this patronage to establish and maintain their political followings. The Koch administration's reorganization of the city's antipoverty program made it difficult for black politicians to continue these practices. Also, many employees of these agencies (and also of the municipal hospitals that Mayor Koch threatened to close) earned more than they would likely receive working in the private sector—if, in the face of high unemployment rates among nonwhite New Yorkers, they could find jobs in the private sector. It is small wonder that many reacted heatedly to proposals that might threaten their very way of life, driving them from the world of steady work at decent pay to a life of irregular work at indecent pay.

Finally, Mayor Koch's shouting matches with black politicians violated a tacit understanding that had emerged in the 1960s. A major concession that white political leaders had made to their black counterparts during that decade was to stand mute when being denounced for racism. (By contrast, the members of New York's political fraternity would have cut off all relations with one of their number who regularly accused them of anti-Semitism or anti-Catholicism.) This concession helped black political leaders retain the support of their followers even when, in the give-and-take of the policymaking process, they were obligated to accept compromises that left their constituents at the bottom of the city's social structure. During his first term, at least, Koch refused to play by these rules, replying in kind when denounced by black political leaders and setting off ever more acrimonious exchanges.[52]

Why did Mayor Koch behave in these ways? Koch argued that the use of antipoverty funds as a source of patronage led to gross inefficiencies in many antipoverty programs—an example he often cited was a scholarship program that devoted a third of its budget to administrative expenses—and that at a time of general austerity the city simply could not afford to ignore waste in any municipal agency. By reducing the number of administrative personnel in antipoverty agencies, it would be possible to maintain or increase the amount of assistance flowing to the poor people who were supposed to be the beneficiaries of these programs, even as the budgets of these agencies were being cut. This may explain why the mayor reacted with indignation, and replied sharply, to charges of racism.[53]

Koch's attacks upon black leaders struck a responsive chord among many white voters being asked to accept cuts in programs that served

180

them, so it is reasonable to infer that these voters regarded the reaction of blacks to the mayor's reorganization of the poverty program as a demand for "special treatment." Moreover, many organizations and organs representing the opinions of upper-middle- and upper-class New Yorkers were prepared to tolerate Mayor Koch's rhetoric on racial issues, even if they did not approve of it. The *New York Times,* which periodically chided Koch for exacerbating racial tensions in the city, nonetheless supported his renomination and reelection because it approved of his fiscal policies. Koch thus found it politically possible—and, indeed, profitable—to say publicly what he felt about those who attacked him, even if this violated rhetorical concessions earlier granted to blacks.

The coincidence—in the sense of simultaneous occurrence—of New York's fiscal crisis and the rise to power of a mayor who withdrew some concessions earlier granted blacks is thus not a *mere* coincidence. It was the fiscal crisis that altered the priorities of many people who formerly had allied with blacks, thereby making it feasible for Koch to forge a support coalition composed not only of those who backed him because of his attacks on black leaders but also of those who were prepared to back him despite these attacks. That such changes in the structure of incentives and constraints confronting public officials were a precondition of Mayor Koch's behavior is indicated by the response of a rather different politician, Governor Carey, to a demand of the state legislature's black caucus in 1975 that he appoint a black to the EFCB. Although Carey was quite liberal on race-related issues, he refused to accede to this demand. The function of the EFCB was to convince New York City's creditors and potential creditors that a total change had occurred in the fiscal policies, practices, and politics that had driven the municipal government to the edge of bankruptcy, and this purpose could best be served if it did *not* represent all major groups in the city. Indeed, it was advantageous to pointedly exclude representatives of the neediest segment of the city's population. The elite civic associations and newspapers, which only a few years before had joined in a call for opening the city's political system to blacks, did not press the governor to accede to the demand of the black caucus. Evidently, they regarded the municipal government's regaining access to the market as more important than the concerns that had animated them in, say, the Ocean Hill-Brownsville controversy.[54]

In addition to changes in the programmatic priorities of important social groups in New York, another set of conditions that were not of Ed Koch's making contributed to his political success. Historically, in the United States, politicians who rely upon rhetoric with an ethnic or racial

181

component to build personal followings for themselves have had the greatest success in cities and states whose governments are unable to do much to remedy the concrete grievances of their residents, because their formal powers are limited, the economic constraints under which they operate are highly restrictive, or their political parties are too weak to overcome the dispersion of authority among different branches of government. In these situations candidates cannot win public support by making promises, which plausibly could be honored, to enact policies that would alleviate the problems of their constituents. Consequently, electoral turnout declines and the advantage in contests for the support of those voters who remain in the active electorate can be seized by politicians who are able to attract attention to themselves in other ways. It was just these conditions in Boston from the 1910s through the 1940s that enabled James Michael Curley to mobilize an intensely loyal political following with appeals to the solidarities and antipathies of that city's "newer races," as he termed them, and to dominate the political scene for more than thirty years. Similarly, the constraints imposed upon New York's municipal government by the steps it had to take to fund its floating deficit, obtain financing from its banks and unions, and regain the confidence of the capital markets, led to a decline in municipal services and facilities in the late 1970s that the mayor could do little to halt. This state of affairs encouraged Ed Koch to appeal for support in other ways.

This is not to say that the constraints under which New York City has labored dictated the precise political strategy the mayor has pursued, or that if Koch had not run for mayor some other politician would have adopted the same persona. Ed Koch is a genuinely creative politician. Prior to his appearance on New York's political stage, who could have foreseen that there could be such a phenomenon as a Jewish James Michael Curley? It was the genius of Ed Koch to recognize that it is possible to manage the city's affairs in a way that meets with the approval of staid investment bankers, while simultaneously winning the support of Jewish and non-Jewish voters alike, by playing the *kibbitzer*— the brash fellow who has an opinion on everything.

The political coalition Mayor Koch assembled is a personal coalition, which has been deployed almost exclusively to advance his own political fortunes. Koch has not sought in any consistent way to transfer his political strength to those members of the Board of Estimate, city council, or state legislature who have consistently allied with him on public issues. The personal character of Ed Koch's following is another way in which his political *modus operandi* resembles James Michael Curley's, and, as with Curley, it has negative implications for the prospect that the coalition Koch has assembled will be able to survive his departure from City Hall.

Mayor Koch's construction of this broad political coalition has had a very important consequence: it has enabled him to reinvigorate the mayoralty and to restore some of the autonomy the municipal government had lost in 1975. Because Koch is so popular, other public officials hesitate to get into fights with him, and this is a significant reason why the FCB has not intervened as much in New York's affairs since Koch entered office as it did when Beame was mayor.

Koch's powerful support coalition has also increased the mayor's control over the city's quasi-independent agencies, especially the hospital and school systems. By including the budgets of these "covered organizations" in the city's financial plan, the Financial Emergency Acts of 1975 and 1978 reduced the autonomy of these agencies. When Stephen Berger was the EFCB's executive director, this loss was largely (though not entirely) the Board's gain. But for the reasons just mentioned, after Koch entered City Hall the FCB was content to let the mayor spearhead the drive to impose fiscal discipline on these agencies. And Koch has undertaken to do so because fighting the community groups and civil service unions that resist cutbacks adds to his political strength more than it detracts from it.

There is another way in which Mayor Koch's popularity has enabled him to gain influence over New York City's school system. Two of the Board of Education's seven members are appointed directly by the mayor and the remaining five are appointed by the borough presidents. Koch is so strong politically that the borough presidents follow his lead in making appointments, and consequently members of the Board of Education who wish to secure reappointment have a strong incentive to do what the mayor wants. One indication of the extent of Koch's influence is that in both 1978 and 1983 the Board of Education selected the mayor's candidate to be chancellor of the city's school system. (In 1983, however, the state education commissioner declared the mayor's candidate, Deputy Mayor Robert F. Wagner, Jr., to be ineligible, because he did not have the required educational credentials.) The upshot of these developments is that the mayoralty under Koch became stronger in some respects than it had been prior to the fiscal crisis.[55]

Racial Minorities

The character of a regime is determined not only by the composition of its prevailing political coalitions and the structure of its political institutions, but also by the way these relate to the groups occupying a subordinate position within the regime. Since 1975 blacks and Puerto Ricans have occupied such a position in New York City's politics.

Signs of the deteriorating political position of New York's racial minorities appeared early in the fiscal crisis. In 1975, Governor Carey refused to accede to the demand of the state legislature's black and Puerto Rican caucus that a nonwhite be appointed to one of the seats on the EFCB. In the municipal elections two years later, blacks lost control of the Manhattan borough presidency—a position occupied by one of their number for twenty-four years. This deprived blacks of a seat in the city's highest governing body, the Board of Estimate, for the first time in a quarter century. In that same election New York's most prominent black and Puerto Rican politicians, Percy Sutton and Herman Badillo, ran in the Democratic mayoral primary and came in fifth and sixth in a field of seven candidates—a sharp contrast to the previous election, in which Badillo had come in second. Also, minority politicians received little support from their upper-middle-class and upper-class allies of the 1960s in fighting against Mayor Koch's reorganization of the city's poverty program, his closing of municipal hospitals, and his efforts to control the costs of redistributive programs. Consequently, minority politicians lost these battles. Recognizing that the great majority of white opinion leaders and voters approved of Koch's conduct during his first term, black and Hispanic opponents of the mayor, along with liberal whites who had not elevated a commitment to balancing the city's budget over their prior concerns, conducted little more than a token campaign on behalf of the obscure state assemblyman, Frank Barbaro, who was the only elected official they could find to oppose Koch's bid for a second term in the 1981 Democratic primary.

There are a few exceptions to this pattern, but they are exceptions that prove the rule. The most noteworthy was a controversy in 1983 over the question of whether there is a systematic pattern of brutality against nonwhites by the New York City Police Department. This charge was made by the minister of the largest church in Harlem and was picked up by other black leaders, who convinced the chairman of a congressional subcommittee to hold hearings in the city to look into this issue. Mayor Koch and Police Commissioner Robert Maguire heatedly denied that there was any such pattern, and the controversy provoked by this issue lasted for several months.

In an editorial on the controversy, the *New York Times* criticized Koch for failing to recognize that the depth of feeling this issue aroused among members of the city's black community was indicative of their profound sense of alienation from the institutions of local government. The paper asserted that the mayor's rather defensive response to these allegations failed to address this problem. Koch was aware that the charge that he was polarizing the city along racial lines could lose him support among the social groups for which the *Times* spoke, so when Maguire resigned he appointed a black, Benjamin Ward, as police commissioner, which was warmly praised by the *Times*. While the black leaders who had raised the issue of police brutality had not demanded that the mayor appoint a black as police commissioner, Ward is the first to serve in this capacity and his appointment surely must be counted as a victory for New York's racial minorities.[56]

This episode suggests that the support of those whites who had had a standing alliance with blacks in the 1960s is a prerequisite for the political victories of nonwhite New Yorkers. Such alliances have been uncommon since 1975, however, and it is important to note that the one that emerged on the issue of police brutality did not involve a question of municipal fiscal policy. It is this political isolation of blacks that has largely neutralized the opposition of nonwhites to the city's post-fiscal crisis regime.

New York's racial minorities have not been completely without ties to the local political system during Ed Koch's mayoralty. A major link between them and the system is provided by the city's black and Puerto Rican representatives in the city council, state legislature, and U.S. Congress. Their shared antipathy to Ed Koch has recently led the city's black elected officials—among whom there has been a long history of factional cleavages—to unite on a number of occasions. One occasion was in 1983 when many black elected officials, clergymen, and community leaders sought to secure the appointment of a nonwhite as chancellor of the city's public schools, by uniting behind the candidacy of Thomas Minter, a black deputy chancellor in the New York school system. The Board of Education followed the leadership of Mayor Koch in making its appointment, however, and the mayor refused to bow to pressure. But when the (white) candidate Koch supported and the Board appointed was declared to be ineligible for the position by the state commissioner of education, the mayor shied away from reopening the racial divisions that attended his original decision and gave his support to a Hispanic candidate. The black leaders who initially had demanded that a nonwhite be appointed as chancellor regarded this as a victory.[57]

The black leaders who were brought together on the chancellor issue decided to form a permanent organization, the Coalition for a Just New York (CJNY), which was chaired by Assemblyman Albert Vann and is dedicated to increasing the representation of nonwhites in public offices. The coalition played a leading role in registering tens of thousands of new black voters in conjunction with Jesse Jackson's campaign in the 1984 Democratic presidential primary, with an eye toward electing a nonwhite mayor in 1985, or at least securing the defeat of Ed Koch. In February 1985 the CJNY endorsed the mayoral candidacy of Herman D. Farrell, Jr., a black state assemblyman from Manhattan.[58]

In its efforts to unite and energize members of the city's black community behind common causes, the CJNY resembles the alliances that have emerged since 1975 within other sectors of New York's public life. Like the leaders of these other alliances, the leaders of the CJNY are not mindless of the constraints under which municipal officials operate or of the compromises it may be prudent to make for the sake of building coalitions across sectoral lines. For example, the candidate the CJNY backed for school chancellor, Thomas Minter, is a low-keyed educational bureaucrat who is worlds apart from the firebrands who ran the Ocean Hill-Brownsville community school district where Albert Vann first gained public prominence. (As one newspaper account of Vann's political metamorphosis put it, "he has traded his dashiki for three piece suits and monogrammed shirts.") In December 1984 a number of black and Jewish leaders organized a group, the Black/Jewish Coalition, dedicated to reducing tensions between their communities. Some observers (among them, the mayor) saw this attempt to overcome divisions that dated back to the Ocean Hill controversy as the first step in an effort to forge an anti-Koch coalition among blacks and liberal Jews in the 1985 mayoral election. The experience of contending with Ed Koch, it thus would appear, is contributing to the incorporation of blacks into New York City's political system under a chastened political leadership.[59]

Another institution linking nonwhites to New York's political system are the city's public employee unions. Blacks compose a majority or near majority of some of New York's largest civil service unions—District Council 37 of AFSCME, the Transport Workers Union, and Local 237 of

186

the Teamsters—and through collective bargaining, grievance procedures, and lobbying these unions represent their black, as much as their white, members. Furthermore, public employee unions should not be seen as simply representing their own members. Positions on the public payroll are one of the most significant benefits that the municipal government distributes to different ethnic and racial groups in the city; along with state and federal jobs, they are a major channel of social mobility for blacks in New York, as elsewhere in the country. Consequently, by advancing the interests of black members, New York's civil service unions are advocating the interests of an important segment of the city's black community.

Since the onset of the fiscal crisis, municipal union leaders have had to walk a narrow line representing the interests of their members—white and nonwhite alike. On the one hand, they regard their mission to be maintaining and improving wages and benefits; on the other, they must avoid pushing the city into bankruptcy. The tension between these two imperatives has created strains between union leaders and the rank-and-file, who cannot help but wonder whether their interests are being sold out when their leaders consort with Messrs. Rohatyn, Rockefeller, and Wriston. These strains are exacerbated in unions where membership is heavily black while leadership is white.

Public officials and other influential figures who wish to see the city remain solvent share an interest with "responsible" municipal union leaders in containing such tensions, helping these leaders remain in office, and inducing rank-and-file union members to ratify contracts their leaders negotiate. Inasmuch as such strains are especially severe in unions with large nonwhite memberships, some of the most extreme examples of collusion between municipal labor leaders and management have involved these unions. For example, in 1980, tensions between the predominantly nonwhite membership of the Transport Workers Union and the TWU's white leader, John Lawe, were so great that Lawe and Richard Ravitch, then chairman of the Metropolitan Transit Authority (MTA), agreed that it would be impossible to secure ratification of any settlement that appeared to involve concessions by Lawe to the MTA. Therefore, at a private dinner prior to the formal negotiations, Ravitch and Lawe worked out a plan that involved an MTA wage increase proposal of 6 percent, which they knew the union's executive board would reject, and a Lawe counteroffer of 7 percent, which Ravitch was prepared to accept. But conflicts within the union were even greater than Lawe and Ravitch anticipated. Lawe's proposed 7 percent counteroffer

187

was shouted down by the executive board and a strike was called. Ravitch and Lawe then agreed that the only way to secure the executive board's approval of a new offer would be to pretend that its terms were proposed by a neutral mediator. This tactic worked, though barely, and Lawe was able to order his men to go back to work.[60]

To the extent that New York's civil service unions exert a measure of control over, as well as represent, their membership, they link city employees to the municipal government in a way that has fewer adverse consequences for the city's budget than was the case prior to the fiscal crisis, when blacks composed a smaller proportion of their membership. (In 1981, for the first time in New York's history, a majority of the city's newly hired employees were nonwhite, a pattern that has continued to the present.) In one of those bitter ironies characteristic of the experience of blacks in the United States, access to a benefit that formerly had been denied to large numbers of blacks has coincided with a decline in the value of that benefit. In the case of civil service jobs in New York City, the rate of increase in the wages, fringe benefits, and pensions that New York's public sector unions have been able to secure for their members has been lower (in inflation-adjusted dollars) in recent years than had been the case when there were fewer nonwhites on the city's payroll.[61] This correlation, moreover, is not spurious. It is precisely because the relative attractiveness of many municipal jobs in New York City has declined since the fiscal crisis that fewer whites are competing for these positions, and hence more are available to blacks.

The 1975 fiscal crisis has thus contributed to the revival of a process formerly conducted through the machine/reform dialectic. In the wake of reform movements, the machine helped recruit members of new ethnic groups onto the municipal payroll, thereby establishing a relationship between the ethnic community in question and the local political system, while taking care not to bankrupt the municipal treasury. The unionization of public employees had interfered with this process of ethnic succession by raising the compensation of civil service jobs enough to make city employment attractive to the members of established ethnic groups, thereby freezing out large numbers of nonwhites. The post-fiscal crisis tightening of the constraints under which civil service unions operate has enabled this process of ethnic and racial succession to resume. Municipal employee unions represent the interests of their increasingly nonwhite membership and provide a link between the municipal government and upwardly mobile elements of the city's nonwhite communities, but they must do so now with greater regard to

188

the city economy's ability to finance the benefits they seek for their members.

Reconciling Fiscal and Political Viability

New York's politics have been remarkably placid since the early years of the fiscal crisis. The city has moved steadily—albeit more slowly than expected—toward the goal of regaining full access to the credit market. Despite the burdens this has placed on most segments of the city's population, the retrenchment process has encountered surprisingly little resistance. Certainly, there have been tensions within and among the city's power centers. Also, the policies generated by these power centers have been opposed by New Yorkers not belonging to the constituencies of any of them. But since 1976 these conflicts have rarely escalated into major blow-ups. Indeed, it is the interactions within and among these centers of power, and the skirmishes between these institutions and the groups excluded from them, that have provided the city's regime with the capacity to secure acquiescense to its policies from most of the major interests having a stake in New York's finances and to isolate politically those who oppose these policies.

The major contribution of the bank/union nexus to the maintenance of political order in New York in the wake of the 1975 fiscal crisis was to reduce the probability that conflicts between its own members would erupt. Another aspect of the entente between the city's banks and public employee unions has also lowered the political temperature in New York. This entente has led each side to move away from previous alliances with other political forces that have opposed many of the city's new fiscal policies. This, in turn, has reduced the scope, intensity, and effectiveness of the opposition with which those who govern New York have had to contend.

Since the formation of the Municipal Union-Financial Leaders Group, commercial bankers have been absent from the ranks of those spokesmen for the business community who have proposed that the city abolish agencies and fire employees performing nonessential municipal services, base wage increases for municipal employees on increases in productivity, and devote surplus revenues to reducing business taxes, retiring debt, or renovating the capital infrastructure. In brief, it is noteworthy that the

189

banks have not attempted to use their leverage as creditors to pressure the city into pursuing the "developmental" policies spelled out in the TCCF's final report. The *Wall Street Journal* has been acutely conscious of the failure of the city's banks to take full advantage of the opportunity the fiscal crisis presented to make New York a more attractive place in which to do business and has criticized them for placing their interest above the common interest—or, one might even say, the interest of their class.[62]

In a similar fashion, public employee union leaders have not attacked the post-fiscal crisis regime on as wide a front as might have been expected. The policies New York has pursued since 1975 have been criticized from the Left as well as from the Right, and because some municipal employee unions are among the most liberal labor organizations in the city (for example, District Council 37 of the State, County, and Municipal Employees), they might have been expected to join in these attacks. A number of prominent reform Democrats, liberal journalists, and minority group politicians have denounced the municipal government's construction of development projects and granting of tax abatements to encourage private investment in Manhattan's downtown and midtown office districts. Public revenues expended or foregone for these purposes, these critics argue, could better be used to improve services and facilities in the city's "neighborhoods."

Had New York's banks joined forces with those who advocated right-wing alternatives to the policies the municipal government has pursued since 1975, had public employee unions joined with left-wing critics of the city's policies, and had the banks and unions used their leverage to fight for the adoption of these very different fiscal priorities, major political conflicts almost certainly would have erupted. But the banks and unions joined forces with one another, rather than with their traditional allies, contributing to the political isolation and impotence of those who oppose existing policies and thereby to the maintenance of political order in a situation that seemed ripe for political turmoil.

The interaction among New York's fiscal monitoring agencies—in particular, the FCB—and other centers of power in the metropolis also has contributed to the stability of the city's regime. The FCB has acted as a mediator between the capital markets and major political forces in the city—not simply as a surrogate for the market. By so doing, the FCB has provided those responsible for the city's affairs with the capacity to meet fiscal and political imperatives that had appeared to be irreconcilable in 1975.

190

The FCB has accomplished this feat by enabling the demands of the market to be factored into the local political process. The Board's insisting that City Hall reduce municipal spending (as it did in 1982), or that it prepare detailed contingency plans for cutting its budget in the event that its revenue and expenditure estimates prove to be too optimistic (as it does every year), has made local officials alter their course, or prepare to do so, well before investors indicate their dissatisfaction with the municipal government's policies by refusing to purchase New York City securities. As the events of the early 1970s indicated, in the absence of the Board, local officials could simply ignore less forceful warnings—critical reports by the Citizens Budget Commission or rising interest rates on the city's securities—that trouble lay ahead.

At the same time, the monitoring agencies enable the market to make concessions to local political forces. As long as the FCB retains the general confidence of participants in the credit markets, it can relax the standards it compels the municipal government to meet, for the sake of avoiding major conflicts in the city that might scare off potential investors in New York securities. The clearest example of this occurred when the Board authorized its initial program of cost-of-living adjustments (COLA I's) for city workers. One of the early sacrifices that had been imposed on municipal employees was the requirement that they contribute more to their retirement programs, thereby suffering a reduction in their take-home pay. The FCB recognized how difficult it would be for city workers to absorb outright pay cuts in a period of inflation, and to prevent their resentment from erupting into labor turmoil the Board lifted the wage freeze authorized by the Financial Emergency Act and granted them COLA I's, which were not contingent upon increased productivity. More generally, the FCB's permitting the municipal government to pursue the set of budgetary policies described in chapter 6 can be understood as a concession by the Board to local forces capable of provoking conflicts that could delay the city's regaining full access to the public capital markets.[63]

The importance of this mediating function is indicated by the turmoil that occurred in 1975 prior to the creation of the fiscal monitoring agencies. The goal of the governor and his fiscal advisors in those months had also been to help the city regain access to the market, but no one knew precisely what it would demand as the price of admission. This uncertainty raised the hopes of some that what had been the entire thrust of municipal policy over the preceding fifteen years could be reversed, and raised the fears of others that everything gained in these

191

years might be lost. This open-endedness fostered the demonstrations and wildcat strikes of the period. The creation of the FCB and the city's other fiscal monitoring agencies, however, made it possible to conduct negotiations concerning—and thereby delimit—the sacrifices that the interests with an immediate stake in the city's finances would be called upon to make, greatly facilitating the restoration of political order in New York.

Interactions between the third of the power centers—the Koch administration—and other political forces have also contributed to the ability of the post-fiscal crisis regime to meet the imperatives confronting it in recent years. Mayor Koch's behavior in office—not least, his "feisty" rhetoric—has provided the regime with popular support despite the erosion of a number of municipal services since 1975. At the same time, Koch's words and deeds have sent signals to businessmen contemplating investments in New York City—namely, that the political climate has changed decisively and that they need not worry about having to face the escalating taxes and other burdens imposed upon businesses by previous administrations.[64] These changed perceptions have contributed to the recovery that the city's economy has experienced since 1978 (although the magnitude of that contribution is impossible to estimate) and have eased the task of balancing the municipal budget.

There is one other way in which Mayor Koch's popularity has helped the city balance its budget. Inasmuch as elected officials in Albany and Washington welcome his support and fear his opposition, they are more inclined than they might otherwise be to grant additional financial aid to New York City.[65]

Finally, the opposition of blacks and Puerto Ricans to the regime that has governed New York City in recent years has been neutralized, and the acquiescence of nonwhites to the policies pursued by this regime has been secured, through a combination of two factors: (1) the political isolation of nonwhites in many policy conflicts and in mayoral elections, and (2) the linkage of racial minorities to the local political system through institutions that simultaneously represent them and impose limitations upon how far they can advance their distinctive interests.

As for the first factor, I argued earlier in this chapter that the dissolution of the coalition among racial minorities and upper-middle-class and upper-class New Yorkers that emerged in the 1960s has facilitated the election and reelection of a mayor whom many blacks have regarded as hostile. It has also made it easier for public officials to limit the growth rate of expenditures disproportionately targeted for this segment of the city's population. And as for the second factor, members of the city's

192

black and Puerto Rican communities are not totally without ties to the local political system, but the elected officials and the municipal labor leaders who link them to that system have reason to contain, as well as to represent, the demands of their constituents. This combination of the stick and the carrot has contributed to the political and fiscal viability of the post-fiscal crisis regime.

8

Fiscal Politics in
New York City:
Past, Present, and
Future

BOTH the content of municipal fiscal policy and the conduct of local politics in New York City have been transformed in a number of fundamental ways since 1975. Nonetheless, some significant continuities exist in both the fiscal and political domains. In the realm of fiscal policy, the municipal government no longer finances any of its operating expenditures with borrowed funds, the size of the city's budget has been cut relative to the local economy, and public officials have allowed inflation to reduce the real income of welfare recipients. However, the range of public services provided to the city's residents, the allocation of employees among different municipal agencies, and the way city services are produced and distributed have not changed greatly since the fiscal crisis erupted.[1]

194

In the political realm, new alliances among important political actors have formed and new power centers have emerged, but changes have not been as far-reaching as many participants in, and observers of, New York politics had expected at the outset of the fiscal crisis. Despite the creation by the state of agencies that possess plenary authority over the municipal government's finances and count prominent businessmen among their members, the city retains a considerable measure of autonomy in setting its fiscal policies. Consequently, its fiscal priorities do not conform exactly to the preferences of many leading members of New York's business community.[2] In addition, although Mayor Koch has had a number of verbal confrontations with city labor and racial minority leaders, the relationship between the municipal government and its employees has not changed as much as it appeared it would in the early months of the crisis, and except on the rhetorical level, the intensity of New York's political conflicts in recent years has been surprisingly low.

The existence of continuities, as well as changes, in New York's fiscal policies and politics since 1975 reflects the alliances formed between some political forces whose influence had increased during the reform episode of the 1960s and more established political participants. Similar alliances were characteristic of the regimes that followed other episodes of reform. In addition, there are some interesting similarities between the structure of politics in New York City today and the structure of the regimes that governed the city after previous reform episodes, particularly the pluralist regime of 1945–60. These patterns of stability and change suggest possible directions in which New York City's politics might move in the future.

Contemporary New York City Politics: Old Wine in New Bottles?

The regime that currently governs New York has endured for the better part of a decade because, like previous post-reform regimes, its political institutions and processes enable it to meet the four major imperatives of urban politics—mobilizing an electoral majority, promoting economic growth, maintaining the city's credit, and moderating political conflicts. The following will compare how these imperatives are met in New York City today with how they were met by the regime that governed the city in the wake of Fiorello LaGuardia's reform administration.

195

Mobilizing an Electoral Majority

Popular backing for New York's current regime has been mobilized chiefly by Ed Koch, who relies heavily on rhetoric and personality to generate support. Beyond this, Mayor Koch and leading party politicians have managed to isolate and neutralize those political forces that had gained influence in the 1960s but now refuse to accept the fiscal parameters within which the city's regime operates. Some of the uncertainties normally associated with competitive elections have also been reduced by the alliances Koch has formed with leaders of New York's Democratic and Republican county organizations.

The reconciliation between Koch and the Democratic county machines made it difficult for any candidate opposed to the mayor's fiscal priorities to threaten his prospects for renomination in the 1981 Democratic primary. And the alliance that Koch formed with the city's Republican party in 1981 assured that any coalition of the mayor's opponents that used a third party (such as the Liberal party) as its political vehicle could not profit from a divided field in the general election.

These alliances were arranged by Koch himself, his great personal popularity providing Democratic and Republican machine politicians with the incentive to go along with him. But in recent years such alliances have involved public figures other than Edward I. Koch. Comptroller Harrison Golden, who entered politics through the Democratic reform movement in the Bronx, was supported by a majority of the city's Democratic machine politicians in his quest for renomination in 1981. And in the early 1980s a majority of the city's Republican state senators received both the GOP and Democratic nominations in one or more of their campaigns for reelection.

These recent efforts to isolate political forces that are unwilling to accept the post-reform political settlement, and to reduce the uncertainties attendant upon competitive elections, resemble those occurring in the aftermath of previous reform eras. In the late 1940s, for example, the Democratic and Republican parties jointly nominated a number of candidates in a successful effort to destroy the leftist-dominated American Labor party, which had provided Mayor LaGuardia with a majority of his votes toward second and third terms but had become an anathema to elements of New York's postwar governing coalition. Also, the number of candidates jointly nominated by the Democrats and the Liberals increased steadily during the 1940s and 1950s, a trend that culminated in both parties endorsing Mayor Wagner when he ran for a second term in 1957. This all but eliminated the possibility that the Democratic ticket could be defeated, and, interestingly, the landslide victory of Wagner in the 1957 general election was not equalled by a mayoral candidate in New York City until Ed Koch ran for a second term in 1981.

Promoting Economic Growth

The imperative of promoting economic growth has been a priority of New York's regime since 1975. This has manifested itself in two ways, each of which had an analogue in New York's postwar regime. First, the Koch administration and various independent authorities—the Metropolitan Transit Authority, the Urban Development Corporation, and the Port of New York Authority—embarked upon massive capital programs involving expenditures of well over $40 billion during the decade 1984–1994, for the purpose of renovating the city's basic physical infrastructure and promoting the development of the local economy. This focus for capital spending stands in sharp contrast to the practice during the late 1960s and early 1970s of using the city's capital budget to finance current expenditures, and, correlatively, the city's failure to maintain, repair, and replace decaying streets, water mains, subway tracks, and sanitation trucks.[3] Conversely, the massive scale and the central focus of the city's current capital program—promoting economic development—resemble the construction program the city pursued during the postwar period under the direction of Robert Moses.

A second way City Hall has sought to promote economic growth has been by reducing the burden of taxation on business firms in the city. Following the eruption of the fiscal crisis, the municipal government reduced or repealed a number of business taxes and froze the general property tax. An Industrial and Commercial Incentives Board was also created, which granted tax abatements on a case-by-case basis to encourage firms to make new investments in the city. In 1983 this program was replaced with one that granted automatic tax abatements to encourage development in the business districts of the outer boroughs. This new sensitivity of the municipal government to the impact of taxation on business firms' decisions to remain or to locate in New York City again contrasts with the 1960s and early 1970s, but resembles the reluctance of the Board of Estimate to increase tax rates during the postwar era.

Maintaining the City's Credit

The regime that now governs New York has made considerable progress toward reestablishing the city's credit. Under its aegis, the municipal government regained partial access to the long-term bond market in 1981, and obtained investment grade ratings for its notes and

197

bonds in 1983. The bond rating agencies and federal bank regulators are now prepared to give their approval to New York City securities because the city balances its budget and conducts its fiscal affairs in a way that assures investors it will be able to repay the money it borrows.

The most explicit guarantee investors have that New York City will be in a position to redeem its securities is the state law requiring that each year the mayor submit the city's budget and financial plan to the Financial Control Board for its approval, and that the FCB certify that the municipal budget is balanced. The budgets of the city's quasi-independent agencies— such as the Board of Education and the Health and Hospitals Corporation—are also included in the financial documents the mayor submits to the FCB to ensure that the expenditures of these "covered organizations" are as closely scrutinized and tightly controlled as the outlays of other municipal agencies.

Formal requirements in state law that the city's budget be balanced, however, are not in themselves sufficient to assure the municipal government's creditors. The formal fiscal controls under which New York now operates were enacted in 1975, yet it was not until eight years later that the two major municipal bond rating agencies and the three federal agencies that regulate banks all gave an investment grade rating to the city's bonds. This was because the city's heavy reliance on borrowed funds to finance operating expenditures in the 1960s and early 1970s indicated that laws requiring a balanced budget could often be evaded. These agencies wanted to be shown that this pattern of deficit financing would not be repeated. Also, if all that kept New York's budget in balance was the FCB's imposing expenditure cuts against the vehement opposition of city officials and other locally influential political forces, the ensuing controversy and turmoil would in all likelihood scare investors away from New York City securities.

For these reasons, regaining access to the public capital markets must also be attributed to those features of New York City's political system that have led local officials to impose restraints on the growth of municipal spending. This, in turn, is related to two conditions discussed in this book—the composition of prevailing political coalitions in the city, and the structure of the city's political organizations and institutions. Specifically, New York City officials have restrained the growth of municipal expenditures as a consequence of: (1) those aspects of the local political system that give important political forces a stake in a balanced budget and that enhance their influence relative to expenditure-demanding interests, and (2) those organizational structures, governmental procedures,

198

and political processes that provide the governing regime with the political and technical capacity to balance the budget.

Today most influential participants in New York City politics have a livelier sense of their stake in fiscal viability than they had prior to 1975, but the greatest change has occurred in the fiscal priorities of the mayor. The constant stream of financial plans and documents that must be submitted to the FCB cannot but remind the mayor of his stake in balancing the city's budget, because these requirements are a standing warning that he will be stripped of his power—as Abe Beame had been in 1975—if he fails to do so. In a striking role reversal, the mayor has become the public official through whom the proponents of fiscal discipline—rather than, as had been the case, the proponents of greater municipal expenditures—find representation. And the collapse of the coalition of expenditure-demanding interests John Lindsay had assembled in the late 1960s, plus Ed Koch's discovery of a political formula for winning widespread electoral support within the constraints imposed by the capital markets, have enabled the mayor to prevail in many confrontations with political forces seeking increased spending on municipal programs. Furthermore, the financing arrangements established to prevent bankruptcy in 1975 gave both the city's public employee unions and the state government an immediate and visible stake in the municipal government's credit-worthiness.

Mayor Koch's ability to dominate politics and prevail in conflicts with expenditure-demanding constituencies is in part a consequence (and in part a cause) of the decay of institutions and organizations that might serve as political bases for potential opponents of the mayor—the Liberal party, the reform faction of the Democratic party, and, in some circumstances, New York's Democratic county machines. In 1969 and 1973, John Lindsay and Abe Beame had been able to win mayoral elections by putting together coalitions in which some or all of these organizations played a significant role, whereas by 1981 these groups were sufficiently weakened that either their leaders calculated that their interests would best be served by joining Koch's camp, or the support they offered the mayor's opponents was not enough to threaten his reelection.

In addition, the mayor's annual financial plan to the FCB provides him with leverage for imposing restraints on the expenditures of quasi-independent agencies as well as of departments more directly subject to his control. The influence of proponents of fiscal discipline relative to expenditure-demanders is further enhanced by the FCB's informal rule of unanimity, which restrains the elected officials on the Board from

199

attempting to strengthen their political position by breaking ranks with colleagues on the FCB and publicly advocating higher levels of spending on one or another popular program.

Finally, a number of changes in governmental organization and procedures have helped to increase the capacity of the city's regime to control municipal spending, by altering the way in which expertise is organized into the local policymaking process. At the insistence of New York's fiscal monitors, the municipal government has revamped its accounting and management information systems and now systematically collects and reports data on its current financial condition and on the services performed by municipal agencies. Numerous reports, audits, and studies of the city's finances and services are conducted by the staffs of the FCB, MAC, the Office of the Special Deputy Comptroller, the CBC, and the SMP project. All of these sources of information increase the knowledge municipal officials and the city's fiscal monitors have regarding the likely impact of their possible actions on the city's finances and on municipal services. These studies, reports, and audits also suggest alternative ways of conducting the business of government that would be more efficient than those the city currently employs.[4]

These reports are not, of course, self-implementing. They do, however, provide useful information—and ammunition—to those in New York politics who are both dedicated to balancing the budget and in a position to influence city policies: members of the FCB; the mayor, his deputy mayors, and his budget director; the city's civic and business elites; and its news media. The policy analysts affiliated with the municipal government, the city's fiscal monitoring agencies, and various nonprofit institutions provide these powerholders with information they can use in deciding when and where to wield their power.

The political institutions and processes that guarantee a balanced budget and maintain access to public credit markets in New York City today are analogous to those in operation during the postwar period. After the reform episode of the 1930s and early 1940s, the city's Democrats developed a formula that enabled them simultaneously to balance the budget and dominate elections, but the power centers which guaranteed that the city government would meet these imperatives were then the county party organizations, the Board of Estimate, and politicians closely tied to those institutions.

During the 1940s and 1950s the Democratic slate for the city's top elective offices was selected in negotiations among leaders of the party's county organizations, with first Ed Flynn and then Carmine DeSapio playing the role of first among equals that Charles Murphy had occupied after the reform era of 1913–17 and that Ed Koch occupies today. In selecting their party's candidates, Flynn and DeSapio saw the wisdom of balancing the Democratic ticket not only ethnically, but ideologically. They backed mayoral candidates—notably, William O'Dwyer and Robert Wagner—who could bring independent strength to the ticket because they enjoyed wide public recognition, were identified with the New Deal, and had close ties to the city's labor movement. Flynn and DeSapio's candidates for city comptroller, on the other hand, had ties to real estate and banking interests in the city.[5]

The Democratic candidates for the five borough presidencies were also creatures of the party organization in their borough and, as such, were responsive to the concerns of the homeowners and small businessmen who, at least in the outer boroughs, were key elements of these organizations' constituencies. The character of their political bases made the comptroller and the borough presidents natural allies against the mayor on issues of fiscal policy. Because they held a majority of votes on the city's highest governing body, the Board of Estimate, the Board ensured that the city's operating expenditures did not exceed its recurring revenues.

Because mayors came and went, whereas the "economy bloc" of the comptroller and borough presidents dominated the Board of Estimate no matter who occupied New York's highest office, the city's budget directors found that they could maximize their tenure in office by serving as agents of the Board rather than of the mayor. The Citizens Budget Commission was another element of the nexus of power centered around the Board of Estimate. The CBC enjoyed privileged access to the Board and the Budget Bureau because some of its top leaders were prominent figures in the city's Democratic and Republican parties, and because it helped rally support through the press for the Board's and the Bureau's efforts to impose restraints on the growth of municipal spending.

A number of formal governmental procedures and informal political practices also helped this nexus dominate fiscal policymaking in postwar New York. During this period New York City operated under an extraordinarily detailed line-item budget which, as political scientists Wallace Sayre and Herbert Kaufman observed, the budget director "in fact prepared, and of which only he and his staff are masters." Because of the incredible detail of the budget, if conditions changed in the slightest during the fiscal year—as they invariably did—the heads of municipal agencies were repeatedly required to secure permission from the budget director and the Board of Estimate to transfer funds from one budget line to another.[6]

201

If these formal procedures placed the Board of Estimate at the center of the city's budgetary process, the Board's informal practices ensured that the economy bloc would usually prevail over the mayor when the Board exercised its powers. The Board made all of its major decisions in executive session; then, in its open meetings its members would unanimously ratify whatever decisions they previously had made. The Board of Estimate's informal rule of unanimity, like the FCB's, prevented any member from seeking political advantage by publicly advocating popular expenditures that would make it difficult for other members to heed the imperative of balancing the city's budget. This practice served especially as a constraint upon the mayor, for it deprived him of the opportunity to make use of one of his major assets—access to the press—in an effort to counter the advantages that the advocates of fiscal restraint experienced when the Board met in executive session.[7]

Although there are major differences between the institutions governing New York City today and during the previous post-reform era, the leaders of both regimes found ways to prevent municipal expenditures from rising more rapidly than the city's revenues. Today's centralization of authority over municipal fiscal policy in the FCB and mayoralty, in conjunction with the predominant role that Mayor Koch plays in New York City's electoral politics, is similar to the postwar period's centralization of budgetary authority in the Board of Estimate, in conjunction with the predominant role that regular Democratic party organizations under the leadership of Ed Flynn and Carmine DeSapio played in municipal elections. Both eras placed at the center of the fiscal policymaking process political leaders—the mayor today, the comptroller and borough presidents in the 1940s and 1950s—with a stake in balancing the budget. In both present-day and postwar New York, individuals possessing technical expertise and committed to budgetary restraint have played a significant role in the city's fiscal policymaking process. In this respect the staffs of the FCB, the Office of Management and Budget, the CBC, and the SMP project are today's functional equivalent of the postwar regime's Bureau of the Budget and Citizens Budget Commission. Finally, the rule of unanimity that the FCB observes today, like that of the Board of Estimate in the postwar period, makes it politically feasible for public officials to live within the constraints imposed upon the city by the capital markets.

Containing Political Conflict

The regime that governs New York City today has established a relationship with groups whose influence had increased greatly during the reform episode of the 1960s—city employees and racial minorities—

202

that contains conflict without throwing the city's budget out of balance. In accomplishing this, New York's present regime resembles the post-reform regime of the 1940s and 1950s more than it does the one over which Mayors Lindsay and Beame presided in the early 1970s.

The regime that governed New York between 1969 and 1975 managed to dampen political conflicts, but did so in a way that was not fiscally viable. It increased benefits to municipal employees and racial minorities without making commensurate reductions in public expenditures bene-fiting other segments of the city's population or increasing municipal taxes enough to finance its expenditures. In contrast, the institutions, alliance patterns, and interactions that characterize New York City politics today have managed to limit conflicts involving these groups without adverse financial consequences. In particular, the practice of coalition bargaining makes it easier for municipal labor leaders to negotiate contracts that the city's fiscal monitors regard as acceptable, and the formation of the Municipal Union and Financial Leaders group (MUFL) reduced the danger that either union leaders or bankers might do something to upset the arrangements that kept New York afloat after 1975. As for the city's racial minorities, their displeasure with Mayor Koch's words and deeds has indeed sparked rancorous political conflicts on the rhetorical plane. But to a considerable degree the reshuffling of political alignments that occurred in 1975 has severed the ties between racial minorities and their former allies. Hence, other political forces have not been drawn into the controversies with Koch, and racial disputes have not generated the intense conflicts that characterized New York City politics in the 1960s.

The city's revised budgetary process also contributes to the dampening of conflicts that might have divided the coalition that has governed the city since 1975. The FCB helps limit conflicts, as discussed in chapter 7, by serving as a mediator between the capital markets and the local political system. The FCB has insisted that the city legitimately balance its budget, but it has not insisted that local officials cut deeply into benefits to political forces, such as municipal employee unions, whose resistance might spark conflicts that could scare away potential investors in city securities. Thus, contrary to the initial expectations of many participants in, and observers of, New York politics, the FCB has not pressed the municipal government to completely alter its expenditure priorities or the way it produces and distributes public services. A consequence is that consumers of municipal services have borne some of the heaviest burdens of the city's retrenchment program.

The role that the Board of Estimate and city council have come to play in New York's annual budgetary process, however, helps reduce some of the resentment this could generate among service consumers. Each year, members of the Board and the council announce with much fanfare that they will approve the budget submitted by the mayor only if additional funds are appropriated for services that are salient to middle-class voters—police and fire protection, education, parks, and libraries. However, the sums added to the municipal budget for these services are quite small—amounting to only one-half of 1 percent of the city's operating expenditures in the 1985 fiscal year, for example.[8] The Board of Estimate and city council make these gestures in an effort to win votes, not in an attempt to stabilize the city's current regime. But if their political judgement is correct, their actions contribute to a sense among the most politically active elements of the city's population that their interests are being represented in City Hall, despite the decline in many municipal services since 1975. To the extent that this pattern occurs it reduces the likelihood that latent tensions among the political forces that support New York's current regime will erupt into open conflicts.

The processes through which conflicts are contained in New York City today resemble the way political institutions and practices in postwar New York helped dampen conflicts between various liberal political forces, whose influence had increased during the LaGuardia era, and more established interests in the city. The mayoral candidates backed by Ed Flynn and Carmine DeSapio in the 1940s and 1950s had solid liberal credentials and proposed many policy innovations and expenditure increases. But in addition to being programmatic liberals, they were also products of New York City's regular Democratic party organizations, and as such they acquiesced to the processes through which the Board of Estimate and Budget Bureau imposed restraints on the growth of municipal spending and protected vested bureaucratic interests. Therefore, although the mayor and his allies in the city's liberal community often were able to secure the enactment of new public policies and increases in expenditures for one or another municipal service—and they had a political interest in publicly trumpeting their successes on this score—the policy innovations the municipal government adopted were limited in scope and its annual expenditure increases were incremental. Expenditure-demanding interests consequently had a sense that they were being represented in City Hall without budget deficits being produced—an outcome similar to that generated by New York City's current budgetary process.

In sum, although the governmental institutions through which New York City is ruled in the 1980s are in many ways historically unique, the

204

political processes and the accommodations between newly powerful and more established political forces that dampen conflicts in the metropolis are parallel to the processes and accommodations that had these effects in previous post-reform eras.

Looking Forward

The regime that currently governs New York has endured longer than the one over which Mayors Lindsay and Beame presided between 1969 and 1975, but its continued survival is by no means assured. There are a number of developments that could lead to its transformation: changes in the health of New York's economy, the political strategy of its mayor, the conduct of municipal labor relations, or the behavior of the city's racial minorities.

The corporate sector of New York's economy, which contracted sharply between 1969 and 1977, has flourished since the late 1970s, as the American economy has become more internationalized and New York has strengthened its position as a world financial capital.[9] The tax revenues generated by this economic growth—along with major increases in state aid—have enabled the municipal government to balance its budget since 1981 and regain partial access to the public capital markets, without cutting the real wages of municipal employees more than they would accept or slashing municipal services more than the electorate would tolerate. Most knowledgeable observers predict that New York's corporate headquarters complex will continue to grow in future years. This would allow the city to raise the real wages of its employees, add workers to its payroll, and increase municipal services, as it has done on a modest scale since 1981. But the possibility exists that New York's economy will not be as robust in the future. Changes in state and federal banking regulations and in communications and information technology have enabled major New York banks to move routine operations to other states, and it is possible that this trend will extend to the "back office" operations of other firms in the corporate headquarters complex. In a period of greater scarcity of resources it might be more difficult for municipal officials to satisfy simultaneously the city's voters, its employees, and its creditors.

Prosperity as well as scarcity has its political perils. As public officials face the task of allocating budget surpluses rather than the burdens of

205

retrenchment, the leaders of municipal unions whose members' real incomes remain significantly lower than they had been in 1975—most notably, unions representing police officers and fire fighters—would like to see the former standard of living of their rank and file restored, as would citizens who now receive fewer public services than they had a decade ago. Public officials seeking to win votes and preserve civil harmony face the temptation of responding affirmatively to these demands in the expectation that the revenues generated by economic growth will finance these expenditure increases.

Thus, in the spring of 1984, with the city's budget running a surplus, the politicians who jockeyed to oppose Ed Koch in the 1985 mayoral election—such as City Council President Carol Bellamy—focused their attacks upon the decline of municipal services under his stewardship. The mayor responded by proposing a budget for the 1985 fiscal year that would add 9,500 workers to the city's payroll, and in the message accompanying the budget he proposed further increases in the size of the city's workforce in the years ahead. As one of the mayor's aides said of the political advice Koch has been receiving, "He's been told many times recently that the fiscal crisis is ten years old and that people are tired of hearing about how he balanced the budget. . . . It's fair to say he now realizes it's time to move on."[10]

In the early years of his mayoral career, while presiding over a reduction in municipal services, Ed Koch managed to create a large and loyal personal following for himself by attacking the political forces—most importantly, city employees—he claimed were responsible for New York's fiscal plight. If, with the passage of time, even Koch has come to regard it as politically necessary to increase the size of the municipal workforce, it is likely that other public officials and candidates for public office will regard this course of action as even more imperative. Other politicians, as much as Ed Koch, will also face the problem of reconciling this imperative with the demand of city employees for higher wages. A statement made by the president of the Patrolmen's Benevolent Association (PBA), when Mayor Koch proposed in his 1985 budget to hire one thousand additional police officers, indicates the tensions with which New York's public officials will have to contend even if the local economy continues to grow. The PBA president warned, "We can't allow the mayor to think he can restore full strength in terms of police services over the economic deprivation of our members." If local officials and the city's fiscal monitors differ in their estimates of whether New York's economy will be able to finance both increases in the municipal workforce and in the wages of city employees on a recurring basis, conflicts could ensue that might make investors wary of New York's securities.[11]

A related threat to the stability of the present regime involves the mayor, who plays a crucial role in reconciling the municipal government's fiscal and political viability. Koch's political following is a personal one, however, and there is a high degree of fluidity in the politics of personalism. The example of James Michael Curley again is apt. Curley, who also had a personal following, was a central figure in Boston's politics for well over thirty years; however, his record in mayoral elections was marred by defeats: he won the mayoral election of 1914, lost in 1917, won the elections of 1922 and 1930, lost the elections of 1937 and 1940, won the election of 1945, and lost again in 1949 and in 1951. So it cannot be assumed that Ed Koch can hold on to the mayoralty for however long he chooses. Even if he can, for the very reason that Koch's following is a personal one, it is unlikely that he would be able to transmit it to a successor. Thus, New York's future mayors might find it more difficult than Ed Koch has to meet the various imperatives confronting them.

Another potential source of instability in New York politics is the city's public employee unions. As the threat of municipal bankruptcy has receded, so has the salience of the concerns that led the unions to join forces and negotiate contracts providing wage and benefit increases lower than the rate of inflation. In 1982 the unions representing the city's uniformed employees expelled the Uniformed Sanitationmen's Association (USA) from their coalition, because the USA's agreement to reduce the number of workers manning sanitation trucks in exchange for a $55-a-week bonus narrowed the wage differential between sanitationmen and public safety personnel, causing the other members of the coalition to seek the restoration of this differential. Prior to the 1984 negotiations the fire fighters' union (UFA) withdrew from the uniformed coalition, and during those negotiations the nonuniformed coalition also fragmented. Such fragmentation makes it difficult for union leaders to acquiesce to wage restraint. For example, when the UFA's president did reach an agreement with the city, the other uniformed unions immediately denounced the contract as unacceptable, leading to its rejection by the UFA's executive board. Thus, the municipal labor talks that were supposed to conclude in June 1984 dragged into April 1985 before the first union settled, suggesting that union leaders and the mayor were having trouble finding contract terms salable to their respective constituencies. With the city's budget running a surplus, the pattern that had prevailed in the early years of the fiscal crisis—modest wage increases that were financed by reducing municipal services—was no longer as acceptable to New York's employees and voters.[12]

Racial tensions within unions are another potential source of instability in municipal labor relations. Unions whose membership is becoming increasingly black but whose leaders are white are finding it increasingly difficult to mediate between municipal officials and rank-and-file city employees, because any concessions they make to management can be cited by their political opponents as evidence of their willingness to sell out the union. This situation helps explain why union leaders facing this problem have put up some of the staunchest resistance to efforts by municipal managers to alter the work routines or prerogatives of their members. In 1984, the newly hired chairman of the Metropolitan Transportation Authority (MTA) and president of the city's Transit Authority (TA) announced that it would be pointless to proceed with the MTA's $6.4 billion capital construction program unless they were granted greater leeway to reward and punish middle-level managers and tighten supervision over transit workers. The leaders of the unions representing transit personnel vowed to fight them every step of the way. John Lawe of the Transport Workers Union—a white leader of a union with a substantial black membership—denounced disciplinary actions taken by the TA's new management against workers who were away from their jobs at one subway car repair shop as "Gestapo tactics." And, fearing that he would be unable to get his members to ratify any contract containing the work rule changes the MTA was demanding, Lawe sought to avoid bargaining over these issues by having the TWU's 1985 contract settled through binding arbitration.[13]

The disaffection of black and, to a lesser extent, Hispanic voters also poses a potentially serious threat to the stability of the city's current regime. Thus far this threat has been contained by low levels of electoral mobilization and the isolation that has characterized the political situation of nonwhites in city politics since 1975. These conditions, however, have been undergoing change.

The election of Harold Washington as mayor of Chicago and Wilson Goode as mayor of Philadelphia in 1983, along with Jesse Jackson's campaign in the 1984 Democratic presidential primaries, galvanized New York's black political leadership and thousands of potential black voters. Registration drives in 1984 added tens of thousands of blacks to the electoral rolls, and the excitement generated by Jesse Jackson's candidacy led to sharp increases in voter turnout in predominantly black assembly districts. Consequently, the proportion of blacks in the city's Democratic

208

primary electorate shot up from 23 percent in 1980 to 31 percent in 1984.[14]

Even if this degree of electoral mobilization is achieved in future municipal elections, a viable black candidate for citywide office—or a white candidate backed by blacks—would have to win considerable support among voters from other racial groups. Hispanic New Yorkers would appear to be the most obvious allies of blacks. However, age distributions, citizenship rates, and electoral turnout rates of Hispanics are such that they composed only 8 percent of the Democratic primary electorate in 1984. Also, the political appeals that are successful in mobilizing blacks—like those employed by Jesse Jackson—do not necessarily succeed with Hispanics. Consequently, a candidate espousing the cause of New York's racial minorities would need to win many white votes.

The necessity of winning the support of whites, plus the fear of providing ammunition to Ed Koch (or to a candidate coveting his political following) would constrain the budgetary policies that any such mayoral candidate could advocate. Nonetheless, a candidate appealing for the support of blacks could scarcely avoid calling for some changes in the municipal government's fiscal priorities and, were he or she elected, this could generate tensions between the electoral imperative and the other imperatives of city officials.

These considerations suggest that there are at least three possible directions in which New York City's politics might move in the years ahead. The most likely can be termed "neopluralism." If the city's economy performs as well in the future as it has in the recent past, a mayor who practices the politics of bargaining and conciliation, rather than the politics of denunciation—a style more similar to Wagner's than Koch's—may be able to satisfy the political and fiscal imperatives city officials must meet.

A neopluralist mayor could appeal for the support of voters by promising to bolster those municipal services that have deteriorated since 1975 and increase expenditures on some redistributive programs. Such a mayor might win an electoral majority by forging a coalition among those social groups least friendly to Ed Koch—blacks, Hispanics, and young, college-educated Jewish and WASP voters.[15] It also is possible that a neopluralist candidate could win a significant measure of support (even if not a majority) among Catholics, Jews in nonprofessional occupations, older voters, and blue collar workers—social groups whose members have expressed the strongest approval of Mayor Koch in

209

opinion surveys. Mario Cuomo, who is more liberal than Koch on social and economic issues, succeeded in doing this, when running against the mayor in the 1982 Democratic gubernatorial primary, by appealing to a sense of shared responsibility within "the family of New York." It is even conceivable that Ed Koch could alter the character of his own electoral appeal.

A neopluralist regime might also be able to dampen conflicts involving the political forces whose influence had increased most substantially during the 1960s—municipal employees and racial minorities. The strategy that has maintained labor peace in recent years might continue to be successful—namely, the municipal government's providing its employees with wage increases that restore some of the purchasing power lost during the fiscal crisis. And if racial minorities help elect an administration they regard as friendlier to their interests, their leaders would acquire a stake in the viability of that administration. Black political leaders would have strong reasons to abjure demands that might drive the administration into bankruptcy or provide issues that could be used to the advantage of either Ed Koch (trying to stage a political comeback) or some other candidate seeking to inherit his base of support.

If New York's economy remains strong and the state government continues to increase financial aid to the city, the municipal government could increase spending on basic services and redistributive programs without raising tax rates to the point that business firms would be driven from the city and without using borrowed funds to finance operating expenditures. Instead, City Hall and independent authorities could use monies raised through the sale of long-term bonds to renovate the city's infrastructure and provide municipal employees with more efficient equipment and facilities. Such expenditures, taxation, and borrowing policies would contribute to the health of the local economy and enable the municipal government to retain its access to the public capital markets.

This is not to say that a neopluralist administration could increase expenditures on every municipal function. If the city were to avoid raising tax rates to the point that it injured the local economy, and if it were to maintain investment-grade ratings for its notes and bonds, choices would have to be made regarding where to spend revenues generated by economic growth, by increases in intergovernmental aid, and from the credit markets.[16] Over the next decade, memories of 1975 will likely remain sufficiently fresh that municipal officials will be prepared to arrange compromises among themselves and the constituencies they represent that do not violate the constraints imposed by the capital markets. If these memories wane, however, and officials are tempted to engage in deficit financing, the fiscal monitoring agencies stand ready to prevent it, just as the Board of Estimate imposed fiscal discipline upon the pluralist regime of 1946–61.

Although this is the path New York City is most likely to follow in the years ahead, it is not the only possibility. A downturn in the local economy could make it difficult for city officials to satisfy all the constituencies that have leverage against them; a mayor lacking the broad political following of Ed Koch could find it harder to heed both fiscal and political imperatives; the mechanisms that imposed limits on municipal labor costs in the aftermath of the fiscal crisis could weaken; and the mobilization of more nonwhites into the electoral arena could increase pressures to restore social programs that were cut during retrenchment.

If these or other developments undermine the viability—or prevent the emergence—of a neopluralist regime, there are two alternative directions in which New York City politics might move in the future. One would be reimposing limitations on municipal home rule. When Mayor Beame's administration proved politically incapable of taking the necessary steps to restore investor confidence in New York City's securities, the state established monitoring agencies with plenary authority over the city's finances. During the remainder of Beame's term these agencies closely supervised the municipal government. Since Ed Koch's election as mayor the fiscal monitoring agencies have not held the city on a short leash, but neither have they been altogether willing to let go of that leash. In 1984, an opportunity to move in this direction arose when MAC accumulated a surplus of $1 billion and Mayor Koch proposed that these funds be used to redeem the city's federally guaranteed bonds—fulfilling one of the conditions for the FCB to enter its passive mode. However, both the chairman of the FCB and the chairman of MAC (Governor Mario Cuomo and Felix Rohatyn) rejected the mayor's proposal. Their refusal to countenance this suggests that New York's fiscal monitors were not entirely confident that the city could be trusted to manage its affairs on its own. Therefore, if any future city administration were to revert to the fiscal practices of the early 1970s, the state would again respond by imposing severe limitations on local self-government.[17]

A second alternative direction would be a further reorganization of the city's politics so that City Hall would willingly observe the fiscal constraints of the FCB. It is difficult to predict how New York's politics might be reorganized if such a conflict between the FCB and local officials were to erupt, just as in 1975 it could not be foreseen that a politician like Ed Koch would discover a formula for winning support among both Jewish and Catholic voters, as well as the city's business and civic elites while implementing a retrenchment program cutting municipal services. But the outlines of one possible coalition of forces that might emerge can be extrapolated from some changes in the organization of interests and the conduct of politics in New York since 1975.

Were conflicts between local officials and New York's fiscal monitors to erupt in the future, the individuals and groups that are most disturbed would, in all likelihood, attribute the problem to political leaders and organizations out to advance their special interests at the expense of the public interest. This was the ideology of the reform movements that followed earlier fiscal crises, so a new period of fiscal strain could lead to the formation of a modern-day equivalent—a "neoreformist" movement.

New York's policy analysts could provide a neoreformist movement with its program. A central theme might be that the public's demand for better services could be met without increasing the city's payroll if the municipal government were to overcome entrenched bureaucratic interests and radically alter the managerial practices of public agencies, the work routines of civil servants, and, in some instances, the entire way in which particular municipal services are produced and delivered. In formulating such a program, policy analysts could play a role similar to that of earlier reform vanguards.

It is true that as the city's fiscal condition has improved, there has not been a harsh tone in the reports and publications of New York's policy analysts. The CBC's research reports, the essays in the annual volumes published by the SMP project, and the FCB's staff reports have praised the progress the city has made in balancing its budget and improving municipal services, acknowledged the burdens placed on municipal employees and the poor by the city's retrenchment program, and indicated that the city might consider using some of the fiscal dividends it expects to collect to increase the monthly allotments and housing allowances granted to welfare recipients. These reports scarcely sound like the denunciations of City Hall and the predictions of impending doom that earlier reform vanguards issued in an effort to rally New York's business elites and taxpayers against machine-backed administrations.

Nonetheless, leading policy analysts have not hesitated to take up some traditional themes and attack some traditional targets of previous reform vanguards when in their judgement such criticisms are warranted. This was most evident in the final report of the TCCF, a central theme

212

of which was that during the years following the 1975 fiscal crisis, City Hall implemented only those retrenchment measures calculated to least disturb vested political and bureaucratic interests. In more recent years, New York's policy analysts have criticized the municipal government on similar grounds. In the introduction to the 1983 volume of the *Setting Municipal Priorities* series, Charles Brecher and Raymond Horton summarized some of these complaints:

A number of studies, including chapters in this and earlier volumes of the Setting Municipal Priorities series, have identified management practices that hinder the efficient production of services. Uniformed employees are used to perform tasks that lower-paid civilians could perform equally well; civil service requirements restrict managerial discretion in the selection and promotion of employees; too few employees are given managerial responsibilities and paid according to their performance, while too many employees are assigned to work during periods of reduced demand or in locations with limited service needs and are paid the same amounts as those who perform in more difficult assignments.[18]

If New York's economic health were to decline in the years ahead and City Hall were to return to the practice of balancing the municipal budget by reducing basic services, or if a mayor were elected whose fiscal priorities resembled those of Mayors Lindsay and Beame, members of the city's community of policy analysts might address a call to action to New York's opinion leaders similar to the one in the TCCF's final report—explaining the perils of the city's current policies and practices and providing an alternative program behind which civic leaders could rally the public. As Brecher and Horton put it:

Until the public becomes sufficiently aroused over the perpetuation of managerial inefficiencies, political leaders will find it easier to go along with organized civil servants than to fight for the interests of uninterested service consumers.[19]

In all likelihood such a program would appeal to New York's business elite and encourage its members to enter the political arena to support a mayor who is prepared to implement it. Such a call to action could also lead the city's bankers to join with other members of the business community and abandon their alliance with municipal union leaders. The bail-out plans requiring banks and unions to purchase New York securities have expired, and the city's fiscal monitors would now prevent the municipal government from engaging in deficit financing so extensive as to require that banks join with the unions again to bail it out. The city's recently centralized and organized business associations—the Chamber of Commerce and Industry and the New York Partnership—

213

might seem available to play a role in a future reform movement parallel to the committees of prominent business and civic leaders that organized the reform campaigns following the fiscal crises of the 1870s and 1930s. In the political conditions of the 1980s, however, it is unlikely that a reform movement organized by such a committee would be able to win an electoral majority. Therefore, a coalition that could win elections, as well as unite and energize the city's business community, almost certainly would have to be assembled by a professional politician like Ed Koch, who is capable of arousing the enthusiastic support of a majority of the city's voters.

If New York City were again to experience serious fiscal strains, such a political entrepreneur could forge together a neoreformist coalition dedicated to bringing about greater changes in New York's managerial practices and expenditure priorities than those implemented after the 1975 fiscal crisis. One major impediment to implementing greater changes in these practices and priorities was the city's financial dependence upon the municipal employee pension funds when it was unable to borrow in the public capital markets. Another impediment has been the adverse impact labor turmoil could have upon the city's ability to regain full access to the credit markets. Now that New York no longer relies upon the pension funds for its financing, the first of these conditions no longer obtains, and there are circumstances in which the second one might be surmounted as well.

One way in which a mayor could attempt to cope with the threat of labor turmoil would be to exacerbate existing cleavages between the city's uniformed employees and nonuniformed personnel. When the unions representing New York's uniformed employees formed a separate coalition in 1980, they asserted that their members should receive larger wage increases than other municipal workers because uniformed forces perform the most vital public services.[20] In large measure, this assertion is correct. A simultaneous strike by the police, fire fighters, correction officers, and sanitation workers (the threat implied when they bargain with the city as a single unit) would be a municipal catastrophe.

Certainly, the coalition of uniformed employees has suffered strains since its formation in 1980. The cohesion of any group, however, is a function not simply of the common attitudes, interests, and identifications that its members bring with them into the political arena, but also of their relationship with other political forces. Mayor Koch played a role in the initial formation of the uniformed employees coalition by announcing in 1979 that if in the months ahead the city had to lay off any personnel, he would lay off only nonuniformed workers, thus signalling to the unions representing uniformed employees that he was prepared to treat their members better than other city workers.[21] In a future period of fiscal stress, a mayor could again find it useful to come to terms with uniformed employees at the expense of nonuniformed personnel. This division in the municipal labor movement could be widened by again making it clear to uniformed employees that they will accomplish more by emphasizing what they have in common with one another and by distinguishing themselves from other city workers than by going their separate ways or expressing solidarity with nonuniformed personnel.

Nonuniformed municipal employees are in a much weaker bargaining position. A simultaneous strike by the city's clerical employees, maintenance personnel, teachers, social workers, nurses, and hospital orderlies (the threat implied when they bargain as a single unit) would certainly cause a great deal of inconvenience. But much of this inconvenience would be suffered by a minority of the city's population—the poor—and as long as it did not turn violent, the municipal government could probably endure the strike for a longer period of time than those on the picket lines could get by without their paychecks. This explains why the coalition of nonuniformed employees was compelled in the 1980 and 1982 contract negotiations to accept a smaller pay increase than the city's uniformed personnel, even though the coalition's leaders had initially insisted that they would not tolerate unequal treatment. True, their pay increases were only 1 percent lower than those granted to uniformed employees, but that the nonuniformed employees were compelled to accept a public humiliation in 1980 and 1982 indicates they are weaker. In the future, this weakness might work to their disadvantage in a more substantial way.[22]

If New York encounters economic or fiscal problems that require slashing the budget in the future, a plausible strategy for the mayor would be to stress the commonalities of interest among public employees whose work is vital to the city, voters who work in the private sector, and business firms that provide the city's residents with these jobs, against the interests of public employees whose jobs are less critical to the city's functioning and the city's poor, who do not work and who consume a major proportion of the municipal government's expenditures.[23] Such a divisive attack could lead the city's nonuniformed employees and nonwhites (from whom the poor are disproportionately drawn) to ally in self-defense. The first of these coalitions, however, would almost certainly prevail over the second in any confrontation, and the resulting polarization could generate the political energy local officials would need to impose severe economies on the city's nonuniformed personnel and

215

the segments of the population dependent upon their services.

It is true that the policy analysts who have evaluated the impact of New York's retrenchment program have uncovered inefficiencies in the city's uniformed services as well as in agencies employing nonuniformed personnel. They have also discerned successful adaptations to budgetary stringency in both uniformed and nonuniformed agencies. Yet the advantages of allying with the city's uniformed personnel and imposing the burden of retrenchment on other municipal employees are not likely to be lost on business and civic elites. The uniformed services could be valuable allies because the victims of retrenchment, if backed into a corner, could stage strikes or violent protests. If the police, out of a sense of solidarity, were to hesitate to intervene against striking teachers, if private sector labor unions were to honor the picket lines set up by striking municipal hospital workers, or if the electorate hesitated to support the use of strong measures to deal with violent protests by the clients of social service agencies, any or all of these tactics could disrupt the public order. But in the wake of a heated election campaign stressing the interests shared by the productive segments of the city's population and how these common interests conflict with those of other groups, disruptive tactics are unlikely to receive much support, and therefore would not likely succeed. This, in turn, reduces the likelihood they will be tried. With the implementation of such a retrenchment program, and the defeat or retreat of its opponents, the concerns of business and its allies would truly become the business of politics in New York.[24]

PART IV

THE POLITICAL
IMPLICATIONS OF
URBAN FISCAL
CRISES

9

Can Cities Be
Democratically
Governed?

NEW YORK is not a typical American city, and the past two decades were not an ordinary period in the history of America's premier metropolis. Nonetheless, this book's analysis of the political sources and consequences of the most recent of New York's recurrent fiscal crises has several implications for an understanding of American urban politics in general, and of the patterns of fiscal politics that characterize major cities in the Northeast and Midwest in particular. This analysis also has implications regarding the prospects for, and limitations on, democratic self-government in American cities.

Political Conflicts and Fiscal Crises: A Restatement

The fiscal crises that have erupted periodically in New York are manifestations of recurrent tensions in the city's politics. These were once expressed as conflicts between machine politicians and reformers, but in more recent years they have been expressed in other ways.

These tensions were discussed in general terms in chapter 1, where I argued that municipal officials must heed a number of imperatives that at times come into conflict with one another. They must pursue policies that will win votes, prevent social and political conflicts from getting out of hand, contribute to the health of their city's economy, and generate sufficient revenues to finance the operations of the municipal government. The precise way municipal officials meet these imperatives is shaped by the composition of the political coalitions they depend on for support and the structure of political organizations and institutions in their city. It is not impossible for municipal officials to heed all of the imperatives confronting them, but any set of policies successful at one point in time may be insufficient later, as changes in the broader economic and political systems of which the city is a part alter the problems and opportunities confronting political forces and public officials in the city.

One consequence of an urban regime's failure to meet its imperatives is a municipal fiscal crisis. Such crises occur when city officials, in an effort to win votes or contain social conflicts, increase municipal expenditures more rapidly than they can increase municipal revenues, and when potential creditors become wary of financing the ensuing deficit because they question the municipal government's economic ability or political capacity to repay the money it borrows. Because municipal governments, unlike the federal government, do not have the constitutional authority to create legal tender, they cannot monetize their deficits—that is, they cannot cover the difference between their revenues and their outlays by printing money—and therefore they can find themselves unable to redeem the notes or bonds sold to finance their deficits. Consequently, municipal bond holders, in contrast to investors in U.S. Treasury securities, cannot protect their investments against persistent budget deficits simply by demanding higher interest rates. Instead, they will refuse to buy the city's securities. Thus, *political processes that on the national level generate currency inflation, on the local level generate municipal fiscal crises.*

Municipal fiscal crises cause bankers and businessmen to conclude that the politicians in power are driving their city to ruin. Those sharing this view, or believing for other reasons that the incumbent administration is fundamentally misgoverning their city, can be united in a campaign to throw the rascals out and, in instances where machine politicians control City Hall, "reform" the municipal government. In this way, fiscal crises historically were associated with reform crusades in American cities.

Machine politicians have often managed to regain power after being defeated by reform coalitions, for two reasons. First, nonpartisan reform movements, whose core support came from upper- and middle-class members of both the Republican and Democratic parties, rarely managed to establish durable organizations—as did the local machines affiliated with national political parties—that would link them to the great mass of the city's voters and enable them to reliably mobilize electoral majorities. To the contrary, the appeals they used to rally core supporters against party politicians often led them to enact policies that were an anathema to the majority of voters. Second, the experience of defeat often convinced the machine's leaders that it would be prudent to make concessions to various groups that had supported reform and made it easier to get their subordinates to go along with these concessions. These concessions could significantly alter the policies, the structure, and the political base of the municipal government—and thereby the conditions under which subsequent fiscal crises erupted.

Many of the conditions that historically had led to the election of reform administrations, including serious municipal fiscal problems, were present in New York in the 1960s and contributed to the election of John Lindsay as mayor on a fusion ticket in 1965. In addition, Mayor Lindsay's conduct in office, like previous fusion mayors, alienated many voters and made him appear headed for defeat when he ran for a second term in 1969. Lindsay managed to win reelection, however, by coming to terms with some of the "power brokers" he had denounced during his first campaign—Democratic machine politicians and municipal labor leaders—and his subsequent behavior in office reflected these new alliances. In this respect, the second Lindsay administration resembled previous post-reform administrations, and the election in 1973 of Mayor Abe Beame, whose ties to New York's Democratic political machines and the municipal civil service went back more than twenty-five years, ratified the results of the 1969 election.

There were, however, important differences between the fiscal policies of Mayors Lindsay and Beame and those of previous reform and post-reform mayors. During his first three years in office, Mayor Lindsay came close to balancing the city's budget, but he did so by raising taxes and relying upon massive infusions of state and federal aid rather than by reducing expenditures. When the city's economy turned sharply downward during 1969–1975, and the growth rate of intergovernmental aid to the city slowed, Lindsay and Beame did not implement commensurate reductions in municipal spending. As a result, the city accumulated an enormous floating deficit, setting the stage for the fiscal crisis of 1975. This crisis erupted only six years after Mayor Lindsay's campaign for a

221

second term, whereas previous post-reform regimes had managed to stay afloat for fifteen to twenty years.

These differences between the fiscal policies of the reform and post-reform regimes of the 1960s and 1970s and their counterparts during the classic era of conflict between the Tammany boss and the reformer were a consequence of a set of interrelated changes in the structure of political organizations and the relationship among major political forces in the city, whose roots were in the reform era of the 1930s and 1940s, and in the accommodations that Democratic machine politicians and public officials made to regain power at the end of that era. The first change was that a political party (the Liberal party) affiliated with an important segment of the city's labor movement became the major organizational vehicle for the fusion forces, supplanting citizens committees dominated by upper-class New Yorkers who were concerned above all with reducing municipal operating expenditures. Second, the system of federal grants-in-aid emerged alongside the political parties as a major link between national and local politics. In the 1960s federal urban programs became channels through which a coalition of upper-middle-class professionals and racial minorities in both the national and local political arenas were able to get the municipal government to increase expenditures that benefited (or purported to benefit) the poor. Third, civil service unions supplanted the political machine as the chief mode of organizing municipal employees, enabling city workers to secure higher wages, fringe benefits, and more favorable work rules, no matter who controlled City Hall. These unions offered protection against the efforts of the Lindsay administration to redistribute public resources at the expense of the city's current employees. This, in turn, meant that the only way Mayor Lindsay could increase the flow of public benefits to the political forces in his coalition was to increase the total level of municipal spending. Finally, the declining power of New York's Democratic party organizations in the 1960s undermined the major institutions and processes through which an accommodation between money-providing and expenditure-demanding interests had been reached during the postwar period. This arrangement had kept municipal expenditures from growing more rapidly than the revenues generated by existing city taxes.[1]

These developments led the municipal government to accumulate such enormous deficits after New York's economy faltered in 1969, and so altered the conduct of politics in the city, that when the public capital markets closed to New York in 1975, the processes through which the city's previous fiscal crises had been resolved were no longer available. The city's major banks did not command sufficient resources to bail out the municipal government, and the members of New York's business and civic elite could not expect that a slate of candidates selected by them and running as reformers would be able to win control of the city's top elective offices and be in a position to reorder the municipal government's fiscal priorities. New York was rescued from bankruptcy only after additional sources of credit were tapped (the state and federal governments and the municipal employee pension funds), and new public institutions were created to monitor the city's finances.

The 1975 fiscal crisis, and the subsequent creation of new financing arrangements and monitoring agencies, has significantly altered the conduct of politics and the content of municipal fiscal policy in New York. Contrary to the claims of many observers, however, the crisis has not placed effective control over the city's finances in the hands of New York's business elite. Rather, as discussed in chapter 7, three centers of power have emerged in New York since 1975 that have directly or indirectly influenced municipal fiscal policy: the city's public creditors and its official and unofficial fiscal monitors; the municipal employee unions and commercial banks that helped finance the city government after the crisis erupted; and the mayor and his political following.

The fiscal policies generated by these power centers differ from the policies the municipal government pursued in the 1960s and early 1970s. Most important, the city no longer finances operating expenditures with borrowed funds. Also, the local public sector has shrunk relative to the local private sector; and, as indicated in chapter 6, changes have occurred since 1975 in the distribution of public benefits and burdens among the city's racial minorities, public employees, municipal bond holders, business community, and consumers of basic public services. *New York City's fiscal crisis and the political coalitions, institutions, and processes that emerged from it have created a new set of accommodations among the political forces whose influence had increased during the reform episode of the 1960s and established interests in the city.* These new relationships have been reflected in the city's recent fiscal policies.

These new patterns of politics and policy enable New York's present regime to win the votes of a majority of the active electorate, balance the municipal budget, preserve the city's credit, promote the growth of the local economy, and keep political conflicts from getting out of hand. That is, they enable City Hall to meet the imperatives of urban politics outlined in chapter 1. During and after previous eras of great demographic, economic, and political change such a process of adjustment had been achieved through conflicts and compromises among the city's machines and the members of fusion coalitions. It is in this sense that *the political sources and consequences of New York's most recent fiscal crisis can be regarded as similar in substance to, and different chiefly in form from, earlier conflicts and compromises among machine politicians and reformers.*

If this analysis of the political sources and consequences of New York's recent fiscal crisis is correct, and the comparison between the 1975 crisis and earlier episodes of the machine/reform dialectic is apt, a number of general conclusions concerning the conduct of politics in New York and kindred cities are suggested. First, it suggests that *in the urban arena political crises often manifest themselves as fiscal crises. Consequently, fiscal crises should be regarded not as aberrations but as an integral part of urban politics.* That is, the events that constitute a fiscal crisis, such as the closing of credit markets to a city, the imposition of a bail-out plan, and the implementation of a retrenchment program, are as much ways in which urban politics is conducted as are the emergence of reform movements, the election of fusion administrations, and the working out of compromises between machine politicians and their former opponents.

A second conclusion from this analysis is that New York City's 1975 fiscal crisis was not simply a consequence of a combination of events unique to the 1960s and 1970s, ranging from changes in the racial composition of the city's population and the spatial distribution of manufacturing plants to John Lindsay's and Abe Beame's efforts to secure election and reelection. The periodic eruption of fiscal crises in New York suggests that the proximate causes of the city's difficulties during the 1970s were manifestations of recurrent strains in the political economy of American cities (analyzed in chapter 1). And if similarities between recent events and those earlier strains can be discerned, then support is lent to the claim here that the model of urban politics outlined in chapter 1 does specify some of the fundamental forces that shape the politics of cities.

A third conclusion that can be drawn from this examination of New York's recurrent fiscal crises is that what political scientist Walter Dean Burnham has said of American politics on the national level applies to politics in cities as well: "Politics as usual . . . is not politics as always." In this regard, it is important to note that in comparing the political sources and consequences of the 1975 fiscal crisis with previous episodes of the machine/reform dialectic, I am asserting not only that there are some important parallels between the power centers and political processes in the city today and the institutions and practices of previous post-reform regimes, but also that there are significant similarities between the entire *sequence* of events in New York during the period 1961–1985

224

and earlier episodes of the machine/reform dialectic. In both the recent and previous episodes, an accommodation among major participants in the city's politics that had endured for some fifteen to twenty years was shattered as tensions among them mounted (most often because of changes in the national or international systems in which these political forces were enmeshed). A period of turmoil and reform ensued as opponents sought to topple the prevailing regime from power. Political order was restored only after party leaders and municipal officials established a new set of accommodations among major political forces in the city, pursued a new set of public policies, and altered existing political organizations and institutions in ways that would enable their regime to meet the imperatives of urban politics in the new environment confronting the city.[2]

This cyclical pattern can be viewed as a process of *serial bargaining*— bargaining conducted over time—among established and insurgent political forces. On a more general level it can be regarded as a process through which the local political order adjusts to changes in the wider demographic, economic, and political systems in which the city is embedded. Fiscal crises and political upheavals are integral to this process of bargaining and adjustment, and the way these crises are resolved establishes the boundaries and practices of political contestation in American cities in more normal times. One can gain an understanding of the boundaries and practices that characterize "politics as usual" in major American cities today only if one is aware of the alternatives precluded by the coalitions and the institutions that restored order in the aftermath of earlier fiscal and political crises.

A final conclusion of this analysis concerns the possibilities of, and prospects for, democratic self-government in American cities in light of the imperatives and constraints confronting municipal officials. Before discussing this question, however, it makes sense to consider the extent to which the recent experiences of New York pertain to other major cities.

New York City as a Polar Case

Changes in the national and international economic and political systems that contributed to New York's 1975 fiscal crisis have generated budgetary problems in other cities. The flight or failure of factories located in central cities, the simultaneous migration from the city of middle-income whites and migration into the city of lower-income blacks and Hispanics, the political mobilization of nonwhites, the efforts of Great Society urban programs to alter prevailing bureaucratic practices and expenditure patterns in cities, the unionization of municipal employees, homeowners' increasing resistance to rising property tax bills, and a decline in the growth rate of federal aid to cities in the 1970s were developments that exerted downward pressure on municipal revenues and upward pressure on municipal expenditures in many cities. On the whole, however, these developments have placed greater strains upon the finances of cities in the nation's Northeast (or "Snowbelt") than of cities in the South and Southwest (or "Sunbelt").

One source of these regional differences is economic: while the number of jobs in many Northeastern cities has declined in recent decades, employment levels in Sunbelt cities have grown. Another source is demographic: whereas the number of middle-income taxpayers living in most central cities in the Snowbelt has been falling, the number in Sunbelt cities has been rising. A third and related source of these differences is juridical: state laws regarding municipal annexation make it easier for central cities in the South and Southwest to annex—and hence add to their tax base—surrounding areas in which new residential construction and commercial development is taking place.

In addition, the impact of recent national and international developments on the finances of any given city varied with the structure of that city's "domestic" politics as it entered the 1960s and with the position it occupied in the national political system. The influx of poor blacks, the mobilization of these relatively new city dwellers as a part of the national civil rights movement, and the effort of federal grant-giving agencies to alter the way municipal bureaucracies dealt with their nonwhite clients all had the potential for unsettling existing relationships among local political forces in cities throughout the country. The extent to which this potential was realized in any given city was a function of the pattern of coalitions and cleavages that prevailed in the city's politics and the structure of its political organizations and institutions when those potentially disruptive developments occurred. Together these aspects of a city's politics determined whether changes in the broader political system presented a threat or an opportunity to various local interests, and whether these interests would be able to protect themselves against the threats or take advantage of the opportunities.

Snowbelt Cities

In most Northeastern cities, as in New York, political machines that received the bulk of their electoral support from working-class and/or ethnic voters and possessed a measure of autonomy from the local business community emerged during the nineteenth and early twentieth centuries. During the New Deal and post–World War II periods Democrats in the White House and in Congress solidified their party's position in these urban strongholds by enacting legislation providing benefits to the major social groups in these cities. This legislation guaranteed the right of labor to organize, provided welfare benefits and social insurance to the working and middle class, and subsidized the construction of public works and the redevelopment of the central business districts in older cities. These federal programs provided urban Democratic machines with an opportunity to extend their political base. As political scientist John Mollenkopf said of urban redevelopment programs, a major discovery of Democratic political entrepreneurs during and after the New Deal

... [was] that they could bring together formerly-feuding urban constituencies around a program of federal intervention into the urban development process. ... The disparate urban constituencies of the national Democratic party— machines as well as reform groups, big business as well as labor, blue collar ethnics as well as minorities—could each find reasons to be united behind a program of growth and development.[3]

Generally speaking, during the postwar period machine politicians in most major Northeastern cities took advantage of these opportunities and reached a series of accommodations with other key political forces that roughly resembled the pluralist pattern characterizing politics in postwar New York. Politicians with ties to the local machine occupied most elective offices, but they pursued redevelopment policies of benefit to the local business community, permitted the municipal civil service to control its own recruitment practices and work routines, strove to keep taxes down, and did not use the police against striking workers in labor disputes.[4]

These regimes, however, were not politically invulnerable. The persistence of machine politics in most Northeastern cities posed a threat to the political interests and values of the upper-middle-class professionals, the elite civic associations, and the newspapers that historically had played a major role in municipal reform movements. As political scientists David Greenstone and Paul Peterson have argued, this led members of these groups to become a self-conscious political force and encouraged them to direct their energies into the urban political arena and be on the lookout for issues and allies that could help their cause.[5]

Another potential source of danger for these pluralist regimes was that many of the bargains binding them together were struck at the expense of racial minorities. In particular, the use of competitive written examinations to prevent politicians from influencing the recruitment and promotion of city employees left nonwhites with less than their share of jobs on the municipal payroll, and the autonomy accorded to welfare agencies and school systems enabled them to deal with their poor clients in ways that served their own bureaucratic interests.[6] Also, the urban renewal projects that cities sponsored to attract firms to their central business districts, or to protect hospitals and universities from encroaching slums, often destroyed low-rent housing occupied by nonwhites. Cities were able to pursue such policies during the postwar period because blacks were politically quiescent. Protest demonstrations, let alone ghetto riots, were all but unknown in the 1950s, and electoral turnout rates among nonwhites tended to be the lowest of all population groups in the city.

The nationwide political mobilization of blacks in the 1960s had a major impact upon politics in Northeastern cities because important political forces in these cities cultivated alliances with blacks. Middle-class reformers tried to discredit machine politicians and municipal bureaucracies by charging that they were insensitive to the plight of blacks and unresponsive to the demands of the black community. Civic associations, charitable organizations, and newspapers with ties to local business elites saw in race-related issues (such as who should control the poverty program in their city) an opportunity to increase their influence relative to the other political forces they had had to contend with during the postwar period. And as political turmoil escalated in the 1960s, elements of the business community in many Northeastern cities, speaking through organization like New York's Urban Coalition, expressed doubts about whether existing municipal policies and political accommodations could preserve public order and were prepared to consider alternative arrangements.

These attacks upon, and tensions among, the political forces that had governed Northeastern cities during the 1950s and early 1960s provided political entrepreneurs with an opportunity to advance their careers in local politics, and/or establish a name for themselves outside their city, by forging coalitions among those who wanted to redistribute the benefits of municipal politics. These cleavages also provided Washington officials who administered federal urban programs with an opportunity to lend support to their local counterparts seeking to alter the ways in which municipal bureaucracies dealt with their nonwhite clients.

These efforts to bring about major changes in the bureaucratic practices and fiscal priorities of municipal governments were furiously resisted by the political forces that would be injured were they to succeed—most important, city employees and groups currently receiving city services. Their countermobilization made it politically impossible for municipal officials to finance increases in the flow of public benefits to blacks by reducing benefits to established political interests. To the contrary, the mayors of Northeastern cities generally found that the only politically feasible way to restore order and remain in office was to boost the level of total municipal spending. When state and federal governments and local taxpayers refused to pick up the tab, the officials of a number of Northeastern cities could not resist the temptation of engaging in deficit financing.[7]

To argue that some of the conditions that led New York's expenditures to grow more rapidly than its revenues in the late 1960s and early 1970s were present in other Northeastern cities, is not to say that the impulse to increase public spending was as strong in other cities as it was in New York. Primarily because of the distinctive position New York occupied in the national system of cities, a wider array of forces participated actively in its politics. Large numbers of professionals, many working for firms providing advanced business services to national corporations, were active participants in New York politics, as were a number of national philanthropic organizations with headquarters in New York, and both sought to get City Hall to enact new policies and expand existing programs. This multiplied the opportunities in the 1960s and 1970s for the formation of coalitions in New York and in Washington by those who wished to alter the municipal government's bureaucratic practices and expenditure priorities. And because public employee unions were unusually strong in New York, the conflicts generated by their resistance to such efforts were especially intense, and the price New York's mayors had to pay to preserve civil harmony was unusually high. This helps explain why New York suffered an especially severe fiscal crisis in the 1970s. But the variety of actors playing an independent role in the metropolis's politics make New York more a polar case than a deviant one among Northeastern cities. Many other Northeastern cities have experienced fiscal strains over the past decade that are similar in kind to (albeit less severe in degree than) those that afflicted New York in 1975.[8]

Sunbelt Cities

The changes in the national economic and political system that placed strains upon the budgets of older Northeastern cities during the 1960s and 1970s had fewer adverse consequences in newer cities in the Sunbelt. These variations were partially a consequence of differences existing prior to the 1960s in the position that cities in these regions occupied in national political coalitions, and relatedly, in the characteristic structure of "domestic" politics in Snowbelt and Sunbelt cities.

For reasons too complicated to detail here, the structure of the American national party system in the late nineteenth century fostered the development of party organizations that were considerably weaker and more narrowly based in the peripheral regions of the country than in the Northeastern industrial core. Consequently, during the Progressive Era, business-dominated "good government" movements managed to overwhelm machine politicians and establish reform institutions (non-partisan, at-large elections and city manager or commission governments) that business interests, operating through slate-making citizens committees, were usually able to dominate. Correlatively, other political actors—party politicians, elected officials, middle-class professionals, and labor leaders—generally did not play an independent and important role in the politics of Sunbelt cities.[9]

Under both Democratic and Republican administrations, the federal government during the 1940s, 1950s, and early 1960s did little to undermine, and much to reinforce, the business-dominated regimes of Sunbelt cities. Section 14(b) of the Taft-Hartley Act, which permitted states to outlaw union shops, was enacted by a coalition of Republicans and Southern Democrats and subsequently accepted by Northern Democrats, making it difficult for organized labor to emerge as a counterweight to business in Sunbelt cities. And, as John Mollenkopf has argued, federal programs promoting economic growth in Southwestern cities were administered in very different ways, and had very different political consequences, from federal programs—such as urban renewal—that were designed to foster growth in Northeastern cities. Urban renewal was administered by public agencies and eventually generated opposition in neighborhoods targeted for slum clearance. In contrast, the military procurement and water development projects that promoted the growth of Southwestern cities were implemented by private firms or directly by federal agencies without being subject to review by local governments. Consequently they provided no opportunities for persons who would be injured by such projects to mobilize against them. Thus, the economic

230

growth fostered by these federal policies and programs was an unalloyed political benefit for the business-dominated regimes of Southwestern cities.[10]

Because the regimes that governed Southwestern cities entered the 1960s with so little in the way of organized or effective opposition, it was difficult for both racial minorities and the federal officials who administered Great Society urban programs to find local allies to support their efforts to alter the bureaucratic practices and fiscal priorites of these cities. An indication of this is that in large Southwestern cities average expenditures on community action and Model Cities programs in the 1960s were significantly lower than in large cities in the Northeast, and community action agencies in these Sunbelt cities were much less likely than their Northeastern counterparts to sponsor the organization of militant community groups in poor neighborhoods.[11]

In the absence of a major challenge by nonwhites to established bureaucratic practices and expenditure patterns, municipal employees and other elements of the white community in Southwestern cities had less compelling incentives than their counterparts in Northeastern cities to mobilize in self-defense. (In addition, the weakness of private sector labor unions in the Southwest had adverse implications for the strength of municipal employee unions, because the legal environment that facilitated the unionization of civil servants in the Northeast, and the political climate that encouraged city officials to respond favorably to their demands, was less prevalent in the Sunbelt.) Consequently, city officials in the Sunbelt were less likely than those in the Snowbelt to boost municipal spending in an effort to preserve civil harmony. This goes a considerable way toward explaining why the gap between per capita expenditures in large Southern and Western cities and large Northeastern cities widened during the late 1960s. And this, in turn, helps explain why cities in the Snowbelt faced more serious fiscal problems when the growth rate of federal aid to cities slowed in the 1970s.[12]

Can Cities Be Democratically Governed?

A final question remains: What does this analysis of urban fiscal politics and New York's recurrent fiscal crises suggest about the possibilities of, and prospects for, democratic self-government in American cities?

A rough way of summarizing the previous section's argument is to say that American cities fall into one of two categories. The first, which is most typical of the Southwest, is composed of cities in which local business elites dominate local politics, and their priorities are reflected in municipal fiscal policy. The second category is composed of cities, such as New York and other major cities in the Northeast, in which the local political system possesses a significant measure of autonomy from the hierarchies of civil society and in which politicians and public officials are at times tempted to engage in deficit financing. In such cities fiscal discipline is imposed upon the local government by the municipal bond-rating agencies and the public capital market, and by the threat that if the market closes to the city, political forces allied with local business elites may be able to wage a successful reform campaign and gain control of City Hall. Such threats provide the city's politicians and public officials with a strong incentive to reach an accord with business and to pursue fiscal policies that are acceptable both to it and to participants in the public capital market. In other words, municipal governments may be subject either to *internally-imposed* fiscal discipline or to *externally-imposed* fiscal discipline, but in one or the other form they cannot evade such discipline over the long run. A municipal government must either impose fiscal restraints upon itself or find itself subject to restraints by outsiders.

The case of New York in the late 1960s and early 1970s is especially telling in this regard, because the political forces encouraging the city's officials to engage in deficit financing during those years were probably as strong as they have ever been in any American city, and the mechanisms through which fiscal discipline traditionally had been imposed on the municipal government no longer were powerful enough to counteract these forces. Nonetheless, a complex of formal institutions and informal political practices and accommodations emerged after the 1975 fiscal crisis that led City Hall to balance its budget, enabled a mayor—Ed Koch—to win the support of a majority of the electorate while presiding over cutbacks of many municipal services, and politically isolated those groups (most notably, racial minorities) that opposed the mayor's conduct in office. That such a reversal could occur in a city whose politics had been so biased in the other direction only a few years earlier, indicates that the imperative cities face of maintaining their credit is powerful indeed. This imperative is, if anything, more powerful than the democratic impulse in American cities, for when it conflicted with the principle of local self-government in 1975, it was the latter principle that was sacrificed. And it almost certainly is true that if such a conflict were to emerge in the future (for example, after Ed Koch leaves City

Hall), the principle of local democracy would again be sacrificed.

But should the restraints that the capital markets place on the fiscal policies cities pursue be regarded as limits on democracy? After all, one would not say that New York, or Chicago, or Los Angeles, is less than a full democracy because its city council cannot repeal the laws of thermodynamics, or decree that every resident of its city will live to celebrate his or her 100th birthday. Is it any more a restriction on democracy that investors will refuse to purchase a city's securities unless the fiscal policies it pursues provide them with reasonable assurances that the money they lend the city will be repaid?

To answer this question it is useful to consider an analogy. Economists and policymakers belonging to the monetarist school of economics advocate that strict controls be placed on the growth of the nation's money supply—that the Federal Reserve abstain from manipulating interest rates or the money supply on a month-to-month basis in an effort either to "fine tune" the economy or, even worse, to accommodate any and all borrowing by the U.S. Treasury. Rather, they want the Federal Reserve to increase the money supply at a slow and steady rate—a rate high enough to permit the economy to grow at a moderate pace, but not so rapid as to foster inflation. Under such a monetary regime, the federal government would not be able to pursue fiscal policies that might generate inflation, because with the supply of money set at a predetermined level at any point in time, any "excessive" borrowing by the U.S. Treasury would automatically increase interest rates and reduce borrowing by the private sector, thereby precipitating a recession rather than an inflationary expansion of the economy. Thus whatever the partisan affiliation or ideological orientation of the president, congressmen, and senators elected by the nation's voters, the federal government would be unable to implement inflationary policies. In similar fashion, the inability of municipal governments to monetize their deficits, and their consequent dependence upon the capital markets to close any gap between their expenditures and revenues, imposes restraints upon the fiscal policies that popularly elected city officials can pursue.

This analogy points to a major difference between national and local politics in the United States. Whereas monetarism is a highly controversial doctrine in American national politics—indeed, it is not unreasonable to say that fully implementing its prescriptions is beyond the bounds of possibility in contemporary American national politics—comparable restraints imposed on the fiscal policies pursued by elected city officials are not subjects of political contention. On the contrary, they are one of the uncontested boundaries within which democratic politics is conducted in

233

American cities, and the great majority of all participants in urban politics regard them as no more subject to challenge or change than are the laws of physics.[13]

That most participants in urban politics regard the imperative of maintaining access to the capital market as akin to a law of nature, and that political contestation occurs within narrower boundaries in American cities than on the national level does not mean, however, that members of the public exert no influence over the governance of their city. Participants in the public credit markets are more concerned that a city's total expenditures not exceed its revenues than they are with how it allocates those expenditures between the producers and consumers of municipal services (that is, whether it has a small, well-paid workforce, or a large, poorly paid workforce); how it deploys its workforce among agencies performing different municipal services; or how it distributes the municipal services it does provide (and the positions on the public payroll of the workers who perform these services) among the city's racial and ethnic groups. Moreover, in addition to providing public services, municipal governments regulate the conduct of a city's residents (for example, they enforce traffic regulations, health and building codes, and criminal laws). The way a city performs these tasks is unlikely to affect its credit rating. When making decisions regarding such policies, municipal officials take into account the views of various segments of their city's electorate, and also the probable reaction of those elements of the city's population that are most likely to disrupt public order. Over the past century and a half this measure of popular responsiveness has led municipal governments to distribute the rewards of city politics to the members of the successive ethnic and racial groups who migrated to America's cities.

Although urban political leaders take into account the preferences of voters in making budgetary decisions, the composition of a city's political leadership and the outlook of its voters are themselves influenced by the constraints imposed upon municipal officials by the capital markets. As discussed in chapter 2, during the nineteenth and early twentieth centuries machine politicians were able to assume the political leadership of successive waves of migrants to the American city because they developed a means of reconciling the imperative of mobilizing an electoral majority with the other imperatives faced by city officials, including the imperative of maintaining access to the public capital markets. And the triumph of such politicians over other contenders for the political leadership of America's cities helped shape the views their

234

followers had regarding which of their interests it was appropriate to pursue in the urban political arena.[14]

In the 1970s, when these political institutions and patterns of political leadership proved incapable of reconciling the electoral and fiscal imperatives confronting municipal officials in many cities, new modes of political leadership—exemplified by mayors such as New York's Ed Koch and Pittsburgh's Peter Flaherty—and, in some cities, new political institutions, emerged that had this capacity.[15] It was not inevitable that this would occur. In the case of New York it was only by the narrowest of margins that the city avoided bankruptcy in 1975, and with it the elimination of local self-government. But for better or worse, it is the genius of the American system that the governance and politics of New York and other major cities have repeatedly been shaped and reshaped so that municipal officials can retain the confidence of the capital markets, as well as the support of a majority of their city's voters.

In light of this, can cities be democratically governed? This book suggests that the patterns of politics and fiscal policy prevailing in New York and other major cities embody an accommodation between those who control credit and capital, on the one side, and the ideal that government should be subject to popular political control, on the other. In American cities, more than on the national level, this accommodation is weighted toward the concerns of creditors—and against the democratic impulse.

235

NOTES

Introduction

1. U.S., Congressional Budget Office, *New York City's Fiscal Problem: Its Origins, Potential Repercussions, and Some Alternative Policy Responses,* Background Paper No. 1, 10 October 1975; Ken Auletta, *The Streets Were Paved With Gold* (New York: Random House, 1979); William K. Tabb, *The Long Default* (New York: Monthly Review Press, 1982).

2. Stephen David and Paul Kantor, "The Political Economy of Change in Urban Budgetary Politics," *British Journal of Political Science* 13 (1983): 270–74; Jack Newfield and Paul DuBrul, *The Permanent Government* (New York: Pilgrim Press, 1981), chap. 12.

Chapter 1

1. For a somewhat different formulation see Frances Fox Piven and Roger Friedland, "Public Choice and Private Power: The Origins of the Urban Fiscal Crisis" (Paper delivered at the Annual Meeting of the Public Choice Society, San Francisco, March 1980).

2. I speak of these as "imperatives," rather than saying that city officials are subject to a number of "pressures," because these four considerations can influence the behavior of public officials even in the absence of any overt efforts by individuals or groups to compel City Hall to pay heed to them. For example, a mayor cannot be utterly indifferent to the adverse consequences a proposed tax increase might have for the city's economy even if not besieged by delegations of businessmen threatening to leave town if the new tax is enacted. A declining economy will generate widespread unemployment, and this can lead to defeat in the next mayoral election. In the vocabulary of recent debates among political scientists and sociologists, the model of urban politics I am outlining in this section is a "structural" rather than a "pluralist" one. This model differs from a pressure-group model in two other respects. I argue that urban regimes help form the interests with which they must later contend and that the way political leaders mobilize support influences the understanding voters and other political participants have of their interests and entitlements. See Stephen Krasner, "Approaches to the State: Alternative Conceptions and Historical Dynamics," *Comparative Politics* 17 (January 1984): 223–48; Theda Skocpol, "Bringing the State Back In: A Review of Current Theories and Research," in *Bringing the State Back In,* ed. Peter Evans, Dietrich Rueschemeyer, and Theda Skocpol (New York: Cambridge University Press, 1985), chap. 1.

3. In recent decades municipal governments have come to rely increasingly on grants from the federal and state governments to finance operating and capital expenditures. The quest for these funds can lead city officials to implement programs that are opposed by significant elements of their city's electorate. See James Q. Wilson, "The Mayors vs. The Cities," *The Public Interest* 16 (Summer 1969): 25–37.

4. Paul Peterson, *City Limits* (Chicago: University of Chicago Press, 1981), 4.

5. Richard Knight, *Employment Expansion and Metropolitan Trade* (New York: Praeger, 1973).

6. Stephen Elkin, "Cities Without Power: The Transformation of American Urban

Regimes," in *National Resources and Urban Policy*, ed. Douglas Ashford (New York: Methuen, 1980), 265–94.

7. This is not to say that the electorate is a *tabula rasa* upon which politicians can draw any line of cleavage. It is most unlikely that a mayor who presides over the economic decline or bankruptcy of his city can expect to win reelection by calling upon all short voters to side with him against his taller opponent. However, at any given time, most of the important limitations upon electoral fluidity are a consequence of earlier political conflicts, for it is these that shape the political loyalties and outlook of voters (especially their understanding of the responsibilities of government) and that lead to the formation of political organizations (most notably, political parties) that acquire a stake in emphasizing some political issues or lines of cleavage and subordinating others. See Ira Katznelson, *City Trenches: Urban Politics and the Patterning of Class in the United States* (New York: Pantheon, 1981), chap. 3.

8. Edward Banfield and James Q. Wilson, *City Politics* (Cambridge, Mass.: Harvard University Press, 1963), chap. 8; Michael Lipsky, *Street Level Bureaucracy* (New York: Russell Sage, 1980).

9. Oliver Williams and Charles Adrian, *Four Cities* (Philadelphia: University of Pennsylvania Press, 1963), chap. 12.

10. If, as a consequence of either national economic conditions or the emergence of low-cost competitors in other cities, local businessmen find it difficult to sell their products, they may not simply resist paying higher taxes to finance relief for the unemployed, but may also press the municipal government to spend additional funds on programs or projects (such as improved transportation facilities) that would decrease their costs and enable them to lower their prices. This would further tempt city officials to engage in deficit financing. Roger Friedland, Frances Fox Piven, and Robert Alford, "Political Conflict, Urban Structure, and the Fiscal Crisis," *International Journal of Urban and Regional Research* 1 (1977): 447–72.

11. This is not to deny that there are economic, if not juridical, constraints upon the federal government's ability to finance its expenditures by printing money. The federal government levies taxes and sells Treasury securities to cover the bulk of its expenditures because printing money to pay all of its bills would be self-defeating. It would generate hyperinflation, cause the national currency to lose all value, and wreck the economy. Although the federal government has never been in the situation New York City experienced in 1975 (it has never been totally unable to borrow money), these economic constraints give its creditors bargaining power against it, the measure of which is the interest rate the Treasury must pay to induce investors to buy its securities.

Chapter 2

1. Amy Bridges, *A City in the Republic: New York and the Origins of Machine Politics* (New York: Cambridge University Press, 1984), chap. 1. See also Sean Wilentz, *Chants Democratic: New York City and the Rise of the American Working Class, 1788–1850* (New York: Oxford University Press, 1984), chaps. 1 and 2.

2. Max Weber, "Politics as a Vocation," in *From Max Weber*, ed. Hans Gerth and C. Wright Mills (New York: Oxford University Press, 1958), 77–128.

3. At various times during the nineteenth century other groups of Democratic politicians challenged Tammany Hall's claim to be the official Democratic organization in New York City. It was not until the turn of the century that Tammany fully prevailed over competing factions. For an account of Tammany's early history, see Jerome Mushkat, *Tammany: The Evolution of a Political Machine 1789–1865* (Syracuse, N.Y.: Syracuse University Press, 1971).

4. Eric Foner, "Class, Ethnicity, and Radicalism in the Gilded Age: The Land League and Irish-America," in *Politics and Ideology in the Age of the Civil War*, ed. Eric Foner (New York: Oxford University Press, 1980), 198 and following. Compare Edward Banfield and James Q. Wilson, *City Politics* (Cambridge, Mass.: Harvard University Press, 1963), chaps. 6 and 9.

5. Martin Shefter, "The Electoral Foundations of the Political Machine: New York City, 1884–1897," in *The History of American Electoral Behavior*, ed. Joel Silbey, Allen Bogue, and

William Flanagan (Princeton, N.J.: Princeton University Press, 1978), 282, 288.

6. Morton Keller, *Affairs of State* (Cambridge, Mass.: Harvard University Press, 1977), 239.

7. Bridges, *City in the Republic,* chap. 8; Herbert Gutman, "The Tompkins Square 'Riot' in New York City on January 13, 1874: A Re-examination of Its Causes and Its Aftermath," *Labor History* 6 (Winter 1965): 44–70.

8. Seymour Mandelbaum, *Boss Tweed's New York* (New York: Wiley, 1965), chap. 7.

9. The "Orange Riot" of 1871 provided members of New York's upper class with an additional incentive to overthrow the Tweed Ring, rally under the banner of reform, and attempt to take control of the municipal government. That year Mayor A. Oakey Hall, a member of the Tweed Ring, denied a fraternal organization of Irish Protestants a permit to stage a march on the anniversary of the Protestant defeat of the Catholics in Ireland at the Battle of the Boyne, claiming that this would inflame the city's large Irish Catholic community and perhaps spark sectarian violence. The governor overruled the mayor and deployed a unit of state militia to protect the Protestant parade. Catholic spectators pelted the paraders and their protectors with stones, and the militia responded by firing into the crowd, killing thirty-seven people. Upper-class New Yorkers felt City Hall was responsible for provoking this episode and concluded that an administration dependent upon the political support of Irish Catholics could not maintain public order. In their view, it was now doubly necessary to overthrow the Tweed Ring. See Anon., "Civil Rights. The Hibernian Riot and the 'Insurrection of the Capitalists,'" cited in David Montgomery, *Beyond Equality* (New York: Knopf, 1967), 378.

10. Martin Shefter, "Party and Patronage: Germany, England, and Italy," *Politics & Society* 7 (1977): 403–52.

11. Martin Shefter, "The Emergence of the Political Machine: An Alternative View," in *Theoretical Perspectives in Urban Politics,* ed. Willis Hawley and Michael Lipsky (Englewood Cliffs, N.J.: Prentice-Hall, 1976), chap. 2.

12. David Hammack, *Power and Society: Greater New York at the Turn of the Century* (New York: Russell Sage, 1982), chap. 5.

13. Ibid., chap. 6.

14. Compare Theodore Lowi, *At the Pleasure of the Mayor* (New York: Free Press, 1964), chap. 8.

15. Hammack, *Power and Society,* 143.

16. Examples are the Meyer Committee investigation of 1921, and the Proskauer and Kefauver investigations of 1951–52.

17. This is not to say that members of the city's downtown business community are the only New Yorkers who have wanted transportation facilities constructed. As Roger Starr has noted, advocating the construction of new transit links between Manhattan and the outer boroughs has long been a cause behind which both businessmen and the residents of those boroughs could unite. Roger Starr, "Power and Powerlessness in a Regional City," *The Public Interest* 16 (Summer 1969): 3–24.

18. Andy Logan, *Against the Evidence: The Becker-Rosenthal Affair* (New York: McCall, 1970), 220–21, 290–91; Martin Shefter, "Economic Crises, Social Coalitions, and Political Institutions: New York City's Little New Deal" (Paper delivered at the Annual Meeting of the American Political Science Association, New York City, September 1, 1981).

19. It is worth noting the implications of this argument for a general understanding of machine and reform politics. Reform movements mobilize against the machine not out of an abstract opposition to the style of politics it practices—as suggested by Edward Banfield and James Q. Wilson—but rather because the concrete policies it pursues or refuses to pursue (such as its failure to balance the city's budget or its refusal to renovate the city's capital infrastructure) lead other groups to conclude that it is fundamentally misgoverning the city. Because opposition to the machine is based on such concrete grievances, when an administration with ties to the machine implements policies that speak to these concerns, many former members of the reform coalition will be prepared to support the new regime. Compare Banfield and Wilson, *City Politics,* chap. 11, and their article "Political Ethos Revisited," *American Political Science Review* 65 (December 1971): 1048–62.

Certainly there are reform ideologues who refuse to be placated by any policy concessions made by machine politicians, but their principled stance cannot be explained by their ethnic heritage (as Banfield and Wilson suggest), because their backgrounds generally are similar to those of the more pliable members of reform coalitions. This reform vanguard can be better understood as one in a succession of would-be leadership groups that have sought political hegemony in the American city over the past two centuries. These groups have always included large numbers of Anglo-Saxon Protestants, yet their attitudes toward patronage have varied considerably from one group to the next. The notables who governed the city in the eighteenth and early nineteenth centuries made use of patronage; the nonpartisan reformers of the late nineteenth century through the 1950s opposed patronage; and the reformers affiliated with the New Politics movement in the 1960s were prepared to tolerate patronage in community action agencies.

20. Robert Caro, *The Power Broker: Robert Moses and the Fall of New York* (New York: Knopf, 1974), chaps. 19–40.

21. Lowi, *At the Pleasure of the Mayor*, fig. 8.4.

22. Ibid., fig. 8.2.

23. Martin Shefter, "Political Incorporation and the Extrusion of the Left: The Organization of Ethnic Groups into American Urban Politics" (Paper delivered at the Annual Meeting of the American Political Science Association, Chicago, September 2, 1983).

24. Wallace Sayre and Herbert Kaufman, *Governing New York City* (New York: Russell Sage, 1960), chap. 11.

25. Stephen Elkin, "Political Structure, Political Organization, and Race," *Politics & Society* 8 (1978): 225–51.

26. James Q. Wilson, *Negro Politics* (New York: Free Press, 1960), chap. 2.

27. In adopting the terminology of interest "articulation" and "aggregation" from Almond and Coleman (who use these terms to mean the representation of interests and arranging accommodations among them), I do not mean to suggest that the institutions of New York's postwar regime passively channeled demands that arose autonomously in civil society. In the case of Robert Moses's public works empire, for example, it was Moses who convinced many of the city's businessmen, bankers, and newspapers that their interests (and the interests of the city) would be served by the construction of a network of arterial highways, bridges, and tunnels in metropolitan New York. Moreover, his public works projects helped create, or at least strengthen, many of the giant construction firms and unions that later supported his program, and once this constituency existed, it was Moses who provided it with leadership. See Gabriel Almond, "Introduction: A Functional Approach to Comparative Politics," in *The Politics of Developing Areas*, ed. Garbriel Almond and James Coleman (Princeton: Princeton University Press, 1960), 3–64.

28. Sayre and Kaufman, *Governing New York City*, chap. 17.

Chapter 3

1. James Q. Wilson, *The Amateur Democrat* (Chicago: University of Chicago Press, 1962), 52–54.

2. Ibid., 60–63.

3. Charles Van Devander, *The Big Bosses* (n.p.: Howell, Soskin, 1944), 21–22.

4. This account of the downfall of Robert Moses is drawn from Robert Caro, *The Power Broker: Robert Moses and the Fall of New York* (New York: Knopf, 1974), chaps. 41–45. Caro is not responsible, of course, for my interpretation of these events.

5. Ibid., 1022.

6. Fred Cook and Gene Gleason, "The Shame of New York," *The Nation*, 31 October 1959, 261–321.

7. *New York Times*, 22 February 1960, p. 14.

8. David Greenstone and Paul Peterson, *Race and Authority in Urban Politics* (New York: Russell Sage, 1973), 41.

9. Richard Cloward and Lloyd Ohlin, *Delinquency and Opportunity* (Glencoe, Ill.: Free Press, 1960).

10. Daniel Patrick Moynihan, *Maximum Feasible Misunderstanding* (New York: Free Press, 1969), 14–15.

11. Frances Fox Piven, "Dilemmas in Social Planning: A Case Inquiry," *Social Service Review* 42 (1968): 197–206; Peter Marris and Martin Rein, *Dilemmas of Social Reform* (Chicago: Aldine, 1973), 20.

12. Greenstone and Peterson, *Race and Authority*, 136–37.

13. Harold H. Weissman, "Overview of the Community Development Program" and Alfred Fried, "The Attack on Mobilization," in *Community Development in the Mobilization for Youth Experience*, ed. Harold Weissman (New York: Association Press, 1969), 24, 139, 143–44.

14. *New York Times*, 24 Aug. 1964, p. 1; 19 Oct. 1964, p. 1; 4 Dec. 1964, p. 53.

15. The New York Police Department's Bureau of Special Services (the "Red Squad") conducted its own investigation of MFY's personnel several months before the *Daily News* published its story, and Mayor Wagner instructed the agency's chairman to get rid of the undesirables on his staff. Before the issue became public, however, the mayor did not monitor the implementation of his directive, and MFY was able to evade it. Fried, "The Attack on Mobilization," 142.

16. Ibid., 144.

17. Ibid., 150.

18. *New York Times*, 4 Aug. 1965, p. 16; 14 Sept. 1965, p. 26.

19. Greenstone and Peterson, *Race and Authority*, 159.

20. *New York Times*, 23 March 1965, p. 20.

21. Greenstone and Peterson, *Race and Authority*, 274–75.

22. *New York Times*, 1 Feb. 1961, p. 28.

23. Raymond Vernon, *Metropolis 1985* (Cambridge: Harvard University Press, 1960), 78–85; see also Dick Netzer, "New York City's Mixed Economy: Ten Years Later," *The Public Interest* 16 (Summer 1969): 188–201.

24. *New York Times*, 13 Sept. 1965, p. 35; 21 Oct. 1965, p. 46.

25. Norman Fainstein and Susan Fainstein, "Stages in the Politics of Urban Development: New York Since 1945" (Paper delivered at the Conference on New York City in the Postindustrial Period, Social Science Research Council, New York City, 4 May 1984), 23.

26. *New York Times*, 24 Jan. 1965, p. 71; 26 May 1965, p. 1.

27. *New York Times*, 5 Sept. 1965, p. 38. Under the leadership of such a czar, Austin Tobin, the Port Authority proceeded quite rapidly with the projects it undertook. See Michael Danielson and Jameson Doig, *New York: The Politics of Urban Regional Development* (Berkeley: University of California Press, 1982).

28. New York Herald Tribune (under the direction of Barry Gottehrer), *New York in Crisis: A Study in the Depth of Urban Sickness* (New York: McKay, 1965), 95.

29. *New York Times*, 9 March 1965, p. 37.

30. New York Chamber of Commerce, *The Coming Crisis in New York City Finances* (New York: New York Chamber of Commerce, 1960); Citizens Budget Commission, *Fiscal Momentum in New York City's Future* (New York: Citizens Budget Commission, 1961).

31. For a lucid account of the various budgetary gimmicks New York City employed in the 1960s and 1970s, see Charles Morris, *The Cost of Good Intentions* (New York: Norton, 1980), 131–36.

32. *New York Times*, 3 June 1963, p. 1.

33. Citizens Budget Commission, *Anatomy of a Fiscal Crisis* (New York: Citizens Budget Commission, 1964).

34. *New York Times*, 9 March 1965, p. 56.

35. *New York Times*, 9 April 1965, p. 38.

36. *New York Times*, 9 July 1965, p. 1.

37. Citizens Budget Commission, *Anatomy of a Fiscal Crisis*, 4–12.

38. Ibid., 12, 17; *New York Times*, 18 Dec. 1963, p. 35; 3 June 1963, p. 3; 25 May 1965, p. 33; 9 July 1965, p. 1.

39. *New York Times*, 3 June 1963, p. 1; 14 Oct. 1963, p. 42; 6 July 1964, p. 28; 7 June 1963, p. 13; 25 July 1963, p. 14.

40. *New York Times*, 8 Sept. 1965, p. 42; New York Herald Tribune, *New York in Crisis*, chap. 10; *Wall Street Journal*, 22 July 1965, p. 16.

41. *New York Times*, 21 July 1965, p. 1; 25 Aug. 1965, p. 32; 16 Oct. 1965, p. 28; 24 Nov. 1965, p. 24; Citizens Budget Commission, *Thirty-Fourth Annual Report, 1965* (New York: Citizens Budget Commission, 1965), 5.

42. *New York Times*, 1 Nov. 1965, p. 1; 14 Oct. 1965, p. 48; 25 May 1965, p. 33; Citizens Budget Commission, *Anatomy of a Fiscal Crisis*, p. 17.

43. Diane Ravitch, *The Great School Wars: New York City, 1805-1973* (New York: Basic Books, 1974), chaps. 23-25.

44. David Rogers, *110 Livingston Street: Politics and Bureaucracy in the New York City Schools* (New York: Random House, 1968), chaps. 4-6.

45. *New York Times*, 7 April 1964, p. 24; 21 April 1964, p. 31; 22 May 1964, p. 36; 16 June 1964, p. 53; 17 June 1964, p. 1; 8 Sept. 1964, p. 58; 9 Dec. 1964, p. 21.

46. *New York Times*, 20 May 1965, p. 1; 17 June 1964, p. 1; 23 July 1964, p. 12.

47. Greenstone and Peterson, *Race and Authority*, 274-75.

48. Rogers, *110 Livingston Street*, 462; *New York Times*, 1 Aug. 1964, p. 1.

49. *New York Times*, 8 April 1965, p. 1.

50. *New York Times*, 28 June 1965, p. 1; 19 July 1965, p. 32.

51. *New York Times*, 21 May 1965, p. 1; 19 Aug. 1965, p. 17; 13 Sept. 1965, p. 34; 22 Oct. 1965, p. 37.

52. Ralph Jones, "City Employee Unions in New York and Chicago" (Ph.D. diss., Harvard University, 1972), 44-46.

53. Theodore Lowi, "Machine Politics—Old and New," *The Public Interest*, no. 9. (Fall 1967): 83-92; Raymond D. Horton, *Municipal Labor Relations in New York City: Lessons of the Lindsay-Wagner Years* (New York: Praeger, 1973), 42.

54. *New York Times*, 12 Sept. 1965, p. 79.

55. *New York Times*, 16 April 1961, p. 46; 13 May 1961, p. 1; 3 June 1961, p. 1.

56. *New York Times*, 15 May 1965, p. 1.

57. *New York Times*, 23 May 1965, sec. 4, p. 10; 14 Oct. 1965, p. 42.

58. *New York Times*, 15 May 1965, p. 1.

59. *New York Times*, 20 June 1965, p. 46.

Chapter 4

1. See Stephen David, "Welfare: The Community Action Program Controversy," in *Race and Politics in New York City*, ed. Jewel Bellush and Stephen David (New York: Praeger, 1971), 25-58; Charles Morris, *The Cost of Good Intentions*, (New York: Norton, 1980), 115; Douglas Yates, "The Urban Jigsaw Puzzle: New York Under Lindsay," *New York Affairs* 2 (Winter 1974): 3-19.

2. Arthur Reiger, "The Corporate Response to the Urban Crisis: A Study of the New York Urban Coalition, 1967-1971" (Ph.D. diss., Cornell University, 1972).

3. See New York City Planning Commission, *Plan for the City of New York: A Proposal* (Cambridge, Mass.: M.I.T. Press, 1969).

4. Robert Caro, *The Power Broker: Robert Moses and the Fall of New York* (New York: Knopf, 1974), chap. 48; Beverly Moss Spatt, *A Proposal to Change the Structure of City Planning: Case Study of New York City* (New York: Praeger, 1971).

5. David, "The Community Action Program Controversy"; Joseph Viteritti, *Bureaucracy and Social Justice* (Port Washington, N.Y.: Kennikat, 1979), chap. 4; C. Peter Rydell, *Welfare Caseload Dynamics in New York City* (New York: Rand Institute, 1974).

6. City of New York, Temporary Commission on City Finances, Eighth Interim Report to the Mayor, *An Historical and Comparative Analysis of Expenditures in the City of New York*, October 1976, Table II; Raymond D. Horton, *Municipal Labor Relations in New York City: Lessons of the Lindsay-Wagner Years* (New York: Praeger, 1973), 80-85.

7. See also Martin Shefter, "Party, Bureaucracy, and Political Change in the United States," in *Political Parties: Development and Decay* (Sage Electoral Studies Yearbook 4), ed. Louis Maisel and Joseph Cooper (Beverly Hills, Calif.: Sage, 1978), 211-66.

8. Jewel Bellush, "Housing: The Scatter-Side Controversy," in *Race and Politics*, ed. Bellush and David, 98-133.

9. Caro, *The Power Broker*, chap. 48.

10. Horton, *Municipal Labor Relations*, 72-80.

11. Viteritti, *Bureaucracy and Social Justice*, chap. 3.

12. *New York Times*, 1 July 1970, p. 41; Peter Szanton, *Not Well Advised* (New York:

Russell Sage, 1981), chap. 4; Viteritti, *Bureaucracy and Social Justice,* 70.

13. Diane Ravitch, *The Great School Wars: New York City, 1805–1973* (New York: Basic Books, 1974), chap. 34.

14. *New York Times,* 17 June 1968, p. 1.

15. Mayor's Advisory Panel on Decentralization of the New York City Schools, *Reconnection for Learning* (New York: Ford Foundation, 1967).

16. David Cohen, "The Price of Community Control," *Commentary* (July 1969): 23–32.

17. Marilyn Gittell, "Education: The Decentralization-Community Control Controversy," in *Race and Politics,* ed. Bellush and David, 134–63; Martin Mayer, *The Teachers' Strikes: New York 1968* (New York: Harper & Row, 1969); Ravitch, *The Great School Wars,* chap. 33.

18. Andrew Hacker, *The New Yorkers: A Profile of an American Metropolis* (New York: Mason/Charter, 1975), chap. 3.

19. *New York Times,* 4 Nov. 1965, p. 50; 6 Nov. 1969, p. 37.

20. James Q. Wilson, "The Mayors vs. the Cities," *The Public Interest* no. 16 (Summer 1969): 25–37.

21. John V. Lindsay, *The City* (New York: Norton, 1970), 25–26.

22. Norman Fainstein and Susan Fainstein, *Urban Political Movements: The Search for Power by Minority Groups in American Cities* (Englewood Cliffs, N.J.: Prentice-Hall, 1974), 229. See also Charles V. Hamilton, "The Patron-Recipient Relationship and Minority Politics in New York City," *Political Science Quarterly* 94 (Summer 1979): 211–28; and Joyce Gelb, "Black Power in Electoral Politics: A Case Study and Comparative Analysis," *Polity* 6 (Summer 1974): 501–23.

23. Horton, *Municipal Labor Relations,* 85–90.

24. *New York Times,* 6 Nov. 1969, p. 1.

25. *New York Times,* 30 Oct. 1969, p. 1.

26. For an analysis of the 1969 electoral returns see Walter Dean Burnham, *Critical Elections and the Mainsprings of American Politics* (New York: Norton, 1970), 159–66.

27. Around City Hall, *The New Yorker,* 7 Feb. 1977, 101–8.

28. Around City Hall, *The New Yorker,* 19 Nov. 1973, 218.

29. This is not to say that the composition and structure of Lindsay's and Beame's support coalitions were completely identical—in particular, the reform vanguard that played a prominent role in Lindsay's two administrations found little comfort in Beame's election. Also, in contrast to Lindsay, who had substantial support among both black and Puerto Rican politicians, Beame's accommodation of black elected officials in 1973 was not duplicated in his relations with their Puerto Rican counterparts.

30. One exception was the administration's efforts to place a low-income public-housing project in the middle-class neighborhood of Forest Hills. For excellent discussions of the administrative reforms Lindsay sought during his second term see Morris, *Cost of Good Intentions,* 159–69, 203–10; Viteritti, *Bureaucracy and Social Justice,* 80–87.

31. *New York Times,* 5 Dec. 1971, sec. 4, p. 1; 28 Sept. 1972, p. 51; 19 Jan. 1975, p. 1; 31 Jan. 1978, p. 45.

32. *New York Times,* 13 Feb. 1975, p. 35; *Village Voice,* 13 Sept. 1976, p. 21.

33. *New York Times,* 19 Jan. 1975, p. 1.

34. An incident that occurred between Beame's election and inauguration illustrates both the extent of factionalism among New York's black politicians and the importance to them that white politicians acknowledge their claims to leadership of the city's black community. During his campaign Beame had pledged to increase black representation at the highest levels of city government. A few weeks after his victory, he indicated he would appoint Wilbert Tatum, a top official in the office of Manhattan Borough President Percy Sutton, as the first black deputy mayor in the city's history. The selection of Tatum, however, caused an uproar among New York's black elected officials. Privately, they complained that it would provide Sutton with privileged access to City Hall, and make all other black politicians in the city dependent upon him. Publicly, they argued that Tatum was not qualified for this position because he was a newcomer to New York, unfamiliar with the problems of the city's black community and unknown to its members, and demanded that the mayor appoint one of their number in his stead. That is, they insisted only someone who had risen through the local political structure could claim to represent New York's black population, and they wanted the mayor to acknowledge this. Faced with

243

this furor, Beame decided not to appoint Tatum. *New York Times,* 22 Nov. 1973, p. 13.
35. *New York Times,* 5 Feb. 1974, p. 31; 15 April 1974, p. 33.
36. *Village Voice,* 30 Aug. 1976, p. 11; 13 Sept. 1976, p. 21; 30 August 1978, p. 1.
37. *New York Times,* 3 Feb. 1966, p. 27; 16 April 1967, p. 1.
38. *New York Times,* 31 May 1974, p. 37; 13 Feb. 1975, p. 35.
39. *New York Times,* 31 Mar. 1974, sect. 4, p. 6.
40. *New York Times,* 7 July 1971, p. 21.
41. *New York Times,* 15 April 1974, p. 33.
42. *New York Times,* 21 Sept. 1974, p. 1.

Chapter 5

1. For an analysis of each New York City budget between 1966 and 1975 see Charles Morris, *The Cost of Good Intentions,* (New York: Norton, 1980), 137–39, 144–46, 150–55, and 218–22. For a prescient analysis of New York City finances from 1960 to 1970 see Dick Netzer "The Budget: Trends and Prospects," in *Agenda for a City,* ed. Lyle Fitch and Annmarie Hauck Walsh (Beverly Hills: Sage, 1970), 651–714.
2. New York State, Municipal Assistance Corporation for New York City, *Annual Report,* 1976, p. 7.
3. U.S. Securities and Exchange Commission, *Staff Report on Transactions in the Securities of the City of New York,* August 26, 1977 (Washington, D.C.: Government Printing Office, 1977), chap. 4, 30–36; chap. 1, 253.
4. U.S. Congressional Budget Office, *New York City's Fiscal Problem,* Background Paper No. 1, 10 October 1975.
5. *New York Times,* 11 June 1972, p. 1.
6. First National City Bank, The Financial Position of the City of New York in Long Term Perspective (New York: First National City Bank, 1970); Moody's report cited in Morris, *Cost of Good Intentions,* 170.
7. Roger E. Alcaly and Helen Bodian, "New York's Fiscal Crisis and the Economy," in *The Fiscal Crisis of American Cities,* ed. Roger Alcaly and David Mermelstein (New York: Vintage, 1977), 20–58.
8. For a discussion of the impact of state politics and policies upon New York City's finances see Peter D. McClelland and Allan L. Magdovitz, *Crisis in the Making* (New York: Cambridge University Press, 1982).
9. See especially John H. Mollenkopf, *The Contested City* (Princeton, N.J.: Princeton University Press, 1983), chaps. 2 and 3; see also Bernard Gifford, "New York City and Cosmopolitan Liberalism," *Political Science Quarterly* 93 (Winter 1978): 559–84. For the impact of federal tax policy see Peter Marcuse, "The Targeted Crisis: On the Ideology of the Urban Fiscal Crisis and Its Uses," *International Journal of Urban and Regional Research* 5 (September 1981), 330–55.
Many of these same policies contributed to the growth of the corporate sector of New York's economy. From 1953 to 1963, job increases in the corporate sector roughly equaled the job losses in manufacturing, between 1963 and 1969 they exceeded those losses by a small margin, and from 1969 through 1975 job increases in the corporate and business-service sector of New York's economy were considerably smaller than the city's loss of manufacturing jobs. However, many of the newly created jobs in the corporate sector required skills that only a small proportion of New York's black and Puerto Rican population possessed. For a discussion of these developments, see City of New York, Temporary Commission on City Finances, Thirteenth Interim Report, *Economic and Demographic Trends in New York City: The Outlook for the Future,* May 1977.
10. Donald Haider, "Sayre and Kaufman Revisited: New York City Government Since 1965," *Urban Affairs Quarterly* 15 (December 1979): 128–29.
11. This section draws upon Martin Shefter, "Party, Bureaucracy and Political Change in the United States," in *Political Parties: Development and Decay* (Sage Electoral Studies Yearbook 4), ed. Louis Maisel and Joseph Cooper (Beverly Hills, Calif.: Sage, 1978), 243–54; see also, Frances Fox Piven, "The Urban Crisis: Who Got What, and Why," in *Urban*

Politics and Public Policy, 2nd edition, ed. Stephen David and Paul Peterson (New York: Praeger, 1976), 318–38.

12. Robert Salisbury, "Urban Politics: The New Convergence of Power," *Journal of Politics* 26 (November 1964): 775–97.

13. Frances Fox Piven and Richard Cloward, *The New Class War* (New York: Pantheon, 1982), chap. 1.

14. See also Frances Fox Piven and Richard Cloward, *Regulating the Poor* (New York: Pantheon, 1971), chap. 9.

15. *New York Times,* 6 May 1972, p. 28.

16. Municipal Assistance Corporation, *Annual Report,* 1976, p. 7; see also Roger Starr, *The Rise and Fall of New York City* (New York: Basic Books, 1985), chap. 12.

17. The categories in table 5.2 are the same as those described in Appendix IIIC of the Final Report of the Temporary Commission on City Finances with the following exceptions: expenditures on training programs for municipal workers and for professional services, fees, and commissions paid to persons who are not city employees were omitted from the category of Wages, Pensions, and Fringe Benefits and included in the category of Contracts, Supplies, Equipment, and Other; and payments to nonprofit agencies and to firms for antipoverty and job training programs were transferred from this last category to the Social Welfare category.

18. Raymond Horton, "Economics, Politics, and Collective Bargaining: The Case of New York City," in *Public Employee Unions,* ed. A. Lawrence Chickering (San Francisco: Institute for Contemporary Studies, 1976), 183–201.

19. Martin Shefter, "Local Politics, State Legislatures, and The Urban Fiscal Crisis: New York City and Boston," in *Territorial Politics in Industrial Nations,* ed. Sidney Tarrow et al. (New York: Praeger, 1978), 170–212.

20. Raymond Horton, *Municipal Labor Relations in New York City: Lessons of the Lindsay-Wagner Years* (New York: Praeger, 1973), 76, 105–11; Morris, *Cost of Good Intentions,* 96.

21. Morris, *Cost of Good Intentions,* 173.

22. The figure of $19,543 for New York's per employee labor costs reported in table 5.3 differs from the one of $22,283 cited on p. 117, because it omits the cost of fringe benefits and is based upon the Census Bureau's definitions and accounting procedures, rather than those of New York City.

23. However, the District of Columbia does receive more federal aid per capita than any city in the nation, enabling it to finance its unusually high expenditures.

24. A portion of municipal labor costs are financed by federal and state aid, but no data are available for comparing the locally financed portion of the wage bills of cities. The residents of most of the nation's large cities must pay taxes to other political jurisdictions to cover the costs of services performed by municipal employees in New York, but this is not germane to the question addressed here—namely, why the municipal government of New York suffered unusually severe financial problems in the mid-1970s.

25. New York's municipal government receives some compensation for performing services that are provided elsewhere by other governmental jurisdictions. New York State passes on federal grants it receives to help finance social welfare programs in the city, and adds additional state monies. Moreover, the general level of state aid to New York City is greater on a peᵣ capita basis than the aid other large cities receive from their state governments. Finally, New York City also does not have to compete with independent school districts or county governments for the right to tax its citizens. Nonetheless, the revenues New York City received from all of these sources in the 1970s did not cover the costs of its unusually high public expenditures. Consequently, New York's per capita expenditures from local sources, and the per capita tax burden borne by its citizens, was the highest of any city in the country in 1975, with the exception of Washington, D.C. See Donald Haider and Thomas Elmore, Jr., "New York at the Crossroads: The Budget Crisis in Perspective," *City Almanac* 5 (February 1975): 4.

26. Paul Peterson, *City Limits* (Chicago: University of Chicago Press, 1981), chap. 10.

27. Locally financed operating expenditures were calculated by subtracting the total state and federal aid received by the city from the sum of the city's expense budget and the operating expenditures included within its capital budget. Because these expenditures were not fully financed by the municipal government's current tax receipts, this is not a measure of the burden city operating costs placed upon the local economy. However, the

use of borrowed funds to finance operating expenditures is precisely what generated the 1975 fiscal crisis, and, consequently, an analysis of the sources of that crisis must take into account expenditures financed in this way. It should also be noted that this measure is not distorted by inflation because its numerator and denominator are measured in dollars of equal value.

28. The decline of New York's economy from 1969 to 1975 also contributed to the growth of the municipal budget relative to the income of the city's residents. It is politically significant, however, that City Hall reacted to this economic contraction not by reducing municipal expenditures, but by increasing them, while relying more and more heavily on borrowed funds for financing these increases. By contrast, in the years immediately following the 1975 fiscal crisis, municipal expenditures declined relative to the personal income of the city's residents despite an equally severe contraction in the local economy.

29. In 1972, Mayor Lindsay was unable to get the Board of Estimate to enact the full package of new city taxes the state legislature had authorized to enable the municipal government to close its budget gap. He encountered even greater resistance in the city council, where the opposition to new taxes was especially strong among council members from districts with high numbers of small property owners. *New York Times*, 25 May 1972, p. 1.

Chapter 6

1. For overviews of the events of 1975 see Robert Bailey, *The Crisis Regime* (Albany, N.Y.: State University of New York Press, 1984), chap. 1; Charles Levine, Irene Rubin, and George Wolohojian, *The Politics of Retrenchment* (Beverly Hills, Calif.: Sage, 1981), chap. 2; Donna Shalala and Carol Bellamy, "A State Saves a City: The New York Case," *Duke Law Journal* 6 (January 1976): 1119–32.

2. *Wall Street Journal*, 14 May 1975, p. 14.

3. Samuel P. Huntington, *Political Order in Changing Societies* (New Haven, Conn.: Yale University Press, 1968), 196.

4. *Wall Street Journal*, 23 May 1975, p. 21; City of New York, Municipal Assistance Corporation, *Minutes of Special Meeting of Board of Directors*, 30 July 1975. I am *not* arguing that the banks either engineered the fiscal crisis or used it as a pretext to compel New York to adopt the policies they favored. The banks would have faced grave legal problems had they underwritten or purchased the securities of a city whose budgetary practices so seriously violated the canons of sound financial management. Also, the banks were correct in their assessment that a necessary condition for New York to regain access to the market was that it balance its budget according to generally accepted accounting principles.

5. Seymour Z. Mann and Edward Handman, "Perspectives on New York City's Fiscal Crisis: The Role of the Municipal Unions," *City Almanac* 12 (June 1977): 10.

6. *New York Times*, 19 June 1975, p. 1.

7. *New York Times*, 23 Nov. 1975, p. 1.

8. Patricia Giles Leeds, "City Politics and the Market: The Case of New York City's Financing Crisis," in *The Municipal Money Chase: The Politics of Local Government Finance*, ed. Alberta Sbragia (Boulder, Colo.: Westview Press, 1983), 113–44.

9. U.S. Securities and Exchange Commission, *Staff Report on Transactions in the Securities of the City of New York*, August 26, 1977 (Washington, D.C.: Government Printing Office, 1977), chap. 1, p. 253.

10. Jewel Bellush and Bernard Bellush, "Collective Bargaining, Leadership, and the Fiscal Crisis." (Paper delivered at the Annual Meeting of the American Political Science Association, New York City, September 3–6, 1981), 12.

11. New York State, Municipal Assistance Corporation for New York City, 1976, *Annual Report*, table III; *The Bond Buyer*, 14 Nov. 1975, p. 5.

12. Around City Hall, *The New Yorker*, 13 Jan. 1975, 67–73.

13. In addition to investment banker Felix Rohatyn, the most prominent members of this group were William Ellinghaus and Richard Shinn, top executives of New York Telephone Company and Metropolitan Life; Simon Rifkind, a former federal judge and a

246

senior partner in one of the city's leading corporate law firms; and a group of advisors who had extensive governmental experience in New York City and/or Albany—Stephen Berger, David Burke, Herbert Elish, Peter Goldmark, Judah Gribetz, and Dick Netzer. See Fred Ferretti, *The Year the Big Apple Went Bust* (New York: Putnam, 1976), 233–86; Municipal Assistance Corporation, *Minutes of Special Meeting of Board of Directors,* 17 July 1975.

14. In 1976 the legislature created a second special account to channel off state financial aid that had formerly gone directly into the city's treasury. The funds in this account are used to meet debt service payments on what are known as "second resolution" MAC bonds.

15. The statute creating the EFCB also established a new Office of the Special Deputy Comptroller for New York City. This official is appointed by the state comptroller and is authorized to review the revenue forecasts and expenditure estimates in the city's three-year plan and annual budget, to monitor the flow of municipal revenues and the pace of expenditures throughout the year, and to conduct performance audits of city departments and recommend how they can increase their efficiency. These forecasts, estimates, and audits are used by the EFCB to decide whether to approve the city's financial plan and its budget, and to determine whether the municipal government is adhering to the commitments outlined in these documents.

16. *New York Times,* 17 Sept. 1975, p. 88; 27 Jan. 1976, p. 1. This demand was identical to the one made by the bankers who bailed out New York following the 1871 and 1933 fiscal crises. In those cases they also insisted that men who enjoyed their confidence (Andrew Haswell Green in the former episode, and George McAneny in the latter) be appointed to top financial positions in the city government.

17. Ferretti, *The Year the Big Apple Went Bust,* 246–47, 272; Bailey, *The Crisis Regime,* 168.

18. Bellush and Bellush, "Collective Bargaining, Leadership and the Fiscal Crisis," 17.

19. City of New York, Commission on Human Rights, *City Layoffs: The Effect on Minorities and Women,* 1976, p. 8.

20. The moratorium was declared unconstitutional by New York State's highest court in 1976. See "New York—A City in Crisis: Fiscal Emergency Legislation and the Constitutional Attacks," *Fordham Urban Law Journal* 6 (Spring 1977): 65–100.

21. See David Grossman, "Intergovernmental Aid," in *Setting Municipal Priorities, 1984,* ed. Charles Brecher and Raymond Horton (New York: New York University Press, 1983), chap. 2; Richard Nathan, "Intergovernmental Aid," in *Setting Municipal Priorities, 1983,* ed. Charles Brecher and Raymond Horton (New York: New York University Press, 1982), chap. 2.

22. The expenditure increase between 1975 and 1976 depicted in figure 6.1 may be explained by the city's adoption of more accurate accounting and financial reporting procedures after the fiscal crisis erupted. Charles Brecher and Raymond Horton, "Expenditures," in *Setting Municipal Priorities, 1984,* ed. Brecher and Horton (New York: New York University Press, 1983), 96. In figure 6.1 and in the text of this section the GNP deflator for state and local government purchases was used to adjust city expenditure data for the effects of inflation.

23. Jac Friedgut, "Perspectives on the New York City Fiscal Crisis: The Role of the Banks," *City Almanac* 12 (June 1977): 1–7.

24. Mary McCormick, "Labor Relations," in *Setting Municipal Priorities, 1982,* ed. Charles Brecher and Raymond Horton (New York: Russell Sage, 1981), chap. 7. The job titles covered by this study are: clerk, nurse's aide, custodial assistant, computer operator, staff nurse, administrative assistant, plumbing inspector, civil engineer, patrolman, teacher with M.A., and teacher with M.A. and 30 additional college credits. McCormick's study was conducted in 1981 and relied upon estimates of the increases in living costs during 1981 and 1982 that turned out to be too high. I have used the actual changes in the consumer price index for urban wage earners and clerical workers in the New York metropolitan area to calculate changes in the real wages of city employees between 1975 and 1984. Salaries for 1984 were calculated by adding the $750 bonus city employees received in 1982 to the 1982 salaries reported by McCormick, and multiplying this sum by the percentage wage increases of 1983 and 1984.

25. That the real wages of many New York City employees were the same in 1984 as

they had been in 1975 does not, of course, erase or restore the loss of purchasing power city workers experienced during the intervening years.

26. Elizabeth Dickson and George Peterson, *Public Employee Compensation: A Twelve City Comparison*, 2nd edition (Washington, D.C.: The Urban Institute, 1981), 141–54. For technical reasons it is necessary to omit hospital workers in calculating the city's per employee labor costs. The 75 percent increase in labor costs per employee between 1975 and 1984 was almost identical to the rise in cost of living during these years. Because of changes in the city's accounting and data gathering practices, however, comparisons between 1975 and post-1975 expenditures must be treated cautiously.

27. McCormick, "Labor Relations," table 7.5. The figure of 273,474 reported in this sentence as the size of the city's workforce in 1975 differs from the one of 294,522 reported in chapter 5 because it relies upon a new definition of full-time equivalent employees adopted by the municipal government in 1977. Improvements in the local economy enabled the city to increase the municipal workforce by 11,727 between 1981 and 1984, but this amounted to only one-fourth of the positions that had been eliminated between 1975 and 1981. See City of New York, Office of the Comptroller, *Annual Report, Fiscal Year 1984*, iv, 244. It should be noted that there is a small discrepancy between the figures given in the Comptroller's report and McCormick's study for the size of the municipal workforce in 1981.

28. Citizens Budget Commission, *Statement by the Citizens Budget Commission on New York City Fiscal Situation* (New York: Citizens Budget Commission, 1975), and *Can New York Make It?* (New York: Citizens Budget Commission, 1976); *New York Times*, 10 April 1976, p. 55; City of New York, Temporary Commission on City Finances, *The City in Transition*, 167–85; City of New York, Mayor's Management Advisory Board, *Personnel*, 1977.

29. The city's efforts between 1976 and 1978 to make wage increases conditional on productivity failed and were abandoned in 1978. More recent efforts to increase productivity have had somewhat greater success, though with one notable exception the savings achieved have been modest. During the 1983 fiscal year, for example, the city's productivity program reduced its $13.9 billion in operating expenditures by $48 million, a saving of three-tenths of one percent. See New York State Financial Control Board, *The New York City Productivity Program, 1983 Review*, 1984, tables 2 and 3. The city's most successful effort to increase worker output was a "gain sharing" agreement with the sanitation workers' union that in 1984 provided workers in smaller crews, (two-person instead of three-person), with bonuses of up to $81 a week.

30. The TCCF urged that the city pursue a "developmental strategy." This would involve reducing operating expenditures; making wage increases of municipal employees contingent upon the city's "regaining managerial control over the deployment and utilization of the workforce" so that expenditure cuts would not lead to reductions in municipal services; and using the savings achieved—as well as any additional state and federal aid received—to retire outstanding debt, reduce taxes, and renovate the city's capital infrastructure for the purpose of promoting economic development. City of New York, Temporary Commission on City Finances, *The City in Transition*, 1977, 14, Part 3. These proposals were endorsed by the major organizations and publications representing the downtown business community. See, for example, Citizens Budget Commission, *Citizens Budget Commission Recommendations on the Final Report of the Temporary Commission on City Finances* (New York: Citizens Budget Commission, 1977); *Wall Street Journal*, 12 August 1977, p. 6.

31. See Citizens Budget Commission, *New York City's Fiscal Crisis: A Redefinition* (New York: Citizens Budget Commission, 1980), and *The City of New York Budget Prospects: Fiscal Years 1983 to 1986* (New York: Citizens Budget Commission, 1982).

32. Raymond Horton and John Palmer Smith, "Expenditures and Services," in *Setting Municipal Priorities, 1983*, ed. Brecher and Horton, 77f.

33. Charles Brecher and Raymond Horton, "Introduction," in *Setting Municipal Priorities: American Cities and the New York Experience*, ed. Charles Brecher and Raymond Horton (New York: New York University Press, 1985), 2.

34. In the late 1970s the largest municipal unions did consent to a policy of "broad-banding"—collapsing a large number of job titles into a smaller number of more general titles—which did increase the control city officials were able to exercise over the composition

and deployment of the municipal workforce. However, collective bargaining agreements and civil service laws would still prevent the mayor from replacing refuse collectors who leave the Sanitation Department's workforce with, say, maintenance personnel or laborers transferred from other city departments.

35. City of New York, Temporary Commission on City Finances, *The City in Transition*, 130, 132.

36. Direct measures of the quantity and quality of the services performed by different municipal agencies would provide a superior indicator of the impact of retrenchment on the consumers of municipal services, but such measures would not be comparable across municipal agencies. The changes in appropriations allocated to different municipal agencies would be another possible indicator of retrenchment, but I chose to look at changes in the payrolls of municipal agencies because they are especially meaningful politically. Most of New York's political leaders believe—as their actions have often shown—that the way to increase the services an agency provides is to increase the size of its workforce. For example, when Mayor Koch's probable opponents in the 1985 election attacked him for failing to improve municipal services during his second term, the mayor responded with a series of press conferences announcing plans for adding employees to various municipal agencies. For an analysis of the impact of retrenchment that relies upon expenditure data, with conclusions that differ from the analysis in this section, see Brecher and Horton, "Expenditures," in *Setting Municipal Priorities, 1984*, ed. Brecher and Horton.

37. Citizens Budget Commission, *Functional Expenditure Priorities in the City of New York, Fiscal Years 1978–82* (New York: Citizens Budget Commission, 1981).

Chapter 7

1. In 1978 the state extended the life of the Financial Control Board until all bonds issued by MAC are redeemed, which is not scheduled to occur until the year 2008. Under a complicated set of conditions the FCB will enter a "passive mode," in which its powers will be reduced somewhat, but if the city gets into financial trouble after this occurs, the FCB will regain its full powers. For an analysis of the formal powers of New York's fiscal monitoring agencies, see Robert Bailey, *The Crisis Regime* (Albany, N.Y.: State University of New York Press, 1984), chap. 1.

2. Charles Brecher and Raymond Horton, "Introduction," in *Setting Municipal Priorities: American Cities and the New York Experience*, ed. Brecher and Horton (New York: New York University Press, 1985).

3. The precise composition of the coalitions participating in these joint negotiations has varied. In 1975 the police and teachers' unions did not participate in negotiations leading to that year's wage-deferral agreement. In 1976 the teachers' union did not formally negotiate with the other municipal unions; nor did the unions representing rank-and-file police, fire, and corrections officers in 1978, but they accepted the same terms as those unions that did bargain as a unit. In 1980, unions representing all of the city's uniformed employees—police officers, fire fighters, corrections officers, and sanitation workers—formed a separate coalition and negotiated their own agreement with the municipal government. In 1982 uniformed personnel again formed their own coalition and negotiated a separate agreement, but this time it included only public safety personnel; the sanitation workers' union bargained independently. In 1984 the fire fighters withdrew from the coalition of uniformed employees. For an analysis of coalition bargaining through 1980 see David Lewin and Mary McCormick, "Coalition Bargaining in Municipal Government: The New York City Experience," *Industrial and Labor Relations Review* 34 (January 1981): 175–90.

4. In 1978 the unions delayed purchasing additional city bonds in an effort to increase their bargaining power in negotiations for a new financing agreement with New York. To minimize the leverage the unions gained by bankrolling the municipal government, the city's fiscal monitors insisted that the 1978 financing agreement make the pension funds' commitment to purchase New York bonds legally binding. This provision in the 1978 financing agreement was not very meaningful, however, because any effort to enforce this commitment in the courts would have taken a great deal of time, and the unions could

have thrown the city into a cash crisis while the issue was being litigated. See *Fiscal Observer* 2, no. 23 (14 Dec. 1978): 12.

5. *Fiscal Observer* 2 (6 July 1978): 1–3, 6–7; and Ken Auletta, *The Streets Were Paved With Gold* (New York: Random House, 1979), 304–315.

6. Fred Ferretti, *The Year the Big Apple Went Bust* (New York: G. P. Putnam's, 1976), 399; *Fiscal Observer* 2 (6 July 1978): 2–3.

7. *Wall Street Journal*, 24 Feb. 1977, p. 22; March 10, 1977, p. 38; and *Fiscal Observer* 2, no. 23 (14 Dec. 1978): 1–5.

8. *New York Times*, 19 Dec. 1979, sec. A, p. 1; Citizens Budget Commission, *1980 Annual Report* (New York: Citizens Budget Commision, 1980).

9. New York Chamber of Commerce and Industry, *Action*, 26 May 1978; *New York Times*, 15 Jan. 1982, sec. B, p. 2.

10. Michael Ball, "Politicians, Managers Team Up to Turn New York City Around," *AMA Forum* 68 (October 1979): 29.

11. Stephen David and Paul Kantor, "The Political Economy of Change in Urban Budgetary Politics," *British Journal of Political Science* 13 (1983): 270–74; Jack Newfield and Paul DuBrul, *The Permanent Government* (New York: Pilgrim Press, 1981), chaps. 2, 7; New York State Chamber of Commerce and Industry, *Action*, 13 Oct. 1977.

12. *New York Times*, 8 Nov. 1982, p. 1; Citizens Budget Commission, *1980 Annual Report*, 3.

13. *Wall Street Journal*, 29 June 1978, p. 18.

14. Governor Carey complained especially of the lack of organized business support for the Westway highway project—despite the wide support for the project privately expressed by leaders of the city's business community—and he and Mayor Koch encouraged members of New York's corporate elite to organize the Partnership. *New York Times*, 19 Dec. 1979, sec. B, p. 3.

15. In 1975 there was a sideshow to the central drama of the fiscal crisis in which New York's good government groups played a somewhat more important role. By coincidence, a charter commission established by the governor and state legislature in 1972 was scheduled to recommend changes in New York City's charter in 1975. Representatives from the Citizens Union and City Club testified before the commission and some of their proposals were adopted; moreover, they urged the city's voters to approve the charter reforms the commission drafted, and their support might have contributed to the substantial margin by which the electorate supported the charter revisions. However, the commission grew out of efforts by Governor Rockefeller to embarrass Mayor Lindsay, as well as the GOP's efforts to provide publicity for the commission's chairman (Roy Goodman, a Republican state senator who had mayoral aspirations), and the reforms proposed by the commission were not very significant. The most important one established community boards to offer advice to city agencies concerning the delivery of municipal services and the construction of municipal facilities in their neighborhoods. Consequently, little significance can be attached to the role that New York's traditional good government groups played in this charter reform effort.

16. Fund for the City of New York, *Public Papers* 1 (January 1982): 1.

17. Raymond Horton and Charles Brecher, "Preface," in *Setting Municipal Priorities, 1980*, ed. Horton and Brecher (Montclair, N.J.: Allanheld, Osmun, 1979), xv–xvi.

18. Eli Ginzberg and Henry Cohen, "Foreword," in *Setting Municipal Priorities, 1980*, ed. Horton and Brecher, xii.

19. See *Setting Municipal Priorities, 1981*, ed. Charles Brecher and Raymond Horton (Montclair, N.J.: Allanheld, Osmun, 1980), xii.

20. Charles Brecher and Raymond Horton, "Introduction," in *Setting Municipal Priorities, 1981*, ed. Brecher and Horton, 7–8; John Mollenkopf, "Economic Development," in *Setting Municipal Priorities, 1984*, ed. Charles Brecher and Raymond Horton (New York: New York University Press, 1983), chap. 5.

21. See, for example, *New York Times*, 7 Dec. 1981, sec. B, p. 3; 29 Nov. 1982, sec. B, p. 4.

22. Citizens Budget Commission, *1980 Annual Report*, 1–3.

23. James Ring Adams, "The Muffle Men," *Empire State Report* 5 (April 1979): 19–23; *New York Times*, 2 Dec. 1980, sec. B, p. 1.

24. *Fiscal Observer* 2 (2 Nov. 1978): 3; Adams, "Muffle Men," 22.

25. In 1978 the banks and unions also joined together to insist that MAC's authority to issue bonds backed by sales tax receipts and state aid payments be limited to $8.8 billion— a stipulation that would enhance the value of the MAC securities in their portfolios, but would restrict MAC's ability to bail out the municipal government if the city failed to regain full access to the public credit markets on schedule. *Wall Street Journal*, 11 Sept. 1978, p. 33. For other examples of how the 1978 financing agreement served the interests of the banks and unions in ways that imposed costs upon the city government, see *Fiscal Observer* 2 (14 Dec. 1978): 5.

26. The final installment of federally guaranteed bonds was released by the Treasury in 1982, and the last new MAC bonds were sold in 1984. However, MAC continues to refund outstanding bonds and to retain discretion over the release of its excess reserves to the city. MAC also issues an annual budget report and is consulted by the FCB as to whether it should approve borrowings by the city.

27. See Herbert Ranschburg, "New York City's Emergency Financial Control Board: An Interim Review of the Record," *City Almanac* 11 (August 1976): 12; Martin Shefter, "New York City's Fiscal Crisis: The Politics of Inflation and Retrenchment," *The Public Interest* 48 (Summer 1977): 127.

28. *Fiscal Observer* 2 (2 Nov. 1978): 2–5.

29. Lewin and McCormick, "Coalition Bargaining," 182.

30. The cost-of-living adjustments referred to in this paragraph are those known as COLA II's. To compensate city workers for the additional contributions they were required to make to their pension plans, the EFCB in 1975 granted them unconditional cost-of-living adjustments known as COLA I's.

31. *Fiscal Observer* 3 (22 March 1979): 2, 4.

32. Ranschburg, "Emergency Financial Control Board," 6–11.

33. Charles Brecher and James Hartman, "Financial Planning," in *Setting Municipal Priorities, 1983*, ed. Charles Brecher and Raymond Horton (New York: New York University Press, 1982), 210–212.

34. *New York Times*, 12 Oct. 1982, sec. B, p. 2; 28 Nov. 1982, sec. 4, p. 6; 23 Dec. 1982, sec. B, p. 1.

35. *Fiscal Observer* 3 (12 April 1979): 7.

36. Shefter, interview of Donald Kummerfeld, Setting Municipal Priorities conference, Harriman, N.Y., December 1981.

37. *Fiscal Observer* 3 (22 March 1979): 5.

38. Ranschburg, "Emergency Financial Control Board," 9.

39. *Fiscal Observer* 3 (22 March 1979): 7.

40. *New York Times*, 5 Dec. 1975, p. 1; 28 Oct. 1976, p. 51.

41. *New York Times*, 5 April 1982, sec. B, p. 2.

42. *New York Times*, 4 March 1978, p. 9.

43. Charles Brecher and Raymond Horton, "Expenditures," in *Setting Municipal Priorities, 1984*, ed. Charles Brecher and Raymond Horton (New York: New York University Press, 1983), 69–81. It should be noted, however, that the increase in appropriations to agencies performing developmental functions during Mayor Koch's first term still left the municipal government spending only slightly more in nominal dollars, and one-third less in inflation-adjusted dollars, on these functions in 1982 than it had in 1975. Even with these additional appropriations, only 7.7 percent of the city's total budget was allocated to developmental agencies in 1982, a share smaller than the 9.5 percent that had been allocated in 1975. Although the $529.4 million in additional appropriations to developmental agencies during Koch's first term represented an increase in their budgets *proportionately* larger than the increase granted to agencies performing other functions, in *absolute* terms this sum was smaller than the $805.4 million in additional appropriations granted to redistributive agencies and the $2.24 billion in additional appropriations granted to agencies performing allocative functions. In other words, slightly less than one-quarter of the city's increased spending during Mayor Koch's first term went to agencies performing developmental functions, and slightly more than three-quarters went to agencies performing other functions.

44. McCormick, "Labor Relations," in *Setting Municipal Priorities 1982*, ed. Charles Brecher and Raymond Horton (New York: Russell Sage, 1981), 215–22; Raymond Horton and John Palmer Smith, "Expenditures and Services," in *Setting Municipal Priorities, 1983*,

ed. Brecher and Horton, chap. 3, especially p. 110; Citizens Budget Commission, *The State of Municipal Services, 1983* (New York: Citizens Budget Commission, 1984), table A; Charles Brecher and Raymond Horton, "Introduction," *Setting Municipal Priorities: American Cities and the New York Experience,* ed. Brecher and Horton.

45. Warren Moscow, *The Last of the Big Time Bosses* (New York: Stein and Day, 1971).
46. *New York Times,* 17 Feb. 1979, p. 26; 2 May 1978, p. 39.
47. *New York Times,* 31 Sept. 1981, sec. B, p. 3; 13 March 1982, p. 28; 16 Jan. 1985, sec. B, p. 5.
48. *New York Times,* 23 Oct. 1979, sec. B, p. 6.
49. Edward Koch, *Mayor* (New York: Simon & Schuster, 1984), 267–70; *New York Times,* 6 June 1981, p. 25.
50. *New York Times,* 28 Feb. 1979, sec. B, p. 7; 27 Feb. 1979, sec. A, p. 1.
51. Martin Shefter, "Political Incorporation and the Extrusion of the Left." (Paper delivered at the Annual Meeting of the American Political Science Association, Chicago, September 2, 1983).
52. See Nathan Glazer and Daniel Patrick Moynihan, *Beyond the Melting Pot,* 2nd ed. (Cambridge, Mass.: MIT Press, 1970), lxxiv–lxxvi.
53. Koch, *Mayor,* 87.
54. When a bill extending the life of the EFCB was considered by the state legislature in 1978, the black and Puerto Rican caucus again demanded that a nonwhite be appointed to it. Because the caucus now held the balance of power in the assembly, Governor Carey agreed. However, the black he appointed—Gilroye Griffin, a vice president of Bristol Myers—did not feel it was his role to represent the distinctive interests of New York's racial minorities on the Board. As he said in an interview, the Board does

not sit in judgment of Mayor Koch. Nor do we examine every city action from the standpoint of morality, but only from the standpoint of fiscal responsibility.... As a private citizen, I would say what I feel about actions the mayor may take to cut the budget of the Health and Hospitals Corporation, for example. How I'd vote on the fiscal prudence of that action may be an entirely different matter.

Fiscal Observer 3, no. 6 (22 March 1979): 5.
55. *New York Times,* 5 April 1983, sec. B, p. 2.
56. *New York Times,* 19 July 1983, sec. A, p. 20; 30 Nov. 1983, p. 30.
57. *New York Times,* 29 April 1983, sec. B, p. 5.
58. *New York Times,* 18 July 1983, sec. B, p. 1; 4 Oct. 1983, sec. B, p. 3; *Amsterdam News,* 16 Feb. 1985, p. 1.
59. *New York Times,* 18 July 1983, sec. B, p. 1; 12 Dec. 1984, sec. A, p. 1; 13 Dec. 1984, sec. A, p. 1. As of 1985, the experience of contending with Ed Koch had not led nonwhites to overcome the factionalism that has long characterized the politics of racial minorities in the city. Herman Farrell entered the mayoral race only when the CJNY was on the verge of endorsing a Hispanic, Herman Badillo, for mayor. Observers regarded Farrell's candidacy as an effort by Manhattan's black politicians to assert primacy over their Brooklyn counterparts, who were Badillo's chief supporters. In addition, Farrell feared that if the CJNY endorsed a Hispanic for mayor, black clergymen might run a candidate of their own, thereby threatening the leadership of black elected officials and party politicians. After being denied the CJNY's endorsement, Badillo, in turn, threatened to withdraw his support of Jose Serrano, a Hispanic running for Bronx borough president, if Serrano, to win the backing of black leaders, endorsed Farrell. *The City Sun,* Feb. 13–19, 1985, pp. 6–8; *New York Times,* 13 Feb. 1985, sec. B, p. 1; *New York Times,* 8 March 1985, sec. B., p. 3.
60. *New York Times,* 7 May 1980, p. 1.
61. McCormick, "Labor Relations," table 7.4.
62. *Wall Street Journal,* 29 June 1978, p. 18; 25 Aug. 1980, p. 4.
63. *Fiscal Observer* 1 (20 October 1977): 1.
64. George Sternlieb, Remarks at Setting Municipal Priorities conference, Harriman, New York, December 1981.
65. See Koch, *Mayor,* chap. 16; see also Citizens Budget Commission, *New York City's Ten Year Plan for Capital Development: An Updated Review,* December 1984, pp. 52–59.

Chapter 8

1. Although the range of public services provided to New York City's residents has not changed greatly since 1975, some services that were formerly performed and financed by the city government are now performed or financed by the state.

2. See, for example, Citizens Budget Commission, *1984 Annual Report* (New York: Citizens Budget Commission, 1985), pp. 4–6.

3. New York's current capital program includes the sort of projects that John Lindsay's supporters in the business community had wanted in the 1960s, but which moved down Lindsay's list of priorities as racial strife and labor turmoil escalated during these years. The post-fiscal crisis reorganization of the city's politics has thus enabled one element of the 1960s reform coalition to secure from New York's current regime policies that the Lindsay administration lacked the political capacity to deliver.

4. For a discussion of the political significance of the social organization of knowledge see Theda Skocpol, "Bringing the State Back In: A Review of Current Theories and Research," in *Bringing the State Back In*, ed. Peter Evans, Dietrich Rueschemeyer, and Theda Skocpol (New York: Cambridge University Press, 1985), chap. 1.

5. Wallace Sayre and Herbert Kaufman, *Governing New York City* (New York: Russell Sage, 1960), 637.

6. Ibid., 368.

7. Ibid., 642–44.

8. *New York Times*, 6 June 1984, sec. A, p. 1.

9. Matthew Drennan, "The Local Economy and Local Revenues," in *Setting Municipal Priorities, 1984*, ed. Charles Brecher and Raymond Horton (New York: New York University Press, 1983), chap. 1.

10. *New York Times*, 27 April 1984, sec. B, p. 4.

11. *New York Times*, 27 April 1984, sec. B, p. 4.

12. *New York Times*, 12 Jan. 1985, p. 24; 22 April 1985, sec. B, p. 3. Also, in 1984 New York's civil service unions scored their first victory in a campaign to restore pre-1975 pension benefits. In 1975 the unions had reluctantly consented to a plan—known as Tier III—providing newly hired city workers with lower pension benefits than their senior colleagues. In 1984 municipal labor lobbyists in Albany secured the restoration of some of these benefits and made no secret of their intentions to work in future years for the full repeal of Tier III.

13. *New York Times*, 7 May 1984, sec. B, p. 4; 1 April 1985, sec. B, p. 4; 2 April 1985, sec. B, p. 2.

14. Data on the race of voters in the 1980 and 1984 Democratic presidential primaries are from the CBS News election day exit polls. I am grateful to Kathleen Frankovic of CBS News for these data. See also *New York Times*, 5 May 1985, p. 42.

15. John Mollenkopf, "The Postindustrial Transformation of the Political Order in New York City." (Paper delivered at the Conference on New York City in the Postindustrial Period, Social Science Research Council, New York City, 4 May 1984), 30–34, 38–43.

16. Charles Brecher and Raymond Horton, "Expenditures," in *Setting Municipal Priorities, 1984*, ed. Brecher and Horton, 88–93.

17. *New York Times*, 18 Jan. 1984, p. 1.

18. Charles Brecher and Raymond Horton, "Introduction," in *Setting Municipal Priorities, 1983*, ed. Brecher and Horton (New York: New York University Press, 1982), 10ff.

19. Ibid., 11.

20. There are additional reasons why the uniformed services coalesced in 1980 and demanded larger wage increases than nonuniformed personnel. First, uniformed employees perform the most dangerous jobs or the most onerous tasks of any city workers, and they felt the city should acknowledge this by paying them accordingly. In addition, labor negotiations in 1975, 1976, and 1978 provided proportionately larger pay increases to those in low-wage brackets than to higher paid city employees. Hence the city's uniformed employees—who are among the city's best paid nonsupervisory personnel—have suffered proportionately larger cuts in their real income since 1975 than most other city workers.

21. See *Fiscal Observer* 3 (25 Jan. 1979): 12.

22. See *New York Times*, 12 Jan. 1985, p. 24.

23. See Edward Koch, *Mayor* (New York: Simon & Schuster, 1984), 221.

24. This scenario, it must be emphasized, is not a probable one. The agencies that monitor New York City's finances, and the budgetary procedures the municipal government now follows, make it unlikely that any fiscal strains the city experiences in future years will reach crisis proportions. Moreover, New York's politicians and public officials—white and nonwhite—are not unmindful of their stake in preserving the confidence of the city's creditors. And because the outcome of confrontational politics is difficult to predict, public officials would probably be reluctant to pursue such a strategy, even if they did find it necessary to cut municipal expenditures drastically.

Nonetheless, for well over a century New York has experienced periodic fiscal strains and even though the observers who have predicted fiscal disasters or political explosions since 1975 have turned out to be wrong time and time again, the possibility that such problems will emerge in the future cannot be excluded. Moreover, in the wake of these previous episodes of fiscal stress, city officials have developed unanticipated methods of reconciling the fiscal and political imperatives confronting them that many New Yorkers regarded as inconsistent with the tenets—or at least the spirit—of democracy. The scenario outlined here is one way these imperatives might be reconciled if New York encounters budgetary problems in the years ahead. In depicting this scenario, it should be clear, I am not advocating it.

Chapter 9

1. By now it should be clear that I am not arguing that political machines are inherently frugal. The eruption of fiscal crises in New York when Tammany and its allied organizations were strong, and the financial problems faced by Mayor Daley's heirs in Chicago more recently, indicate that machines are not immune to the forces that can lead city officials to spend more than the municipal government collects in tax revenues and intergovernmental aid. After suffering the consequences of a municipal fiscal crisis, however, the leaders of New York's Democratic machines were not only astute enough to learn the lessons of defeat, they also had the capacity to implement those lessons—imposing limits on elected officials who might again be tempted to accumulate large budget deficits. By contrast, the leaders of New York's Democratic county machines in the 1960s and 1970s were not in a position to do this.

2. Walter Dean Burnham, *Critical Elections and the Mainsprings of American Politics* (New York: Norton, 1970), 4.

3. John Mollenkopf, *The Contested City* (Princeton, N.J.: Princeton University Press, 1983), 43.

4. Robert Salisbury, "Urban Politics: The New Convergence of Power," *Journal of Politics* 26 (November 1964): 775–97.

5. David Greenstone and Paul Peterson, *Race and Authority in Urban Politics* (New York: Russell Sage, 1973), chap. 8.

6. Richard A. Cloward and Frances Fox Piven, "Welfare for Whom," in *Urban Government*, ed. Edward C. Banfield (New York: Free Press, 1969).

7. Frances Fox Piven, "The Urban Crisis: Who Got What and Why?" in *Urban Politics and Public Policy*, 2nd edition, ed. Steven David and Paul Peterson (New York: Praeger, 1976).

8. It should be emphasized that the pattern of relations among the participants in a city's political system is at least as important as their sheer number or the resources they command in explaining their impact upon the municipal government. During the decade and a half following World War II, an unusually large number of expenditure-demanding groups were active in New York politics, but because the public official through whom they characteristically obtained access to City Hall—the mayor—was also beholden to the city's regular Democratic party organizations, which represented tax-conscious homeowners and small businessmen, their ability to influence municipal fiscal priorities was tightly constrained. As noted in chapter 5, Mayor Wagner's break with Carmine DeSapio and his associates in 1961 and the election of a fusion mayor in 1965 altered the pattern of relations among the major forces in New York politics, and weakened this constraint upon budgetary inflation.

9. Martin Shefter, "Regional Receptivity to Reform: The Legacy of the Progressive Era," *Political Science Quarterly* 98 (Fall 1983): 459–83.

10. Mollenkopf, *The Contested City,* chap. 3.

11. Ibid., 246–49; Michael Aiken and Robert Alford, "Community Structure and Innovation: Public Housing, Urban Renewal and the War on Poverty," in *Comparative Community Politics,* ed. Terry Clark (New York: Wiley, 1974), 243–44.

12. George Peterson, "Finance," in *The Urban Predicament,* ed. William Gorham and Nathan Glazer (Washington, D.C.: The Urban Institute, 1976), chap. 2.

13. The Federal Reserve Board's decision in October 1979 to set targets for the growth of the money supply instead of trying to control interest rates directly is consistent with this argument. Despite that announced policy change, the Fed has since presided over massive fluctuations in the monetary aggregates, much to the chagrin of orthodox monetarists. It is true that during 1981 and the first half of 1982 the Fed pursued restrictive monetary policies in an effort to fight inflation; in mid-1982, however, it abandoned that course. There were a number of reasons for this change, but one was almost certainly that by the summer of 1982 the central bank had exhausted its political capacity to pursue this policy further. This was evidenced by the proposals of both Democrats and Republicans in Congress, and even by members of the Reagan administration, to place restrictions on the independence of the Federal Reserve system. The Fed's shift in policy averted this threat. See *New York Times,* 27 December 1983, sec. D, p. 4. Economist Albert Wojnilower has argued that similar considerations led the Fed to ease monetary policy in late 1984. *New York Times,* 18 Dec., 1984, sec. D, p. 20.

14. Ira Katznelson, *City Trenches: Urban Politics and the Patterning of Class in the United States* (New York: Pantheon, 1981), chap. 3.

15. Terry N. Clark and Lorna C. Ferguson, *City Money: Political Processes, Fiscal Strain, and Retrenchment* (New York: Columbia University Press, 1983), chap. 7.

INDEX